Titanic **Century**

Titanic Century

Media, Myth, and the Making of a Cultural Icon

Paul Heyer

 PRAEGER

AN IMPRINT OF ABC-CLIO, LLC
Santa Barbara, California • Denver, Colorado • Oxford, England

Library of Congress Cataloging-in-Publication Data

Heyer, Paul, 1946–
    Titanic century : media, myth, and the making of a cultural icon / Paul Heyer.
        p. cm.
    Includes bibliographical references and index.
    ISBN 978–0–313–39815–5 (hardback) — ISBN 978–0–313–39816–2 (ebook)
1. Titanic (Steamship) 2. Shipwrecks—North Atlantic Ocean. 3. Disasters—Press
coverage. I. Title.
G530.T6H48   2012
910.9163'4—dc23   2012000372

ISBN: 978–0–313–39815–5
EISBN: 978–0–313–39816–2

16 15 14 13 12   1 2 3 4 5

This book is also available on the World Wide Web as an eBook.
Visit www.abc-clio.com for details.

Praeger
An Imprint of ABC-CLIO, LLC

ABC-CLIO, LLC
130 Cremona Drive, P.O. Box 1911
Santa Barbara, California 93116-1911

This book is printed on acid-free paper ∞

Manufactured in the United States of America

IMAX® is a registered trademark of IMAX Corporation

For Carole

And, behold, I, even I, do bring a flood of waters upon the earth, to destroy all flesh, wherein is the breath of life, from under heaven; *and* everything that is the earth shall die.

—Genesis 6:1

Now small fowls flew screaming over the great yawning gulf; a sullen white surf beat against its steep sides; then all collapsed and the great shroud of the sea rolled on as it rolled five thousand years ago.

—Herman Melville, *Moby Dick*

Contents

A photo essay follows page 99.

Preface

It is now 100 years and counting since that unforgettable night in April of 1912 when the great ship went down and an incredulous world tried to fathom how such an unthinkable tragedy could have happened. In 1995 an earlier edition of this book appeared in response to renewed interest in the sinking resulting from the discovery of the wreck during the previous decade. By the turn of the millennium, however, I thought closure would finally be brought to one of the defining events of the twentieth century. I assumed that the public and the media's almost century-long fascination would have ebbed, finally putting an end to my role as a chronicler of that phenomenon. I should have known better. Much has happened since. I was warned at the time that one of the consequences of any writerly engagement with the *Titanic* is that she will never let go.

Shortly after my book appeared I followed with interest events leading up to the release of James Cameron's *Titanic* in 1997. I shared the general opinion of film cognoscenti in believing that movies had exhausted the *Titanic* as a subject and public interest was on the wane. "Cameron's folly," the film was called in the press. It seemed like another *Waterworld* or *Ishtar* waiting to happen, only in this case foreshadowed in the most obvious of ways by the resounding box office failure in the early 1980s of *Raise the Titanic*. Quite the opposite happened. And in one of those strange quirks of fate I was invited to appear in the film as an extra. Circumstances and caution precluded my acceptance. I was in the middle of a teaching semester and found it hard to justify taking a two-week leave to appear in a film that seemed ill fated, was already running over budget and schedule, and contained no A-list stars—Kate Winslet and Leonardo DiCaprio were barely known at the time. My screen debut would have to wait until the year following the film's release and would be on television, when I was asked to be a consultant and on-camera commentator for the A&E prime-time documentary *Beyond Titanic*.

Post-2000 events relating to the *Titanic* started off slowly but have continued to escalate: new theories relating to her demise, the ongoing exhibition of the salvaged artifacts, the re-release of Cameron's *Titanic* in 3D, and the various cruises and commemorative services planned around the centenary of the tragedy. It seems we cannot let the great ship rest in peace—nor she us. I began to feel that my obligation as a chronicler of the legacy was not yet fulfilled and that my earlier work was in need of substantial revision if I wanted to account for what has transpired since. At Praeger, a wonderfully encouraging editor, Michael Millman, was of a like mind. Together we mapped out a plan to raise and completely refit, if you will pardon the maritime terminology, the original plan I conceived almost 20 years ago.

My interest in the story of the *Titanic*, or in terms of this book the story of her stories, derives from an encounter between a childhood fascination inspired by films such as *Titanic* (1953) and *A Night to Remember* (1958) and a career writing and teaching in the field of media studies. They converged unexpectedly in the 1980s when I joined countless others in being enthralled by press and television coverage of the search for the wreck. This prompted a desire to research aspects of the disaster, particularly its influence over a variety of communication media and the media's role in immortalizing the event. The book that followed was well received, but by millennium's end I had put it behind me, or so I thought. What happened later can be expressed somewhat by inverting the famous promotional moniker used for *Jaws II*, "just when I thought it was safe to get out of the water...."

Many commentaries have been written about the *Titanic* disaster. Most deal with what happened, why, and all the "what ifs" that will forever cling to it. My concern here is not to provide another such account nor to overly speculate on the many mysteries surrounding the ship's demise, save for what I feel is the greatest one: not why she struck an iceberg on a cold April night once-upon-a-time, but the hold that the event still has over us.

In exploring this question, I examine how the *Titanic*'s abortive four-day voyage turned into a 100-year journey in the history of U.S. popular culture and its attendant media. Her fate has prompted endless reflection and influenced established institutions. For example, it showcased the promise and the limitations of the new medium of wireless telegraphy, making Marconi a household name and launching David Sarnoff into a career as head of RCA; it helped raise the stature of the *New York Times* to the eminence it has today; and for a century it has been represented in and has influenced a variety of media, especially motion pictures—without the success of James Cameron's *Titanic*, there would have been no *Avatar*. Finally, I suggest that the cautionary lesson provided by the ship's fate has given her story a mythic status comparable to what we find with great works of literature, from the *Bible* to Shakespeare. At the time she was built the *Titanic* was said to be "unsinkable." Had someone said this of her legacy, the truth of it would have been borne out a century later.

Throughout the research and writing of the first edition of this book I found support everywhere I turned, and it has been no less so the second time around. Blair Davis has provided relentless encouragement, and Michael Dupuis' interest was so informed by his own research into Canadian press coverage of the sinking that I invited him to write Chapter 7. Some individuals who assisted me in the past when I first began to think "*Titanic*" deserve another vote of thanks before I bring a new list onboard. I owe a great debt to the Titanic Historical Society (THS), located in Indian Orchard, Massachusetts. The THS is a treasure trove of *Titanic* information, and its quarterly magazine, the *Titanic Commutator*, is of incalculable value to anyone interested in the great ship and her era. THS president Edward Kamuda graciously took time to answer my correspondences and helped me secure difficult-to-find material. I also wish to thank *Titanic* archivists John Booth and Sean Coughlan and historian Stephen Kern for kindly agreeing to read portions of my initial research material.

My *Titanic* odyssey has led me to many places, from the New York Public Library—may the powers that be grant that venerable institution longer operating hours—to a small museum in rural Australia. Whenever I publicly presented aspects of the project, response was enthusiastic, whether the context was the broadcast media—CBC (Canada), and ABC (Australia)—or an academic setting. The interest and support shown for my work in Australia was especially heartwarming, and much thanks are owed to Hart Cohen, Terry Guthridge, Harry Irwin, Brian Shoesmith, Collette Snowden, Sue Turnbull, Virginia Nightingale, Kate Warren, and Gretchen and Julian Weaver.

Since my move "back East" from Vancouver 10 years ago to Wilfrid Laurier University in Waterloo, Ontario, colleagues and friends have been enormously supportive of my unusual academic pursuits and especially encouraging when informed that I would again attempt to "raise the *Titanic*." Hopefully my labors will not be as ill fated as the film bearing that title. Sincere thanks must go to Bill Buxton, Michael Cheney, Natalie Coulter, Martin Dowding, Elin Edwards, Jonathan Finn, Sandra Gabrele, Philippa Gates, Jenna Hennebry, Andrew Herman, Sylvia Hoang, Penelope Ironstone-Catterall, Barbara Jenkins, Naveen Joshi, Russ Kilbourn, Ute Lischke, Martin Morris, Susan Muck, Judith Nicholson, Greig de Peuter, Herbert Pimlott, Julie Pong, Ian Roderick, Lior Samfiru, Brad Skelton, Katherine Spring, Paul Tiessen, Sivan Tumarkin, Peter Urquhart, and Darren Wershler.

Working again with Praeger has been a delight. Editor Michael Millman has been my ship's quartermaster extraordinaire. The production process was greatly assisted by Bhuvaneswari Rathinam and her team at PreMediaGlobal and the copy editor Daniel Nighting, who showed an informed awareness of how style should relate to the specific content under discussion.

Introduction: From Triumph to Tragedy

It is Sunday, April 14, 1912, 400 miles southeast of the coast of Newfoundland in space, 11:40 p.m. in time. The North Atlantic sits dark and motionless, like a great pool of oil. The air is as cold and sharp as a razor. In seconds the renowned creation of an era is going to collide with an anonymous fragment of nature.

And so it began. Although it is not my concern to provide a detailed assessment of the event, relevant facts pertaining to it will inevitably emerge in subsequent discussions. The reader, however, might benefit at the outset from the following brief summary of what happened and when.

On April 10, 1912, the *Titanic* set sail on her maiden voyage from Southampton, England, to New York, where she was due to arrive on April 16. She was the largest liner ever built, 882 feet in length, 92 feet wide, and 46,328 tons in weight. Prior to the collision the ship had been steaming at her fastest speed of the voyage, 22-1/2 knots (almost 25 miles per hour), into a region where several reports had warned of the presence of ice. When the lookout spotted the iceberg, at perhaps 500 yards, it was to late to do more than attempt evasive maneuvers. Most onboard felt the collision as a mild shudder. What resulted was a glancing blow that cut a 300-foot slit below the waterline on the starboard bow. Five or six watertight compartments were breached (perhaps semiwatertight would have been a better term since they did not extend all the way to the top deck). The ship could only stay afloat if no more than four were flooded. As the ship settled, further compartments were filled, gradually pulling her down by the bow. She vanished at 2:20 a.m.

There were 2,227 passengers and crew on board; 705 survived in lifeboats. The number of lifeboats was inadequate because of a British Board of Trade regulation that based the number of lifeboats a ship carried on her tonnage, not the number of passengers; nevertheless the available lifeboats could have held 1,200 people if properly deployed. Shortly after the collision the wireless operators began sending an SOS, followed by the ship's position. Morse lamp was also used when a nearby ship, possibly the *Californian*, came into view. Signal rockets were also sent up. The first ship on the scene was the Cunard liner *Carpathia*. She arrived shortly after 4:00 a.m., having been 58 miles away when she first picked up the *Titanic*'s distress call. The *Carpathia* took the survivors to New York, where they arrived on the evening of April 18.

On April 19 a committee of the United States Senate chaired by William Alden Smith began an inquiry into the causes of the disaster. It released its report on May 28. The document was critical of established maritime practice in the North Atlantic; the comportment of the Titanic's parent company, the White Star Line, before, during, and after the sinking; and the captain of the *Californian*, Stanley Lord, for not responding to the *Titanic*'s distress rockets. The inquiry was not empowered to lay charges, but its findings had a major influence on subsequent regulatory policy regarding shipping and wireless use.

On May 2, a British Board of Trade inquiry was launched. It was led by a judge, Lord Mersey, and released its report on July 30. This inquiry was more technically minded than the American effort. It was also less critical of established maritime practice and not as severe in its condemnation of the White Star Line; however, the position taken on the *Californian* and her captain paralleled the U.S. judgment. Numerous commentators, then and now, have argued that the British inquiry was a "whitewash" that protected both the Board of Trade and White Star from the severe censure they should have received. No charges were laid, although the inquiry was empowered to do so, but a number of regulations were changed, most immediately the one pertaining to the number of lifeboats required on a ship.

These raw facts pertaining to an event that occurred a century ago disrupted a dream that by coincidence began exactly 100 years before the *Titanic* was built. The first application of steam to commercial travel by ship occurred in 1811 when Robert Fulton put his *New Orleans* into service on the Mississippi. In the decades that followed, oceanic horizons loomed and inspired the application of steam to make crossings not only much faster but also more luxurious than had been possible under sail. In 1912 the *Titanic* represented the culmination of this desire and the latest salvo in the transatlantic passenger trade rivalry that saw her parent company, White Star, facing off against domestic and foreign competitors. Ocean travel had come a long way from how it was described by that eminently quotable eighteenth-century man of letters, Dr. Samuel Johnson, who likened it to "being in jail with the chance of being drowned." By the early twentieth century, the odds of being drowned on an ocean voyage had diminished considerably, and even third-class ("steerage") passengers had accommodations substantially better than most prisons. First-class passengers could travel in a state of nirvana unthinkable only a generation earlier.

Although the *Titanic* showed that nothing could or should be taken for granted in pursuing this dream, it did not come to an end because of tragedy but from a different kind of competition. During the 1950s, the Cunard Line, facing increased competition from the airlines that would soon end the glory days of ocean travel between Europe and North America, coined the slogan, "Getting there is half the fun." It was a "back to the future" idea that would eventually be done in by the turboprop. The slogan would have certainly had relevance in 1912 as a lure for travel on the jewels of Cunard's fleet, the *Lusitania* and *Mauritania*. Even then competition was severe. Cunard's main rival was White Star, which could offer the *Olympic* and, at least for one voyage, her sister ship the *Titanic*. These vessels, especially the *Titanic*, had appointments so sumptuous that today's advertising hype might promote them with the phrase, "Getting there is more fun than being there."

Both White Star and Cunard had continental challengers, most notably Bremen's North German Lloyd and the Hamburg-Amerika Line, or HAPAG (Hamburg-Amerikanische Packetfahrt Actien-Gesellschaft). The paying customer could elect to travel a little bit faster (Cunard/North German Lloyd) or with a touch more luxury (White Star/HAPAG), or simply according to a convenient time and place of departure. It was if there was a conscious attempt to push behind the historical horizon all memories of those dank and uncertain crossings that had so often plagued ocean travel in previous centuries. While White Star, Cunard, and their German rivals strove for a new standard of comfort in ocean travel, a high priority was also placed on precise and reliable schedules. Previously the model for temporal consistency had been the railways. Shipping timetables, in contrast, had been subject to the vicissitudes of the North Atlantic, and during much of the nineteenth century they were guesstimates at best. In the days of sail, arrival times could be off by several weeks. Early steamers, although not as tyrannized by the weather, were nonetheless affected by it.

Up until the 1890s, or only about a decade prior to the planning of the *Titanic*, virtually all transatlantic liners carried auxiliary sailing gear; ironically, earlier in the century it had been the steam engines that were considered auxiliary. The sail rigging could be deployed in the case of engine failure or to conserve fuel by taking advantage of exceptionally favorable winds. When a ship was late during the nineteenth century, weather was usually assumed to be the culprit, with mechanical breakdown an additional possibility if the ship was a steamer. After about one week's delay serious thoughts might be entertained regarding the possibility of a disaster.

To implement what had been a long-cherished dream—a transatlantic schedule based on same-day weekly departures—White Star conceived the *Titanic* as part of a triumvirate. Her sister ships were the *Olympic*, launched in 1911, and the *Britannic*, launched in 1915. Three ships were necessary for the service, given a five- to six-day travel period and layovers that might last as long as a week. The *Titanic*'s demise thwarted the company's attempt to be first with this transatlantic shuttle operation, but they would have been beaten by Cunard in any case. In 1914 the *Aquitania* joined the *Lusitania* and *Mauritania* in finally achieving this impressive breakthrough.

Cunard had tried to accomplish the feat several years earlier by teaming the *Campania* with the *Lusitania* and *Mauritania*, but the plan was ill advised. The *Campania*, built in 1893, was an old-style twin-screw steamer that simply could not weather the weather like her larger turbine-driven half-sisters. It soon became apparent that for consistent travel time and ease of maintenance, three well-matched ships were required for reliable weekly departures.

These ambitious plans seem all the more so when we consider how rapid were the transformations that made them possible. In the 1850s—a time when steam auxiliary engines and iron ships were just exiting their prototypical phase—the vast majority of crossings still took place in wooden sailing vessels. Under optimum conditions the trip could be done in five weeks. However, steam was clearly the future, and the handwriting must have been on the wall in bold. Yet, as Carl Cutler has pointed out in his history of American sailing ships, the extraordinary though brief success of the American clippers during the early 1850s yielded a number of editorials proclaiming sail over steam. The latter was deemed to be too dangerous, uncomfortable, expensive, and at times even slower than those new wind-powered "greyhounds of the sea." But technological improvements in engine and ship design would soon make it no contest. By 1901, passage on the *Campania*, *Kaiser Wilhelm II*, or *Celtic* had reduced the time to 5-1/2 days, and even third-class accommodations included fresh meals, clean (if crowded) quarters, and decent sanitary facilities, assuming individuals had the patience to wait their turn.

More recently, travelers in our jet age who remember crossing the Atlantic in the 1950s during the last golden age of the great liners, perhaps on either of the two *Queens* or the *SS United States*, rarely hesitate to speak of the experience with nostalgia. Time lost by choosing sea over air, or gained vice versa, seems rarely significant in later life. Air travel tends to be forgettable unless something goes wrong; ocean voyages are almost always memorable. When a contemporary airline uses the by-now generic motto, "The only way to fly," the phrase might prompt us to hark back to a time when flying was not the only way.

Nevertheless, ocean travel persists. The growth of the cruise ship industry indicates that a means of transport need not be thought of as solely a way of getting from point A to point B. Such voyages have become, at best, pleasant parodies, theme parks recalling an era that looms larger in our historical rear view mirror the more we move into the new millennium. As the great maverick American economist and social theorist Thorstein Veblen prophetically noted almost 100 years ago, when modern technological capacities render obsolete what was once a widespread and essential activity, that activity often resurfaces as a pastime for leisure or amusement.

The first steam-assisted crossing of the Atlantic began with the *Savannah* in 1819. She was steam assisted at least during those highly visible and newsworthy moments of departure and arrival—media events are not just a post-twentieth-century phenomenon. The available paddle-wheel technology was bulky. It consumed so much fuel that the modest gain in speed—it took four weeks to cross—was offset by diminished space and a ticket price limited to the affluent, who in any case would have had to possess a degree of courage to risk their lives in such an unproven vessel. By 1838, ships such as the *Great Western* were using paddle wheels to reduce the crossing time to two weeks, with most of the voyage under steam rather than sail. Passenger space, however, was limited to 80, with enough soot to cover everyone.

By the next decade, two developments helped improve both space and speed: the switch from paddle wheels to screw propellers and the use of iron in a ship's construction. In 1843, the *Great Britain* became the first vessel to employ both. Understandably there were reservations regarding the use of iron, especially as to its buoyancy relative to wood. But as a new generation of ship engineers pointed out time and again, an iron ship is not only stronger, it is also lighter than a wooden one of the same dimensions because it does not have to be as thick in either the hull or beam. This consequent lightness aids speed. Also, wooden ships, laden as they were with iron and brass fittings, were not renowned for their flotation capacity when breached.

Cunard, which started service in 1840, had by the end of the decade become the success story of the passenger ship industry. Reliability and an exemplary safety record were the primary reasons. What an America challenger, Collins, offered in response was speed. In 1852 this dream of speed led to the Collins liner *Pacific* pushing down the time to cross to just under 10 days. But in 1856 Collins also offered something else: a navigation lesson the *Titanic* seems to have forgotten. The *Pacific* entered an ice field and vanished. Two years earlier her sister ship, the *Arctic*, had foundered after colliding with another vessel off Cape Race, Newfoundland. In 1858, after only eight years of service, the Collins Line went the route of its two prized vessels.

The Collins ships had not only offered speed, they also contained hitherto untried luxuries, such as large cabins, steam heating, and ornate decor; some of these frills, however, had to be packed away shortly after the ships left port so as not to be damaged by rough seas or seasick passengers.

The idea of outfitting a ship in the manner of an elegant hotel would be a precedent very much on the minds of the builders of the *Titanic*, but it did not have to wait until the Gilded Age for further elaboration. In 1858, after four years in the building, the *Great Eastern* was launched into the Thames. She was the most ambitious ship, relative to her time, that had ever been or probably ever will be conceived. Her near 19,000 tons made her five times larger than any previous vessel and would not be exceeded until the completion of the *Celtic* and *Kaiser Wilhelm II* in 1901. In contrast, the *Olympic* and *Titanic* surpassed the gross tonnage of the previous largest vessels of their era, the *Mauritania* and *Lusitania*, by a factor of "only" 50 percent. At almost 700 feet from stem to stern, the *Great Eastern* would not be nosed out in length until the *Oceanic II* entered service in 1899.

The *Great Eastern* was to have been called the *Leviathan*. The name *Titanic* would have been just as appropriate. Although the infamous *Titanic* was 200 feet longer, the *Great Eastern* was designed to carry 800 more passengers, giving her a maximum capacity of 4,000—or up to 10,000 as a troop ship. The audaciousness of the vessel was not approached until 1907, when White Star and the shipbuilder Harland and Wolff drafted plans for the *Olympic, Titanic,* and *Britannic.* It is not certain if those involved in this project studied the history of the *Great Eastern* when so engaged. If not they should have. Lessons, both positive and negative, could have been gleaned.

Isambord Kingdom Brunel was the *Great Eastern*'s creator, a renowned civil engineer whose bridges and railways crisscrossed Britain. His previous venture in ship design had yielded the successful *Great Western.* Brunel conceived the *Great Eastern* as a combination paddle-wheel and screw-driven vessel with a 15 knot cruising speed. She also carried the obligatory sail rigging: six masts, five of which were of sheet iron and doubled as funnels. Add to this a complement of five large funnels, or one more than the *Titanic,* and the ship cut an awesome figure at the time and by the standards of any subsequent era.

As would be the case with the *Titanic,* the builders of the *Great Eastern* declared her to be "practically unsinkable." She had a double hull from waterline to keel—the *Titanic* only had a double bottom—with 2 feet 6 inches between the platings. Had the hull of the *Titanic* been built along such lines she might have survived the gash the iceberg cut just below her waterline. (After the *Titanic*'s demise the *Olympic* was recalled from service and refitted with a similar double skin.) Like the *Titanic,* the *Great Eastern* had her structure severely tested. In 1862, en route from Liverpool to New York, the ship struck a submerged rock off the coast of Long Island, and the outer hull was breeched. Although she did not founder, the cost of repairs bankrupted the owners, and in 1864 they consigned the ship to the auction block.

The *Great Eastern* was not simply ahead of her time, or even at the leading edge, as was the *Titanic,* but completely outside it. Conceived in 1851 as the "Floating City" or "Crystal Palace of the Sea" (After the famous Crystal Palace Exposition in London the same year), it was hoped she would turn large profits on the eastward run to Australia and points between. Her prodigious fuel capacity seemed to favor such long voyages, but her equally prodigious appetite for fuel consumption made operating her expensive. At every step of her history she was beset with problems: the launch took almost three months and resulted in several deaths, a rash of injuries, and the destruction of expensive equipment; the maiden voyage attracted only 55 paying customers; and in her final days of service, during the 1870s laying submarine telegraph cables, she lacked the maneuverability to even make this a permanent métier. The list goes on, and when tallied yields one of the nineteenth century's most notorious white elephants.

Like the *Titanic* and *Olympic*, the *Great Eastern* was appointed with lavish staterooms, lounges, and dining areas. These features, along with the luxurious upholstery and teak and walnut decor, were unlike anything yet seen on a ship and were harbingers of what the Gilded Age would eventually bring to maritime travel. In that sense she was ahead of her time. Another link with the later White Star liners was the ship's bulkiness and slow response to the helm. Several near misses at sea and a few wrecked wharves were the result. In the case of the White Star's dream machines, the deficiencies led to the *Olympic*'s collision with the *Hawke* in 1911—both ships made it back to port for repairs—and the *Titanic* pulling the liner *New York* loose from her moorings as the former was leaving Southampton, resulting from an ominous near miss. When it came to general seaworthiness, however, the *Great Eastern* was clearly inferior to her giant successors. Storms were not merely an inconvenience; they tended to dislodge fixtures, flood state rooms, and make life miserable for many on board.

Ironically, the *Great Eastern*'s career ended as it began, dockside, with paid sightseeing excursions. In 1886, the ship that was inspired by the London Exposition of 1851 became part of the Liverpool Exposition and attracted half a million paying customers. A year later she was sold for scrap and perhaps demonstrated a modicum of revenge on her detractors when she proved to be extraordinarily difficult to break up.

Despite the failure of the *Great Eastern* to be a viable leap forward in size, comfort, and speed, the trend in this direction proceeded, albeit in a less quantum fashion. Success in the competitive shipping business often meant knowing how far previous standards could be exceeded while still maintaining the public's confidence. Thomas Henry Ismay understood this formula when he entered the shipping business in 1867. Two years later, with financial backing from Gustavus Schwabe, a Hamburg investor, he organized the Oceanic Steam Navigation Company and purchased a small line known as White Star.

White Star's flagship, the *Royal Standard*, had regularly transported immigrants and cargo to Australia. Unfortunately the company's record carried one noteworthy blemish that can be seen as an eerie harbinger of what would happen in April 1912. In April of 1863, sailing east across the South Pacific on the homeward journey, the *Royal Standard* struck an iceberg. The damage was severe, but unlike the Collins liner *Pacific* the ship survived. Several anxious weeks were spent completing the crossing before she made port in Rio de Janeiro for repairs.

Schwabe convinced Ismay that greater economic possibilities lay in the North American run. The United States and Canada were teeming with raw materials such as wheat, timber, minerals, cotton, and tobacco. Travel in the other direction seemed assured, with the dynamism of the New World providing an ongoing lure for a new generation of Europeans contemplating emigration. Ismay's vision was to commission ships large enough to handle this traffic comfortably and then endow them with the type of luxury appointments that would also attract an elite cadre of high-paying first-class passengers.

Under the management of Ismay, along with his partner William Imrie, the company began its new steamer service in 1871. Their flagship was the just-completed *Oceanic*. She was 420 feet in length, weighed 38,000 tones, and had the capacity to make the crossing in just under 10 days. The *Oceanic* was slightly larger than the Cunard liners and almost as fast. Where she had a decided edge was in the domain of luxury appointments. Her large grand saloon and great parlor had spectacular high ceilings, were located amidships rather than aft (at the rear), and ran the entire width of the ship. This reduced engine vibration and roll. There were also fireplaces with marble mantles and plush staterooms equipped with water taps and oil lamps. Such ostentation was not without risk since comparisons with the *Great Eastern* would be inevitable. Although the *Oceanic* had a passenger capacity of 1,200, only 64 were present on the maiden voyage; mechanical problems did not make them happy customers. Within a month the problem was rectified, and the public gradually came to accept the new ship, and White Star, as a viable alternative to Cunard.

With the success of the *Oceanic*, Ismay and Imrie were not about to throw away the mold that created her. It was used to generate siblings that were similar, such as the *Atlantic*, *Baltic*, and *Republic*, and then enlarged to accommodate the *Adriatic* and *Celtic*. The company's early success, however, was punctuated by one massive failure: the loss of the *Atlantic*.

She was wrecked on the rocks off Nova Scotia in April 1873. There were 942 on board, of whom 481 perished, making it the nineteenth century's worst ocean disaster. Omniscient hindsight invites us to see this tragedy as a harbinger of what would happen during the same month 39 years later. The parallels are uncanny. Like the *Titanic*, the *Atlantic*'s misfortune occurred on a clear, calm night. In both scenarios the presence of danger—rocks in 1873, ice in 1912—was well known. Other similarities include the captain not being at the helm and both ships traveling at almost full speed. The incident became a media cause célèbre. Speculation was rife that the *Atlantic* was low on coal and trying to take a dangerous shortcut. The captain behaved heroically by helping the passengers until he became exhausted and was pulled from the sea into a lifeboat. Such valor led to "only" a two-year suspension, after which he was back at the helm for White Star.

We can only wonder how thoroughly the lesson of the *Atlantic* was imparted from Thomas Ismay to his son Bruce, who took over management of the line in 1899 and went on to become the *Titanic*'s most notorious survivor. Although he was, in his own words, "just a passenger," he nevertheless consulted regularly with the captain whenever navigational decisions were at issue.

A major factor in White Star's success was its liaison with the Harland and Wolff shipyards of Belfast. The Belfast shipbuilding industry had started in 1792 with the construction of the 300-ton *Hibernia*. In 1849 facilities were expanded to accommodate the construction of iron ships. In 1854 Edward James Harland arrived on the scene to become manager of a small local shipyard; it signaled a new beginning. Sailing ships, freighters, naval vessels, and tankers would continue to be built, but now the Belfast repertoire would include liners, which would bring the shipyard more notoriety than all other types of vessel. In 1858, Harland took complete control of the yard, along with his assistant, Gustav Wolff, who would become a full partner in 1861.

In 1863, William James Pirrie, a Canadian of Scottish-Irish parentage, joined Harland and Wolff as an apprentice draftsman at age 15. By 1874 he had become a full partner, and following the death of Harland in 1895, Pirrie became managing director. It was Pirrie who, in collaboration with Bruce Ismay and White Star, would plan the *Olympic*-class liners. Illness prevented him from making the *Titanic* voyage, which was all to the good: he would have perished or been chastised for having survived a disaster that partly resulted from assumed shortcomings in the design of his ship. Pirrie nonetheless weathered the aftermath and continued to build ships. He became Lord Pirrie in 1909 and died of pneumonia in 1924, appropriately enough at sea.

When Harland and Wolff built the *Oceanic* for White Star in 1871, it marked the beginning of a long and mutually beneficial collaboration. They remained the shipping line's sole builder throughout White Star's history until the merger with Cunard in 1934. The marriage was not without its ulterior logic. Gustav Wolff was the nephew of Gustavus Schwabe, who had provided the primary capital for Thomas Ismay to purchase and revamp White Star. The fortunes of the two companies were also drawn together by the trust White Star had in Harland and Wolff's contractual policy. Instead of charging a fixed price for the building of a ship—which, given the fluctuations in the cost of material and labor, would entail a risk on their part—the arrangement was "cost plus." In other words, the shipping company paid for the building of the vessel, ceding complete jurisdiction in that area to Harland and Wolff, and then added a four percent commission to the total.

The quality of the Harland and Wolff ships helped make White Star competitive with Cunard. Cunarders were normally built in Glasgow, which had less costly access than Belfast to coal, timber, and steel, which by the turn of the century had displaced iron as the primary medium for ship construction, being stronger and 15 percent lighter. Belfast had lower rents and labor costs. It was a balanced competition and a near monopoly for the two giants until, in 1899, Germany decided to enter the game as a major player.

On a visit to England that year, Kaiser Wilhelm II, grandson of Queen Victoria, was so impressed by the White Star's *Teutonic*—certainly the name must have appealed to him—that he decided to commit substantial resources to bolstering his nation's mercantile fleet. Previously, many German vessels had been built at British shipyards, including Harland and Wolff. During the 1890s the Germans instead imported British engineers and craftsmen, who were lured by high salaries and became instrumental in establishing a major shipbuilding industry in Germany. The results of this enterprise were not long in coming.

In 1897 North German Lloyd launched the 650-foot *Kaiser Wilhelm der Grosse*. Capable of carrying 2,300 passengers at 21 knots, she soon snatched from Cunard the coveted Blue Riband for the fastest Atlantic crossing. British observers were also further shocked when in 1900 she became the first transatlantic liner to be equipped with wireless, especially since early breakthroughs applying this medium to maritime communication had been made by Marconi, working in England.

Before Cunard had a chance to recapture the Blue Riband, another German vessel, HAPAG's *Deutschland*, laid claim to it in 1900. Back it went to North German Lloyd in 1903 via the *Kaiser Wilhelm II*. Cunard bided its time until 1907 and then responded with the *Mauretania* and *Lusitania*. The former streaked across in 4 days, 10 hours, and 41 minutes and enabled Cunard to rule the realm of speed for the next 22 years.

In 1929 North German Lloyd, having made a remarkable recovery from the devastation of World War I, recaptured the prize with the *Bremen*. The *Mauretania*, like an aging fighter with a few good moves still left, tried for the title one last time. She gave it her all, bettered her previous best, but still came up four hours short. This glorious competition of the great liners ultimately resulted in the current record set in 1952 by the SS *United States*, of 3 days, 10 hours, and 40 minutes, which was done at an average speed of 35 knots. Her true top speed, a closely guarded secret during her years of service, was close to 40 knots.

Although speed obsessed the German ship industry at the turn of the century, Germany also wanted to make its vessels luxurious. Just as North German Lloyd and Cunard were competitors with respect to record setting, so were HAPAG and White Star in the realm of elegant appointments. HAPAG's director, Albert Ballin, commissioned architect Charles Mewès to design interiors for the *Amerika*, slated to go into service in 1903. Mewès brought to this project his extensive experience working with hotel magnate César Ritz. He came up with a decor that was both refined and understated; it included a stylish à la carte restaurant operated by Ritz personnel, which garnered rave reviews.

Despite the high profile the transatlantic ship industry enjoyed at this time, it was becoming increasingly vulnerable economically. The competition from various companies, which a decade earlier had seemed to benefit all players, now threatened any of them showing signs of weakness. The government-assisted German industry had Cunard and White Star looking over their shoulders when they were not looking sideways at each other. The race would still have its winner, or even winners, but also-rans could accrue financial losses and wind up insolvent.

There rivalries kept passenger fares low and threatened profit margins. In addition, the emigrant trade, which had partly inspired the large ships, was in a slack period. The lavish vessels had to be filled with all classes of passengers for the industry to remain healthy. They also had to be increasingly lavish to continue attracting the elite clientele we so often think of when we conjure up images of La Belle Epoque. But it was not, of course, "belle" for everyone. The unfettered accumulation of fabulous entrepreneurial fortunes was accompanied by considerable poverty, low-paying jobs, and economic fluctuations leading to high unemployment—a situation not unfamiliar to us a century later.

One way of stabilizing the situation, tempering the intense competition, and further developing the industry's public profile, was regulation. Not along government lines—this period was, after all, still dominated by the theory and practice of classical capitalism—but by drawing as many rivals as possible into a conglomerate. It was an intricate and potentially risk-laden project but one that inspired American financier John Pierpont Morgan. In 1902 he had expanded one of his more modest holdings, the International Navigation Company of Philadelphia, into International Mercantile Marine (IMM), a trust devoted to acquiring as many shipping lines as possible. Morgan played monopoly in a way that made the concept represented in the later board game seem tame—indeed, the game itself was inspired by his machinations and it is Morgan's likeness we see in the logo of the mustachioed character wearing a top hat and holding a bag of money.

Those in control of the British government, always resentful of any incursion into their realm of maritime dominance, found Morgan anathema for two reasons. First, he was symptomatic of the transference of industrial wealth from Europe to the United States that had started following the Civil War—by the turn of the century the United States was emerging as the world's leading industrial power. Second, as an individual, Morgan was disdained for his acquisitive megalomania. In the dominant ideology of late Victorian and Edwardian Britain, power and privilege were supposed to be not only hereditary but also *responsible*. This is not to suggest that self-made wealth and nonaristocratic entrepreneurs were uncommon; they existed in the very industry under discussion. But what was rare, prior to Thatcherism three-quarters of a century later, was the notion that one individual, Morgan for example, could or should control a vast empire composed of diverse and sometimes unrelated companies. Many Americans at the time labeled him an audacious predator. The British were hard pressed to find a relevant term in their vocabulary. Nevertheless, a major portion of their shipping business would become willing prey.

Morgan evidenced acquisitive inertia when he formed IMM. A year earlier he had celebrated the turn of the century by buying out Andrew

Carnegie to form the World's first billion-dollar holding company, U.S. Steel. Steel was crucial to the railroad industry, which comprised another Morgan empire; to have easy access to it made entry into the realm of shipping business a logical next step.

In quick succession IMM grabbed the Red Star, Leyland, and Dominion lines; then Morgan cast for bigger fish—While Star and Cunard. The former proved to be the more vulnerable, largely because of the intercession of William Pirrie of Harland and Wolff. Pirrie was a member of the British board of IMM and had previously assisted Morgan in several acquisitions. The arrangement assured further contracts for Pirrie's firm. White Star was his biggest customer, and its future seemed more secure inside than outside the combine. Using this argument, he persuaded a reluctant Bruce Ismay to sell. Ismay retained his chairmanship and within a year was persuaded by Morgan to assume the presidency of IMM. He accepted, with reservations, perhaps feeling the taint of tokenism. Nevertheless his background and organizational skill helped save the trust from collapse when bouts of panic selling by stockholders plagued its early years. Not until 1927 would White Star be returned to British ownership.

To aid the negotiations between IMM and the British companies it sought to acquire, Morgan made a magnanimous but calculated gesture. Even though U.S. owned, their ships could be co-opted by the British navy in case of war. From our vantage point in history this can seem an unenviable commitment in the event of, say, a possible war between Britain and a continental rival—Germany, for instance—in which the United States might wish to remain neutral. The concession might have been a peace offering aimed at mending fences between Britain and the United States, which had been notably disturbed several years earlier when, in 1895, the Americans had claimed that Britain, in her Guyana colony, was overextending that nation's frontier into Venezuela and therefore violating the Monroe Doctrine.

It has been said of Genghis Khan that the extent of his conquests was due partly to not knowing when to stop. Morgan is an equally apt candidate for this observation. With White Star in one hand and reaching for Cunard with the other, he eyed the German shipping industry. Securing Albert Ballin's help, IMM acquired 51 percent of HAPAG and then worked out a similar arrangement with North German Lloyd. The terms allowed the German companies to maintain considerable autonomy—more than was ceded to White Star. The Kaiser saw—or at least rationalized—the deal as a way of ensuring that British shipping would never dominate German.

The one prize that eluded Morgan was Cunard. He made generous overtures. He then tried force, by cutting fares on the IMM routes over which he had effective control. Cunard held fast and continued the daunting task of flying the flag of British shipping in the face of American corporate expansionism. The head of the line, Lord Inverclyde, handled the situation deftly. He used each upping of the ante by Morgan as leverage to convince the government to step in. The government argued instead for the formation of a British combine to counter the American, but Inverclyde knew that this would cost Cunard significant autonomy. The press was in his corner; Morganaphobia had fueled national pride, and Cunard was seen as a sterling example of Britain's maritime accomplishment. A loan from the British government to bolster Cunard's fleet and make it competitive with IMM was finally secured: £2.2 million at 2-3/4 percent. There was one chauvinistic string attached: no foreigners could serve as directors, masters, officers, or engineers on Cunard ships.

The money was well spent, helping to bringing into service in 1907 the *Lusitania* and *Mauritania*. The new Cunarders were not only the fastest liners yet built but also the largest, exceeding White Star's biggest vessels in gross tonnage by 50 percent. Their arrival sent shock waves through IMM. For Pirrie and Ismay it meant going back to the drawing board, or at first, to be more precise, the drawing room.

On a pleasant summer evening in 1907—the exact date appears to have gone unrecorded—the two men and their wives enjoyed a soirée at Pirrie's elegant Belgravia home. The occasion produced pleasant conversation, dinner, and finally serious conversation and a plan. Cunard's lead could not go unchallenged. To try building anything faster than her two superliners would be folly on two counts. First, the fuel cost necessary to operate such a vessel would be exorbitant. Each knot of extra speed over about 21 knots requires a disproportionate increase in the amount of coal consumed; at 25 knots the Cunarders were, in contemporary parlance, gas guzzlers. The second reason to forgo a sprinter's mentality was that such ships were prone to annoying vibration, which a few knots less speed greatly reduced.

By evening's end a plan emerged that favored the building of three liners designed to be larger and more comfortable than the Cunarders. The decision was an extension of the legacy that Thomas Ismay and William Imrie had started in 1871. The increase in size of the liners, although substantial, was of the same magnitude by which their previous liners had just been surpassed by Cunard, but, at 45,000 tons and a length of almost 900 feet, they would be pushing what was at the time regarded as the theoretical size limit for conventional liners. Docks, especially in New York, would have to be modified to accommodate them, but more immediately, so would construction facilities at Harland and Wolff.

The plan was bold, but all parties involved had the kind of experience that evokes confidence. It certainly inspired J. P. Morgan. Grandiosity was his forte, and perhaps still miffed by his failure to acquire Cunard, he seized this opportunity to exert competitive superiority by quickly approving the plan.

In December 1908 construction began on the *Olympic*, and in March 1909, in the adjoining slip, the *Titanic* followed suit. The third member of this triumvirate was to have been called the *Gigantic*, but after the loss of the *Titanic* the name was changed to the *Britannic*. White Star denied that it had ever conceived the original name, but a promotional flyer shows otherwise. Like the *Titanic*, the *Britannic* had a very short life. In 1915 she went into service during the war, and while on duty as a hospital ship less than a year later either hit a mine or was torpedoed. Despite sinking in less than an hour with 1,100 on board, only 30 lives were lost—the *Titanic*'s lifeboat lesson had been learned.

Progress in the construction of the *Olympic* and *Titanic*, and speculation regarding how closely the reality would match the promise, was avidly discussed in trade and technical journals, with the press occasionally weighing in. On October 20, 1910, without fanfare or formal christening (White Star's disinterest in this ritual would give the superstitious something to ponder after the sinking of the *Titanic*), the *Olympic* was launched and towed to another venue to be fitted for service. Then, on May 31, 1911, with a little more pomp, which included the presence of Morgan and numerous other VIPs, the *Titanic* slipped majestically into the harbor and prepared to be fitted. That day also saw the *Olympic* handed over to White Star; and with Ismay, Morgan, and the rest on board, she steamed to Liverpool.

Both ships offered enormous interior space within an overall design that suffered only slightly in comparison with their sleeker and faster rivals. Largely forgotten today by the public at large, the *Olympic* was a vessel that served long and dutifully. She did almost everything her wayward sister was reputed to be capable of doing and has become the darling of maritime historians—perhaps the leading candidate for the title of "greatest liner ever." Her passenger capacity was 2,400, and on her maiden voyage she took a respectable 50 percent of that number to New York. The highly touted facilities functioned well. Passengers dined heartily; they could then burn off the calories in a gym endowed with the latest high-tech equipment, go for a swim in the pool, or have a Turkish bath. The less energetic could take an elevator to the spectator's gallery of the squash courts and watch others work up a sweat.

During World War I, the *Olympic* made a successful transition from luxury liner to troop carrier. In this service she survived several submarine attacks. In one instance she turned around and rammed the offending U-boat, which promptly sank. This bit of derring-do earned her the sobriquet "Old Reliable." In 1919 she became the first large liner converted from coal to diesel. In 1934 she was involved in another collision, this one less heroic. She accidently rammed and sunk the Nantucket lightship, resulting in the loss of all seven crewmembers and a lawsuit against White Star. Add to this the *Hawke* incident of 1911, and her collision total stands at three. Her final violent confrontation would be at the hands of the wrecker in 1935. With the *Queen Mary* on the way, the newly merged Cunard White Star Line decided to cull its fleet. Ironically, the *Olympic*'s great rival, the *Mauretania*, was also on this death list. As befitted her legendary speed, she went to the block first.

The *Titanic* was designed to be an ultradeluxe version of the *Olympic*. She started with the same basic plan: spacious dining areas and lounges, pool, gymnasium, and a labyrinthine interior that caused even crew members to occasionally lose their way. Ismay's experience on the *Olympic*, however, led him to conjure several modifications: passenger capacity was increased to slightly over 3,000 by converting excess deck space into cabins; exquisite carpets and hardwood furniture were added to the grand saloon and several smaller venues; glass paneling was installed on the first-class promenade deck; and two opulent first-class suites were constructed, one for J. P. Morgan (who, although present at the launch, was prevented by illness from making the maiden voyage). This list was augmented with dozens of other changes, the two most notable (in light of postdiscovery interest in the ship and the interest in her decor prompted by James Cameron's film) were the lavish grand staircase of polished oak, which was illuminated by a glass dome framed in wrought iron, and the café Parisien and adjoining boulevard.

At 46,000 tons, the *Titanic*'s extra frills made her 1,000 tons heavier than her elder sister. In terms of power the two ships were virtually identical, transferring 50,000 horsepower to a conventional two-screw setup with a third turbine-driven shaft in the center. They also shared the same inadequate complement of 20 lifeboats, which had only between 1,100 and 1,200 places. This was not an oversight. It complied with, even exceeded, the British Board of Trade regulations that based the number of lifeboats a ship carried on her tonnage. Discussion had been given to increasing the number of boats, but Ismay vetoed the idea in order to permit more recreational space on the decks in question. The general feeling on the part of those concerned with the building of the ship was that she was as close to unsinkable as any vessel could be. This sentiment, when transmogrified into folkloric legend, became "the ship that God himself cannot sink."

The question of the ship's unsinkability, a minor issue prior to the voyage, has now become a central theme in almost any discussion of the disaster. White Star has always denied making the claim, attributing it to the media. Later evidence indicates otherwise. A White Star flyer promoting the *Olympic* and *Titanic* was brought to light by Geoff Robinson and Don Lynch in the February–April 1993 issue of the *Titanic Commutator*. It notes that "as far as possible to do so, these two wonderful vessels are designed to be unsinkable." Ismay himself had the courage to admit to the British Board of Trade inquiry that prior to the sinking he did believe the ship to be "practically unsinkable . . . a lifeboat unto herself."

This confidence was no doubt a result of the ship's design. She was divided into 16 watertight compartments that could be sealed with electrically operated sliding doors. The problem was that these compartments were, in effect, only semiwatertight. Although extending above the waterline, these transverse bulkheads did not reach to the top deck. When more than two became flooded at the bow after the collision, the weight pulled the ship down headfirst, causing water to spill over to the next compartment, and the next, and so on.

Postsinking hindsight has lead to the speculation that, given the ship's design, a better course of action might have been to ram the iceberg head-on instead of reversing the engines and turning the helm. The *Arizona* in 1879, and several other vessels prior to the *Titanic*, had survived encounters with ice by doing just this, although it was not a conscious strategy. Another, more recent bit of speculation emerged from a 1998 article in the *JOM* (formerly *Journal of Metals*), which, after a highly detailed analysis of a recovered plate, made a case that the steel used in the construction of the *Titanic* was vulnerable at low temperatures. This led to some media speculation that it was substandard. However, the article indicated that such steel, although not viable today, was the best available at the time; indeed, workers at

Harland and Wolff referred to it as of "battleship quality." Techno-theorists can now also ponder the rivets, which, to allow for easy heating, might not have been the strongest available, although none of this would seem to have mattered to the iceberg, which outweighed the ship by an enormous factor.

Omniscient hindsight also claims that it was a mistake to close the electrically operated collision doors on the watertight bulkheads. This allowed water to accumulate too rapidly in the bow, thereby exacerbating flooding in the rest of the ship when the bow started to go under. By letting the ship flood evenly it might have been possible to gain another hour or two. Add to this bit of "what-ifery" the decision at the helm that was made—to reverse engines—versus the one that "should" have been, to simply steer at speed. Most recently (2010), a variety of media sources have reported comments by Louise Patten, granddaughter of the ship's second officer, Charles Lightholler, who was the most senior officer to survive the tragedy. She claims that the helm was turned the wrong way when the iceberg was spotted; the damage was then compounded when the ship resumed course after the impact.

All this second-guessing converges on First Officer Murdoch, who was in charge of the bridge that night and for whom we should have considerable sympathy. If only he had been given world enough and time. The agonizingly brief interval—probably less than a minute—between when lookout Frederick Fleet sighted the iceberg and relayed the information to Murdoch, and when the collision occurred, will likely yield another 100 years of speculation.

PART ONE

Wireless World

It seemed as if the stars above saw the ship in distress and had awakened to flash messages across the black dome of the sky to each other.

—Lawrence Beesley, *Titanic* survivor

CHAPTER 1

Enter Marconi

On a brisk January morning in 1986, the *Challenger* lifted skyward from Cape Canaveral while millions watched on live television. Within moments curiosity and anxiety turned to confusion and shocked fascination. The ambitiously conceived spacebound vehicle exploded like a Roman candle. It filled our screens with an image that might have been dazzling were it not for the horrifying implications. The *Challenger* was designed as a technological womb for a handful of intrepid explorers whom the media had presented as intriguing and contrasting personalities. It became a blazing tomb that interred itself in the North Atlantic, 200 miles from where the *Titanic* had come to rest 74 years earlier.

Watching the *Challenger* self-destruct on live television imparted an involvement with the event to a mass audience. This kind of experience is sometimes referred to by media scholars as "co-presence" or "simultaneity"—things distant in space are perceived at the same moment in time regardless of the location of the observer. Early examples familiar to North Americans date from the Golden Age of radio. They include the crash of the *Hindenberg* (1937)—although many accounts cite this broadcast as a live transmission, it aired on 7 May, a day after the hydrogen-filled dirigible was consumed in flames, but it still gave listeners a sense of being there. A year later Orson Welles' infamous *War of the Worlds* broadcast, done as a live late-breaking news report, panicked thousands who believed that a Martian invasion was actually taking place. Shortly thereafter, real attacks were broadcast from London by Edward R. Murrow, whose resonant voice calmly described the chaos with the sound of bombs bursting in the background. Even before these moments of co-presence, the phenomenon was experienced in England when in 1936 a young reported named Richard Dimbleby was sent to cover the Crystal Palace fire. He ducked into a phone booth within earshot of the action and went live to air on the BBC.

The transmission of all these events was anticipated, although on a smaller scale, by the circumstances that surrounded the *Titanic* during the early morning hours of 15 April 1912. As would be the case with the *Challenger*, individuals thousands of miles away knew something was amiss even before the drama played out to its conclusion. Wireless communication made this possible.

Like the telegraph and telephone, wireless was a medium for rapid point-to-point communication. Morse code rather than voice was the dominant format for messages prior to the 1920s. Wireless communication did not constitute broadcasting, as we now understand the term, but it was far less discrete than using the telegraph or telephone. A message radiated in all directions—hence the term *radio-telegraphy*, and then simply *radio* after 1912. Anyone with an adequate receiver could listen in.

With the *Titanic*'s distress call and its subsequent ship-to-ship-to shore relays, the listening network included marine, commercial, and military operators as well as a growing legion of amateurs. It was the largest "audience" ever to have, up to that time, received a series of related transmissions. As a result, wireless communication attained a visibility and significance that had only been hinted at on the several previous occasions where its use for rescue at sea had made headlines. Never before had so many lives been at stake; never before had the medium performed so nobly; and never before had it fallen so short of its true potential. In the aftermath of the disaster, changes in wireless policy were demanded by the press and at both formal inquiries.

And, just as wireless became a major player in the *Titanic*'s bizarre theater of tragedy, so too did the event become a pivotal moment in the history of the new medium. In the midst of it all, the name Guglielmo Marconi (1874–1937) achieved the proverbial household status, both for his invention of wireless and his involvement in the events of April 1912. This involvement was so intimate that he almost succumbed to the disaster that would help valorize his name.

On 10 April 1912, Marconi's wife Beatrice and three-year-old daughter Degna—who recounts the incident in a biography of her father—longingly watched the *Titanic* steam past their country cottage near Southampton. The entire family had been invited by the White

Star Line to be special guests on this maiden voyage. Circumstances intervened. Marconi had left three days earlier on the *Lusitania*, passing on the *Titanic* invitation since he was in a hurry to get to New York and had a pile of business correspondences to attend to. The *Lusitania* had an excellent stenographer, and this also factored into his decision. Beatrice and family were expected to follow on the *Titanic*, but when baby Giulio came down with a fever, they were forced to delay their travel plans. Marconi's return to England was also supposed to be aboard the *Titanic*. The tragedy intervened, rearranging his schedule and, as it would turn out, the fortunes of his company as well.

Thus unfolds a chapter in a story that begins in 1894 in Beillese, Italy, with the youthful Marconi engaged in a series of electrical experiments. His goal: to send Morse code without the use of wires, in others words, through the airwaves. The advantages of this kind of telegraphy? It would be a means of communication whereby messages could travel at the speed of light to and from places where it was not feasible to run wires, such as ship-to-ship and ship-to-shore. A warm, supportive mother, the Scottish-Irish Annie Jameson, overrode the influence of a dour, skeptical father. She took the precocious Marconi to England, where more interest and funding could sustain his work.

In 1896 Marconi filed a patent for his wireless. Throughout his life he would continue to upgrade his invention, but his attention now turned to its practical application and commercial potential. He envisioned a global communications empire based on his wireless. This dream would be almost fully realized following the sinking of the *Titanic*. It would also be vulnerable to regulatory decisions aimed at limiting the extensive control that one company should have over such a strategic technological resource.

In July 1897, Marconi and a small coterie of supporters set up the Wireless Telegraph and Signal Company, Ltd. Up to that point he had been working under the auspices of the British Postal Service, which had offered continued support, but the entrepreneurial freedom of going the private commercial route seemed worth the risks. The immediate goals of the new company were twofold: to set up a viable network of marine communications and then, after further development of the apparatus, to establish trans-Atlantic communication of sufficient reliability that regular service would follow. Today, when we think of using the airwaves, and more precisely the electromagnetic spectrum, for communication, we usually think of broadcasting—the aural and video dissemination of information and entertainment to a mass audience. It is sometimes difficult to imagine that the early history of this form of telecommunications was tied to point-to-point exchanges between ships and shore stations using Morse code. A brief look at the world of transportation and communication around and shortly after the turn of the twentieth century reveals why this was so.

The transoceanic ship industry was big business. It moved an ever increasing volume of goods and people around the world. North Atlantic routes were particularly busy. The immigrant trade was a lucrative aspect of this enterprise, and even the *Titanic*, despite her splendor and the rich and famous passengers she attracted, was expected to earn most to her income this way. The ships involved were relatively fast. A top liner could span the Atlantic in about six days, or about the same amount of time it took to cross the North American continent by train. The major problem with these ocean voyages was the complete isolation that enveloped a ship when she was out of sight of land or other ships. Visual communication was limited to about 100 yards using semaphore flags, and a few miles at best when using Morse lamp at night; sometimes carrier pigeons were employed, but the practice never became widespread.

Compare this situation with overland travel by road or rail, where the telegraph and telephone provided an accompanying information network and lifeline. When a train was late the reasons could be signaled down the line, often in a matter of minutes. When an ocean liner was late, patience was strained and anxiety resulted. She could be off course, perhaps experiencing bad weather. Mechanical difficulties might be the culprit, or it could be more serious. The ship might be foundering because of a collision or fire. But where? Marconi's wireless promised deliverance from this centuries-old dilemma. Ships could now be monitored like trains, not only for safety and navigation but also to prepare ports for their arrival and to relay relevant news.

Before Marconi could sell his service to commercial and government interests, however, he had to sell them first on the idea and its feasibility. Not all great inventors were adept at dealing with those they wished to convince, but Marconi had the "right stuff" when it came to this kind of interpersonal communication. He spoke fluent English and was neither the wild-eyed, unkempt stereotype of an inventor nor its antithesis, the dull abstract theorist. His public persona, especially when dealing with the press, was that of a humble and creative young man who, although exceedingly well dressed, was always modest and cordial—the embodiment of understated brilliance. The many positive depictions of him in newspapers and magazines converged in the aftermath of the *Titanic* disaster. As a result his image easily weathered the potentially scandalous and well-founded accusation that his corporate machinations with the *New York Times*—to guarantee the paper an exclusive interview with the *Titanic*'s surviving wireless operator—were not in the public interest.

Behind the scenes Marconi was somewhat more aloof and obsessive. He was both the wizard and the warlord of wireless—a wizard not in the sense of pure inventive genius but because of his ability to improve on and make practical the work of numerous predecessors. The warlord aspect of his character derived from an ambition to see the Marconi version of wireless become the world's standard and from the accompanying strategies he developed to protect his lead and keep at bay competing organizations who wanted a piece of the pie. Consistent with Marconi's more tempered public image was his opposition, in 1900, to his company's name change. His sole dissenting vote was overridden, and the Wireless Telegraph and Signal Company became the Marconi Wireless Telegraph Company, Ltd.

Marconi's campaign to make wireless an indispensable aspect of maritime communication began in earnest in 1898. The Italian navy adopted his system, thus rewarding a native son whose early experiments were done in that country, although he had been denied funding by its government. More relevant to potential British investors, however, was Marconi's coverage of the Kingston Regatta for the *Dublin Daily Express*. He followed the races in a motor launch and transmitted late-breaking developments. The press was impressed. That summer he was given the opportunity to install his system on the royal yacht *Osborne*, where the Prince of Wales (later Edward VII) was recuperating from a twisted knee The shore unit was set up at Ladywood Cottage on the grounds of Osborne House. The yacht was two miles out and blocked from view by intervening hills. The experiment succeeded, and Queen Victoria was able to monitor the progress of her son's recovery. On 4 August, the *Osborne* sent the first medical bulletin in wireless history.

Events moved with increasing rapidity in 1899. In January, after a month-long trial, regular wireless service was adopted by the East Goodwin lighthouse and lightship. When the *Elbe* ran aground in March, the new medium saved lives and cargo. The admiralty expressed interest and began testing the system for possible adoption by the British Navy. By this time, both sides of the Atlantic were aware of Marconi's efforts, a situation facilitated by his deft rapport with the press. Several Americans, among them the editors of the *New York Herald* and the *Evening Telegram*, began to suspect that Marconi might someday enter the hallowed pantheon of inventive renown that included the likes of Morse, Bell, and Edison. They made him an offer he could not refuse: $5,000 to cover the America's Cup sailing races for them in October. What made Marconi acquiesce was not the money but the potential publicity.

The significance of the America's Cup as a test of wireless cannot be underestimated. The competition, pitting the American ship *Columbia* (the eventual winner), against the British representative, *Shamrock*, was both a sporting and cultural event. It made headlines for half the month, not only in the *Herald* and *Telegram* but also in the *New York Times*. Other notable ongoing stories, such as the Boer War and Dewey's visit to New York, were often consigned to secondary status.

The logistics of coverage entailed that three ships be equipped with wireless. At first the *Ponce*, and later the *Grande Duchesse*, followed the races and relayed coverage to the *MacKay Bennett* (in 1912 she would be involved in a search for bodies following the *Titanic*'s demise), which was anchored offshore and linked by cable to the news networks of a now "wired" world. Marconi's enterprise was noted. Wireless worked. After the races he transferred the sets that were used to the Navy for further testing and possible adoption, then set up the Marconi Wireless Telegraph Company of America—in this context, unlike in Britain, he did not question the wisdom of trading on his name.

In 1900, the Marconi expanding parent company spawned another subsidiary, the Marconi International Marine Communications Company, and signed its first commercial contract, to put wireless aboard the German steamship *Kaiser Wilhelm de Grosse* and, with the permission of the German governments, to also equip a lighthouse and lightship. Germany at this time was Britain's chief rival for seagoing supremacy. She also had a fledgling wireless company, Telefunken, which used the Marconi-inspired Slaby-Arco system. The decision to go with the Marconi system in this instance was based on commercial rather than national considerations. On one hand, Marconi Marine had an already established network of shore stations; on the other, it limited the effectiveness of its smaller rivals by invoking the controversial "no-intercommunications" policy.

"No intercommunications" meant that Marconi Marine forbade its operators to relay or respond to the messages of other companies, *save in an emergency*—and, as we shall see, this policy would come under severe scrutiny following the *Titanic*'s sinking. The public rationale was that rival companies, such as Telefunken, should not be allowed to make use of the Marconi network of shore stations since they did not contribute to their maintenance. In 1902, "no intercommunications" created an international incident when Prince Henry, brother of the Kaiser, while returning from the United States aboard the *Deutschland*, a Telefunken ship, could not get his diplomatic communiqués forwarded. This incident, according to historian Susan Douglas, was a major factor in the convening of the first international conference on wireless in Berlin a year later.

By 1900, the Royal Navy and Cunard had subscribed to the Marconi service. In 1901 Lloyd's of London came on board—pun intended, since marine insurance was a major part of their business. Lloyd's advocated that ships holding policies with them adopt the Marconi wireless, which would link them to a worldwide network of Lloyd's offices being conjoined this way.

Not only did large companies, like the White Star Line, subscribe to this service, but also those of more modest means who felt it was a worthwhile and affordable option. The reason is one familiar to many of us: purchase of the (expensive) apparatus was not necessary. Marconi leased his equipment, along with a trained operator, and did not charge for individual messages. To further ensure control he, unlike other companies, refused to sell his equipment. Exceptions were made in the case of the Italian and British navies, but they had to pay an annual royalty after the initial purchase. Marconi made a similar offer to the United States Navy. They were leery, and negotiations did not go as smoothly as with his other contracts. In 1903, after failed talks with Marconi and several tests of competing equipment, the U.S. Navy went wireless by purchasing the Slaby-Arco system and training its own operators.

The successful expansion of marine wireless began to demonstrate conclusively what Marconi had insisted when he first went into business: wireless signals were not limited to line-of-sight transmission. He believed they followed the curvature of the earth and had a range that was potentially limitless, given the use of low-frequency long waves and a high-power transmitter. Why this was so was not clear, nor did a lack of electromagnetic theory perturb him. What counted was what worked; high-level theoretical explanations could be left to the physicists. In 1899 he spanned the English Channel, and soon after ships were picking up transmissions hundreds of miles distant. Concessions from early naysayers, which included some of the world's most eminent scientists, gradually came.

Further evidence for the long-range capacity of wireless came in December 1901. A successful transatlantic signal made it from Poldhu, in the West of England, to the receiving station manned by Marconi on Signal Hill near St. John's Newfoundland. It was a simple message, a static-filled letter *S*: three dots in Morse code. When the event was reported almost everyone lauded the achievement, except the cable companies, who claimed infringement on their international telegraph monopoly when cable stocks dropped as a result. The press, as usual, was on Marconi's side. So was Alexander Graham Bell, who invited Marconi to set up shop on his property in Cape Breton, Nova Scotia, which, unlike Newfoundland, had no cable company contract. One year later a full message was sent, followed in January 1903 by greetings from President Theodore Roosevelt to King Edward VII.

Not only Bell but Thomas Edison as well expressed admiration for this aspirant to their ranks. In the *au courant* journal *The World's Works*, Edison remarked: "Give Marconi ten years and he will be sending 1,000 words a minute by wireless." It never happened, but in 1907 regular transatlantic service did. At five cents per word for the press and ten cents for others, he undercut the monopoly of the cable companies. They had been charging twenty-five cents per word and now had to reduce their rates to remain competitive. That same year the *New York Times* became an enthusiastic subscriber to the new service, beginning a relationship that would play a strategic role in its coverage of the *Titanic* disaster. In October a new supplement was introduced to the Sunday *Times*: the "Marconi Transatlantic Wireless Dispatches."

The more that marine wireless was used in the early years of the new century, the more various uses for it were envisioned. Navigation and shipping dispatches began to be interspersed with late-breaking news, European or North American, depending on the ship's proximity to either continent. Should a vessel be beyond the range of shore stations, important information could be relayed, ship to ship, to almost any point in the North Atlantic.

Newsletters on larger liners began to include current world news in their pages, a trend started by the *Cunard Daily Bulletin* with its supplement "Marconigrams—direct to the ship." It was claimed, and with some validity, that passengers halfway across the Atlantic were often more in touch with world events than many people on land. And when wireless was not engaged in any of these functions, it could be used to send personal telegrams, a service that, given the *Titanic*'s illustrious and wealthy passengers, kept both her operators regularly engaged.

With such maximal use of the medium almost from its outset, some kind of international consensus had to be reached regarding wireless regulation.

The First International Wireless Telegraphy Conference was held in Berlin in 1903. Although the meeting was convened primarily to sort out issues rather than to mandate specific policy, it did ask participating nations to recommend to their governments that it should be obligatory for all coastal stations to receive and transmit messages from all ships, regardless of their wireless company affiliation.

This challenge to the Marconi no-intercommunications policy was restated at the 1906 International Conference on Wireless Communication at Sea, also held in Berlin. Britain acquiesced to the policy by a one-vote majority in the House of Commons (Marconi was opposed, and he had many supporters in the house), and in 1908 it became law. Was it obeyed? Rarely. Non-Marconi transmissions, except for emergency messages, were snubbed. Telefunken was frustrated since many of their ships used the English Channel. To make matters worse for Germany, two of its shipping lines, HAPAG and Bremer Lloyd, were Marconi subscribers; they could not, therefore, access most German shore stations and other German ships. Reconciliation came later that year when a new German company was formed. It was controlled by Telefunken, which had a 55 percent majority, with Marconi holding significant minority interests. The two giants could now intercommunicate.

Marconi's chief American competitor at this time, United Wireless, was still subject to the now unofficial no-intercommunications rule. The rivalry between them eventually went to the courts, but over another issue, patent infringement by United. Marconi won most of the decisions, and United went bankrupt. Interestingly, Marconi was in New York in April 1912 to consummate a takeover of what remained of United when the *Titanic* went down. With his stock soaring after the disaster, Marconi absorbed United's 70 shore stations and 500 ship installations. This gave him a dominant presence not only on the eastern seaboard but in the Great Lakes as well.

Besides dealing with the no-intercommunications issue, the 1906 Berlin conference proposed other legislation, which in turn was ratified by other nations within two years. All ship stations and operators had to be licensed by their home countries. The minimum performance standard at the key was 12 words per minute—by this time auditory reception was the norm, having displaced the use of a printout paper strip that characterized both the Marconi and Slaby-Arco system during their first years. Each ship was to have a three-letter call signature for easy identification: in the case of the *Titanic* it was what would become the legendary MGY. Also under negotiation were the call letters for an international distress signal. The British preferred CQD (— • — • / — — • — / — • •), for "seek you," the general call, with the addition of D for danger. This was a staple of their railway-influenced telegraph service. The Germans found this solution to complex and chauvinistic. They suggested SOE (• • • / — — — / •), but it was pointed out that the final E could be obliterated by strong interference. Eventually SOS (• • • / — — — / • • •) was adopted, not because, as many later believed, it refers to "save our souls" or "save our ship" but due to its distinct nature and ability to cut through overlapping transmissions and interference.

Not until 1912 would SOS be accepted in practice as the official distress call, largely because of the *Titanic* disaster. In the years between the Berlin Conference and 1912, despite its ratification, SOS was eschewed in favor of alternatives—CQD in the case of Marconi operators. In 1909 this call, coupled with the idea of a ship in distress being dependent on wireless for the survival of her passengers, made front-page news in the most publicized ocean liner accident of the pre-*Titanic* wireless era.

On the fog-enshrouded morning of 23 January, at 5:30 a.m. in the coastal waters off Nantucket, the White Star liner *Republic* was accidently rammed by the *Florida* of the Lloyd Italiano line. The *Republic* was outbound, taking 461 passengers on a Mediterranean cruise. The *Florida* was inbound, loaded with nearly 1,000 immigrants. The collision ripped through the side of the *Republic*, causing serious structural damage and impeding the function of her wireless. The *Florida* was less imperiled but did not have wireless. She limped back to help the endangered vessel, which by this time had closed her collision bulkheads. As the doomed *Republic*'s passengers were transferred to the *Florida*, her wireless operator, Jack Binns, who would later join them, remained on board. He valiantly and successfully struggled to repair the apparatus and send out a distress call. Several ships responded, among them the White Star's *Baltic*. She took passengers from both stricken vessels to New York.

It was a sensational news story, almost miraculous in tenor given the many lives saved that could just as easily have been lost: the final tally of fatalities was two on the *Republic* and three on the *Florida*. A similar collision several years later, involving the Canadian Pacific ship *Empress of Ireland* in the Gulf of St. Lawrence on 29 May 1914, would claim 1,012. She sank in approximately 15 minutes, thereby rendering a wireless-assisted rescue "too little, too late."

The *Republic*'s misfortune produced two heroes: wireless and the ship's Marconi man, Jack Binns. Both were championed by the *New York Times*, which took the lead in presenting the story in considerable and often repetitive detail. Their coverage is worth a brief assessment here since it became an unsuspected dress rehearsal for the *Times*'s performance in the epoch-making maritime drama that would follow in April 1912.

On Sunday, 24 January, the *Times*'s headline noted the plight of the *Republic*. The subheadline read: "A Whole Company of Might Ships Called by Wireless to Her Aid." The lead article explained the call letters CQ and CQD; no mention was made of the "official," but as yet untried, signal SOS. The general manager of American Marconi, John Bromley, was interviewed. He modestly noted how wireless had done its job, then went over the sequence of transmissions that had been received. His comments give the impression that wireless communication was considerably more efficient and well organized than was the case either in 1909 or 1912.

The *Times* followed this with a bit of audacious self-promotion that would have been in exceedingly bad taste, or probably omitted altogether, had casualties been higher. Readers were reminded of the paper's coverage of the fire on board the Phoenix line's steamship *St. Cuthbert*, which had occurred on February 4, 1908, 200 miles off the coast of Nova Scotia. This incident was also characterized by a wireless assisted rescue at sea, whereby the White Star's *Cymric* saved 38 of the 50 crewman caught in the blaze. Since the *Times* had been in direct contact with the *Cymric* by wireless, they proudly noted how it was possible to have exclusive coverage at a time when not a word about the event appeared in other New York papers. These comments and the accompanying story about the *Republic* and *Florida* appeared in a Sunday edition of the paper. The third section contained the weekly feature, "Marconi Transatlantic Wireless Dispatches," which must have further drawn readers' attention to the new medium and the *Times*'s wisdom in using it.

The edition of January 25 noted how the *Republic* had been in tow when she finally sank, with the captain and crew barely managing to escape. On January 26, coverage included a statement from Marconi. He was pleased with the performance of his wireless, hoped more ships would adopt it, and mentioned that future instruments would have increased range. Another article introduced Jack Binns as the courageous wireless operator who, with failed engines having killed the generator, waded through the icy waters of the storage room to get batteries so he could restart the apparatus.

On January 27, Binns's heroics became the headline. An article told of him holding the transmitter together with one hand and signaling with the other while battling frigid conditions. In another entry, he recounted his own version of the events in a modest "Ah shucks, it was nothing," manner, which endeared him to the public. By January 29 he had become a national celebrity. The *Times* described how, while attending a musical review, he was forced onstage to make a speech and was mobbed by chorus girls. The French government recommended to the United States that he be given a special tribute.

Binns emerged as his era's version of the great American hero, a real-life version of Horatio Alger. Various commentators have likened him to Tom Swift, the young inventor depicted in a series of popular novels at the time, and Charles Lindbergh, who would become a champion for the next generation. He also became known as "CQD Binns," and in this capacity he encouraged a legion of youth, primarily white, middle-class males, to take up wireless as a hobby.

These amateurs often made their own sets, many with the hope that they too might one day play a role in reporting some dramatic event and thereby attain celebrity status. It rarely happened, and perhaps out of frustration a number of them turned to less honorable pursuits: They began interfering with or jamming commercial shipping and naval transmissions. This sometimes took the form of obscene messages and, on several unnerving occasions, false alarms about sinking ships, a practice that was suspected when early reports of the *Titanic*'s plight were relayed to shore. A contemporary parallel to this can perhaps be seen in the case of computer hackers, who possess information technology that can access the data banks of large institutions. Their virus implants and other mischief recalls the efforts of the unscrupulous amateurs during the early prebroadcasting days of radio.

After the *Republic* incident, Binns left the wireless business and parlayed his fame into a successful career as a writer on maritime topics. In April 1912, he was in London as the *Titanic* was being readied for her maiden voyage. He gave thought to returning on the celebrated liner. Captain Smith was an old acquaintance—Binns had served with him for two years aboard the *Adriatic* before his posting on the *Republic*. A new job assignment intervened and decided his fate. Anxious to get there, he left on the *Minnesota* several days before the *Titanic* departed Southampton.

CHAPTER 2

Wireless at Work

The bizarre sequence of events that immortalized the *Titanic* gave wireless communication the greatest challenge of its brief history. At first it was believed that the medium performed up to expectations. But as the magnitude and contingencies of the disaster were revealed, so was the failure of wireless to perform the full miracle of coordinating an immediate and complete rescue. The lesson of the *Titanic* demonstrated what the near tragedy of the *Republic* had suggested to a handful of critics: the procedures governing wireless communication had to be more comprehensive, given the volume and complexity of the transportation it monitored.

To understand the resulting changes in regulations governing wireless, we must first consider the circumstances, and some of the messages, that were a part of the tragic event. Such an examination can also help us grasp one of the *Titanic*'s great enigmas and a paramount factor in her enduring fascination: the relationship between what was and what might have been.

When the *Titanic* departed from Southampton on April 10, she was endowed with the latest in wireless technology and two young but proven operators. Her Marconi equipment had a daytime range of 400 miles and a nighttime limit that occasionally approached 2,000 miles. We sometimes notice this difference in electromagnetic capacity when we tune our car radios at night to find a station that is interesting and audible, and soon discover that it is not local but hundreds of miles distant. Our failure to pick up the same station in daylight is due to the interference of solar radiation, a phenomenon little understood in 1912. Marconi and his operators left explanation of the discrepancy to scientists and used a practical understanding of it to schedule their longer-distance exchanges at night.

Power for MGY, the call letters of the *Titanic*'s station, came from the ship's electrical system. A battery-operated backup system was located nearby should the primary source fail. High above the top deck a large antenna ran three-quarters of the length of the ship and was suspended between two towering masts; it can be seen in most reproductions of the ship.

In charge of MGY's wireless transmissions were Jack Phillips, the senior operator who turned 25 on April 11, and Harold Bride, 22. Phillips had served Marconi Marine on the *Teutonic*, *Campania*, *Oceanic*, and *Lusitania*; Bride had also seen duty on the *Lusitania* and on the *Haverford*, *Lanfranc*, and *Anslem*. The two men were never formally part of the crews on the ships they served but wore the uniform of Marconi Marine. Their life on board was largely confined to the wireless cabin. It had a tripartite structure, with two sections for equipment and one for sleeping. Phillips and Bride did not dine or socialize with the ships' officers, several of whom were unknown to them, and Phillips was said to have a preference for the more personal atmosphere of a smaller vessel. Nevertheless, the status of working on the *Titanic* was unmatched. Not so the salary: the low pay of $15 to $20 a month was thought to be offset by the glamour of the calling. During the U.S. inquiry Senator Smith questioned this. Given the importance of wireless operators as a liaison between shipping companies and the outside world, he felt they should be paid a salary commensurate with their responsibilities.

Phillips, Bride, and the other operators on giant liners that carried two Marconi men worked staggered shifts so that one of them would be on duty at all times. Most of the vessels within several hours of MGY when she sent her distress call, including the smaller Leyland ship *Californian* and the Cunarder *Carpathia*, carried but one. Despite the division of labor between Phillips and Bride, they worked shifts that were often exhausting.

A typical mix of MGY messages included information about the position of nearby ships, weather bulletins, time signals, congratulatory messages for the maiden voyage, and comments about floating debris—in this last category at least a half-dozen ice warnings were received prior to the fatal collision. During selected hours the wireless was also used for personal telegrams, which occasionally included business transactions worth thousands of dollars. On the evening of April 14 a backlog of personal messages faced the two Marconi men.

Another important assignment for the wireless operators was to monitor the news of the day at scheduled intervals. It was received from the Marconi station at Poldhu in the west of England when the ship was within range and from Cape Cod when signals from North America were easier to capture. A ship caught somewhere between the range of these two stations could have the information relayed to her by vessels that were closer. On White Star ships this information was incorporated into an attractive magazine, the *Atlantic Daily Bulletin*. Most of its 12 pages were prepared ashore, with updates added en route. The publication contained essays on literature, the arts, science, and business. Minus the news entries, it can be seen as a forerunner of the general-interest magazines put out by today's larger airlines.

Marconi operators were a dedicated breed and their labor a true vocation. An extraordinary amount of time was spent at the headphones, and not just in the handling of official dispatches. Operators would often scan the airwaves to monitor the plethora of transmissions always present, thereby exploring the limits of the new technology. Operators were so skilled that many could distinguish a station by the tone of its signal or a fellow operator by his style in sending the dots and dashes of Morse code.

Like today's computer and mobile communication aficionados, wireless operators used many contractions and abbreviations to economize communication. For example, CQ (seek you) was the general call; QRA meant "what is the name of your station"; QRA MGY, "the name of my station is *Titanic*"; TU OM GN, "thank you old man, good night" (an irony given the youth of most of the operators); QRT, "keep quiet, I'm busy"; and sometimes, GTH OM QRT, "get to hell old man, I'm busy." The latter is but one example of the off-color language that was occasionally used. It could be downright obscene when the receiving station belonged to a different wireless station, at times escalating to the point of willfully jamming a competitor's signal. This practice was less prevalent with Marconi operators than among their smaller rivals.

Part of a wireless operator's responsibility included the maintenance of his equipment. This turned out to be crucial in the case of the *Titanic*. According to Bride, in a postrescue exclusive to the *New York Times*, the transmitter began to act up late on Friday, April 12. The problem was traced to the leads running from the transformer to the transmitter. They had burned through, making contact with the iron bolts that supported the apparatus, thus depleting its power. In the 24 hours prior to the collision, Phillips and Bride (mostly

Phillips) put in nearly 7 hours of crucial repair work. Bride's account suggests that had they failed to resolve this problem, later transmission of the distress signal would have been impossible. When Bride relieved Phillips on that fateful night, it was 12:00 midnight (Bride had slept through the collision, which had occurred at 11:40 p.m.), rather than the regularly scheduled 2:00 a.m., because of the long hours Phillips had already spent fixing the short.

Bride later speculated that the reason he survived and Phillips did not—both were thrown into the water and found their way to lifeboats—was because Phillips was already exhausted when the crisis began. It might have also been more than a coincidence that Bride's account to the press of that wireless repair effort by Phillips recalled the one performed by Jack Binns on the *Republic* three years earlier.

One of the great controversies surrounding wireless and the *Titanic* concerns her reception of ice warnings, which began coming in at the start of the voyage. Despite this, on April 14 the ship was steaming at her fastest speed of the voyage, 22-1/2 knots (just over 24 miles per hour, or close to 40 kilometers per hour). As later testimony would show, this practice was not unusual given a clear sky and calm sea. Captain Edward Smith, when informed of the presence of ice in the vicinity, rather than curb the ship's speed, inquired about the visibility. He stated that if questionable in the slightest, the ship would have to slow down. This was not good enough, according to several recent postmortems that have questioned his competence via the benefit of hindsight. With popular belief that the *Titanic* was speeding through dangerous waters to set a transatlantic record finally laid to rest (the Cunarders were faster), the haste can be more plausibly linked to her schedule. In other words, there was great media expectation surrounding her expected arrival time in New York—a day or even a half day late might have put a damper on the party. Recent computer simulations have shown what some suspected at the time: that a reasonable slowdown, to perhaps half speed, would have probably created a soon-forgotten near miss.

What Captain Smith, with all his experience, and most of the ship's officers did not realize was that conditions were in a sense "too good to be true." Movement by or around an object helps in the perception of it against a neutral background. Had there been waves from even a slight swell breaking against the base of the iceberg, which allegedly had its darker, or black ice, side (where it broke off from land) facing the ship, the waves might have reflected the available light and allowed the lookout, Fred Fleet, to see the iceberg several seconds sooner.

Transcripts from the two later inquiries include testimonies from several crewmen stating that the conditions of sea and air on that night were calmer than any they had ever experienced. Despite these unusual circumstances, and the posted ice warnings, none of the officers suggested to the captain that the ship's speed be curtailed.

Some of the ships involved in sending dispatches about ice were the *Caronia, Amerika, Baltic, Noordam, La Touraine, Mesaba,* and *Californian.* (Thanks to John Booth and the Booth *Titanic* Signal Archive, many of these messages, and others occurring before, during, and after the sinking, have been preserved and published.) Most of the ice warnings were acknowledged, and some posted. Any of the ship's officers who understood their meaning must have realized that entry into ice-infested waters was inevitable. It is almost certain that the first sighting of ice would have resulted in the ship curbing her speed. In an ironic way this was the case. After Fred Fleet called to First Officer Murdoch on the bridge, "Iceberg right ahead," the ship's evasive maneuvers proved inadequate. Thus the first ice the *Titanic* sighted turned out to be the last.

What I interpret from this scenario is that prior to the *Titanic* disaster and especially during the first decade of wireless, seamen put supreme trust in visual verification of phenomena. Wireless messages about hazards such as icebergs were often less a call to take action regarding the ship's physical operation than a call for greater vigilance. Given the presence of ice in her route, the *Titanic* could have slowed down or changed to a more southerly route (which, because of the curvature of the earth, would have added distance and delayed her arrival in New York). She did neither but preferred to wait and *see* before acting. This suggests that prior to the sinking, when large companies like White Start routed their vessels, wireless played a supplemental rather than a determining role.

Another aspect of this maritime communications drama concerns the ice warning the *Titanic* received at 10:30 p.m. on April 13 from the Furness Withy ship *Rappahannock,* wherein wireless was not the medium. Using a Morse lamp as she passed *Titanic* eastbound out of Halifax, she signaled about the ice field ahead and that in negotiating it the ship had damaged her rudder. First Officer Murdoch acknowledged the message but still held to his previous course and speed.

The last wireless ice warning the *Titanic* received—partially received would be more accurate—came from the *Californian* at 11:00 p.m. on April 14. It precipitated a debate that still rages over where that ship was located with respect to *Titanic* and what its captain, Stanley Lord, should have done in the hours that followed.

The scenario begins with the relatively inexperienced operator on the *Californian*, Cyril Evans, age 20, starting to send the aforementioned message indicating the presence of ice. He signaled that it had caused the *Californian* to shut down her engines and drift for the night. Phillips was at the key working Cape Race (Newfoundland) when Evan's transmission cut in. Since the *Californian* is alleged to have been 5 to 20 miles away–the exact distance is still debated–her signal was loud, clear, and an unwelcome interruption. Phillips responded with, "Keep out! Shut up! You're jamming my signal. I'm working Cape Race." Evans did not try again. He turned off his equipment and went to bed a short time later and within minutes of the *Titanic*'s fatal collision. According to British maritime historian Geoffrey Marcus, blame for the failure of Evan's message to be acknowledged resides with both the young operator and Captain Lord. Marcus argues that what Evans should have done was to send a formal master's service message (MSG). Phillips might have then acknowledged and replied to it, or at least put Evans on hold, since an MSG required a response. As it was Evans had sent an unofficial dispatch. For his part, Captain Lord should have insisted on an answer, even if the initial dispatch was unofficial, since he had suggested that Evans send it. In defense of Evans and Lord, it should be noted that the reason they signaled to *Titanic* about their predicament was partly due to the knowledge that the ship was nearby and worth contacting. Although an MSG would have been prudent, the presence of ice in the region was common knowledge to any vessel with wireless.

Marcus also contends that Evans should have stayed at his post and not retired for the night since "emergency conditions" prevailed. Perhaps; there was ice, but the sea was calm and the air clear. Furthermore, Evans was the *only* operator on board and, like Phillips, he had put in a long day, longer than the seamen who worked eight-hour shifts or those on watch who served four. Normal sign-off time for a station having one operator was 11:00 p.m., and Evans had already overstayed it by half an hour. As Senator Smith would discover during the U.S. inquiry, Marconi operators were overworked as well as underpaid.

John Booth and Sean Coughlan, in their meticulous analysis of *Titanic*-related wireless messages, suggest that this infamous information gap between the *Titanic* and *Californian* can be blamed partly on maritime law of the time, regulated in this case by the British Board of Trade. Normal safety precautions, such as the maintenance of a 24-hour watch, were not extended to include wireless. As a result, the divided loyalty of the operators—between messages relating to navigation and private dispatches, from which the Marconi Company earned most of its profits—was generally unquestioned. It could also be argued that some culpability for the "*Californian* incident" was due to the Marconi Company itself. Given the near tragedy of the *Republic*, it could have developed more efficient procedures for ship stations having only one operator.

What happened on the *Californian* after Evans went to sleep has compounded the debate and given the ship an unsought immortality. In the distance loomed another vessel, her lights clearly visible. Was it the *Titanic*? Was the *Californian* the nearby ship several of *Titanic*'s officers observed? Was there a third ship in the vicinity? Other studies have grappled with these enduring questions. For purposes of the wireless assessment presented here, we should note the following sequence of events. At 12:15 a.m., Third Officer Groves of the *Californian*, on his way to bed after his watch was relieved, stopped off at the Marconi cabin. He knew some Morse code and put on the headphones, but he did not know how to start the magnetic detector that powered the transmitter. Rather than further disturb an already half-asleep Evans, he abandoned the idea of a late-night listening session, and in so doing almost certainly missed hearing the *Titanic*'s distress call.

Captain Lord had also noticed the nearby ship before he retired, as did the new watch, Second Officer Stone, who signaled her using Morse lamp—assuming that her lack of motion was a result of her shutting down for the night because of the presence of ice, as his ship had done. No answer came. Eight white rockets were sighted (the *Titanic* had fired eight while in her death throes). Captain Lord was informed of the rockets via speaking tube. He asked their colors and if they were company signals (white was for distress, but company signals, which employed a variety of colors, could also use it). Stone replied that he did not know if they were company signals but was trying to establish contact through Morse lamp. At 2:00 a.m. the ship appeared to steam away. Stone sent an apprentice, Gibson, to inform the captain, and then did so himself via the speaking tube 45 minutes later.

Despite the unusual events of the evening, no one had the presence to wake Evans and bring wireless into the investigation—no one, that is until Chief Officer Stewart came on watch at 4:00 a.m. When informed by Stone regarding what had transpired, he immediately roused Evans, who quickly found out about the tragedy. The *Californian* arrived on the scene shortly thereafter, as the *Carpathia* was picking up the remaining survivors. It turned into a case of "better never than late," given what followed when word about the *Californian*'s earlier inaction broke in the press and was later pursued at the U.S. and British inquiries.

The *Californian* incident and the debate surrounding it continues to divide *Titanic* scholarship into at least three factions: those who believe Captain Lord was negligent; those, sometimes known as Lordites, who argue that he has been a scapegoat unfairly maligned for acting in ways that were not inconsistent with established maritime practice in 1912; and those who contend that neither case has been sufficiently proved to allow us to pass judgment. Most in the latter two categories have favored a formal and comprehensive re-examination of all the facts of the case, a courtesy denied Captain Lord in 1912 and one that he sought until his death in 1962 at the age of 84. In 1992 the case was reopened by a British maritime tribunal. Captain Lord was exonerated of the charge that he failed to respond to a ship in distress but held accountable for not fully investigating the distress rockets.

When Phillips snubbed the *Californian*'s transmission, he had not only been at work for 16 hours repairing the apparatus; when this was done he started on the backlog of messages before Bride could relieve him. Several hours earlier he had received a message from the *Mesaba* reporting "much heavy pack ice and a great number of icebergs" at coordinates close to the *Titanic*'s position. He acknowledged the message. The *Mesaba*'s operator stood by for an acknowledgment from Captain Smith, whom he assumed would be privy to the information. It never came. Phillips put the dispatch under a paperweight and continued working Cape Race to reduce the backlog of private messages that were the company's bread and butter. Exhausted and impatient by this time, perhaps he forgot about the priority status of navigational dispatches. Another, though purely speculative, reason for his inaction might have been the belief that, despite its importance, similar messages had been coming in all day and had been delivered to the bridge. What Phillips must have failed to realize was how close the coordinates of latitude and longitude in the *Mesaba*'s ice warning were to the *Titanic*'s position; given the ship's course and speed, she would be there before his shift was over at midnight.

When Bride joined Phillips for the shift change, Phillips remarked that they must have struck something. Captain Smith soon entered the Marconi cabin and told them about the collision. He said the damage was being assessed and to stand by to send a call for assistance.

Not believing the ship vulnerable, the two operators joked about the situation. Ten minutes later the captain returned and told them to transmit. Phillips began sending CQD. Bride suggested he also try SOS: "It's the new call and it might be your last chance to send it." Popular tradition, and several commentaries, often cite this as the first SOS in maritime history. It was not. Although the *Titanic* might have been the first British ship to use SOS, continental vessels had already employed it. Earlier that month the call was used by the French liner *Niagara* when she was damaged in the same region for the same reason.

With the Titanic's plight looking more desperate each minute, her distress call did not go unheeded. Unfortunately, given the rate at which she was succumbing, the only ship close enough to attempt a rescue of the numerous passengers for whom no lifeboat space was available was the *Californian*. The first response to Phillips's transmission was from the *Frankfurt*. Her operator took the message to the captain. The signal also reached Cape Race. Their reaction was one of disbelief, followed by shock when repeated transmissions confirmed the worst. Numerous ships eventually formed a network of recipients, among them the *Caronia, Mount Temple, Yipiranga, Cincinnati, Celtic, Baltic, Olympic, Birma, Virginian, Asian*, and most notable the *Carpathia*, which was 58 miles to the southeast. Given her position and top speed, she was the vessel that could get there most quickly.

The situation with the *Carpathia* and her wireless operator, Harold Cottam, contrasts with that of Evans and the *Californian*. Cottam, age 22, was the only operator on board and was preparing to turn in for the night. He decided to linger at the headphones a bit longer to get news of the coal strike in England. Earlier during his shift he had also picked up ice warnings, including the one the *Californian* tried to send to *Titanic*. Cottam took off the headphones and started to undress, thereby missing the *Titanic*'s initial CQD and SOS. He then put them back on to ask the *Titanic* if she knew that messages were being held for her at Cape Race and was greeted by the distress call. After verifying the *Titanic*'s plight and position he informed the captain, Arthur Rostron.

Rostron reacted decisively. He fired his ship to full speed in the direction of the disaster and prepared her facilities for a rescue at sea. The *Carpathia* arrived on the scene shortly after 4:00 a.m. and gathered unto her what remained of the *Titanic*'s passengers and crew. It was a courageous effort, one that earned Rostron the Congressional Medal of Honor. It was also a calculated risk and fraught with danger since the *Carpathia* had to maneuver through an ice field lethal enough to give her a share in *Titanic*'s fate.

With the *Carpathia* on the way, Phillips kept signaling. News of his ship's plight ricocheted around the North Atlantic. The *London Times* would later liken the scenario to a great wounded animal summoning help from its kin. Most respondents tried to help in any way they could, and a number of ships altered course to come to *Titanic*'s aid. However, the magnitude of the disaster was not understood by all who received the distress call. The *Olympic* asked if the *Titanic* was steering a course to meet them. Phillips patiently reiterated MGY circumstances and was in turn notified that the *Olympic* was headed toward them at full steam. But she was an agonizingly distant 500 miles.

Another misconstrued interpretation of the distress call came from the first ship to receive it, the *Frankfurt*. When she responded, it was without a sense of urgency. She asked "What is the matter?" whereupon Captain Smith was supposed to have said, "That man is a fool." We do know what Phillips tapped back in response: "You fool stand by and keep out." Since the *Frankfurt* was a Telefunken ship, this seems a case of the old wireless rivalry resurfacing, compounded by the tensions between two nations that would shortly be at war. The incident became newsworthy just over a week later. Germany cited it as a gross example of British inefficiency at sea, and at the U.S. inquiry Senator Smith saw it as yet another example of the questionable way Marconi Marine conducted its business.

The *Titanic*'s wireless functioned almost until the end. The drama of the last few minute in the Marconi cabin was recounted by Bride at the U.S. inquiry and has become one of the enduring legends of that infamous night. What follows is a brief summary:

Phillips keeps signaling. The captain enters and releases the operators under the "Every man for himself" declaration. Phillips will not let go of the key. Bride fastens a lifebelt to him. A crewman enters the cabin and tries to steal it. They dispatch him in a way that has never been made clear—nor is it of sufficient concern to Senator Smith to explore further when he has Bride on the stand. With water almost to the level of the Marconi cabin as *Titanic* descends by the bow, the power fades to nil. Phillips and Bride leave and eventually wind up in the water. They are pulled aboard lifeboats (Phillips's presence in a lifeboat has not been verified by subsequent witnesses). Phillips dies of exposure exacerbated by exhaustion and is later resurrected as one of the heroes of the disaster. Bride survives to narrate the harrowing events in an exclusive to the *New York Times*.

As the *Carpathia* steamed to New York with the survivors, the world became privy to news of the disaster but not the details. Newspaper accounts ranged from the *New York Times*' somber estimate that 1,250 had perished to the *New York Sun*'s report that all had been saved. By April 18, the former estimate, the one nobody wanted to believe, turned out to be close to the truth—agonizingly closer since the actual number of fatalities now appeared to exceed 1,500. The confused reporting resulted from the way the two Harolds, Cottam and Bride, handled communications from the *Carpathia* and the way transmissions from a variety of other sources were interpreted.

Cottam began sending the names of survivors shortly after they were taken on board and made comfortable. Given the limited range of his apparatus, he had to relay the list to the *Olympic*. The list was subsequently forwarded to Cape Race and then direct to New York by wire as well as wireless. An exhausted Cottam was assisted by Bride, who, recovering from exposure as well as a leg injury, had to be carried to the Marconi cabin. They worked tirelessly, and as it turned out conspiratorially. All requests for further information—from the press, the White Star Line, President Taft, and even Marconi at the urging of the United States government—went unheeded. On April 15 the following message to International Mercantile Marine was composed by the *Titanic*'s most notorious survivor, Bruce Ismay, chairman of White Star: "Deeply regret advise you *Titanic* sank this morning after collision with iceberg, resulting in serious loss of life." According to Captain Rostron, who Senator Smith interviewed about the incident, the message was given to the purser, who took it immediately to the Marconi cabin. It was not sent until April 17.

When Ismay was somewhat recovered he drafted another dispatch, which was also sent on April 17. It was signed "YAMSI," a personal code reversing the letters of his name: "Most desirable *Titanic* crew aboard *Carpathia* be returned home earliest moment possible. Suggest you hold *Cedric* sailing her daylight Friday." This concern was partly motivated by a concern for the crew but also by the desire to leave the United States before all hell would break loose in the inevitable media storm to follow. The message, and two others that were similar, were intercepted by the U.S. Navy and forwarded to Senator Smith, who made sure that what was intended did not come to pass.

Responsibility for what was sent from the *Carpathia*, and whether the messages she received were acted upon or not, was in the hands of Cottam and Bride, with Bride having seniority. Several factors can be invoked to explain their behavior. The two most compelling are loyalty to the Marconi Company and its business associates, such as White Star, and thoughts that the two operators might have entertained a notion to profit personally from their experiences by giving as yet undisclosed testimony to the press upon their arrival in New York. At the U.S. inquiry they defended their actions by insisting that the American operators who were sending inquiries, often non-Marconi Navy men, could not use continental Morse code properly. They also claimed that it was not Marconi practice to send important or official transmissions via a relay using other ships—this was given in defense of their failure to send Ismay's first message, which was conceived when the *Carpathia* was too far at sea to reach any shore station with her equipment. They also noted how, since they were under so much pressure, Captain Rostron told them to handle only "official" messages and those relating to the survivors.

Senator Smith soon found that the first two reasons could not be supported conclusively. Navy operators, although not stellar at the apparatus, were competent enough to send and receive with those in the employ of the Marconi Company. As to the second reason, Marconi Marine had no official policy prohibiting the relay of important dispatches, save the lingering influence of the no-intercommunications rule, which would discourage but not necessarily prohibit the use of other wireless companies in such a relay.

The final reason Cottam and Bride gave for their failure to release more information—that they were following Captain Rostron's orders—was to Smith's mind taking a suggestion too literally in order to cover ulterior motives. Later testimony from Rostron indicated that he did support the sending of official messages, along with the survivors' names and related information, by the "most convenient means." Several intercepted dispatches to the *Carpathia* before she docked shed embarrassing light on the reasons Cottam and Bride were such retentive communicators.

The first one was, "Say old man Marconi Company taking good care of you. Keep your mouth shut and hold your story. It is fixed so you will get big money." It was followed by, "Arranged for your exclusive story for dollars in four figures. Mr. Marconi agreeing. Say nothing until you see me." Both messages were signed by Frederick Sammis, Marconi's chief engineer in New York. They were sent on April 18 as the *Carpathia* was about to dock, thus encouraging but not causing a strategy Cottam and Bride had already adopted. Whatever prompted them to be less than thorough operators following the disaster—perhaps they were inspired by Jack Binns of the *Republic*, who had turned misfortune into a fortune—now seemed to be sanctioned by their own commander-in-chief.

Senator Smith would eventually put Marconi and Sammis on the stand. Marconi denied ordering the messages but conceded that he knew about the planned exclusive and the payment involved. Sammis took full responsibility for the messages but claimed the wording transmitted differed from the original. He defended his intent by claiming he wanted to pick up the spirits of his beleaguered operators.

The senator eventually got to the heart of the matter by following a series of revealing facts. Marconi had a business arrangement with the *New York Times* that dated from 1907; it provided the paper with an exclusive transatlantic news link. He was also one of the few VIPs allowed on board the *Carpathia* after she landed at a time when the press was kept dockside. When Marconi boarded he took with him Jim Speers of the *Times*, with advice from and assistance of Carr Van Anda, the paper's managing editor. Bride dictated his riveting story to Speers while Cottam left the ship and made his way to the nearby Strand Hotel, where the *Times* had set up temporary facilities, and gave his version of the *Carpathia*'s role in the rescue. It was a major scoop for the paper and an embarrassment for Marconi when the senator made the famous inventor's actions public.

According to Wyn Craig Wade, who has made a thorough study of the role of the Michigan senator in the U.S. inquiry, Smith pursued the popular inventor with zeal. When Marconi commented that the money paid Bride ($1,000) and Cottam ($750) for their stories was a just reward for their heroic work, the outspoken senator suggested that he pay them a decent wage. Smith used his interrogation of Marconi as a platform for his crusade against the way monopolies and trusts often violated the public interest. He found the practices of the Marconi Company cavalier and self-serving, although he was somewhat more forgiving of the Marconi operators and the *New York Times*. Despite Smith's belief that Marconi was lying and evasive when questioned, pressure from other committee members and the public's adoration of the inventor prevented him from going as far as he wanted in his exposé. He settled for a statement from Marconi discouraging any future attempt on the part of his operators to withhold information so that it could later be sold as an exclusive.

The journalistic piecing together of the story of the sinking—which we will explore in the next section—became an exercise in "creative" news making utilizing a small number of not always consistent wireless messages. The fact that messages had to be relayed three or four times added to the confusion, especially for those messages that filled the airwaves the night of the sinking. This was the case at some point on April 15, when the news everyone wanted to hear—the *Titanic* was safe and in tow to Halifax—became the basis of several headlines, including one in the venerable *New York Evening Sun*. A train was even charted to go from New York to Halifax to retrieve the passengers. Confirmation of the worst forced its return.

A plausible explanation for this misleading message later emerged. Somehow an operator spliced together an inquiry asking if the *Titanic* and her passengers were safe with information sent several times that night by the *Asian* indicating that she was towing an oil tank to Halifax; another version has the *Virginian* doing the towing. At the time, amateur operators were thought to be responsible for this mis-communication reaching New York, and the weight of *Titanic* scholarship favors this view. However, it is possible that a commercial operator receiving signals at the limits of reception, who would be naturally biased toward the believable rather than the unthinkable, might have interpreted signals this way and forwarded such a message.

From April 15 to 18, amid sporadic and fragmentary transmissions circulating among numerous stations, an unlikely location emerged as a source of late-breaking news: Wanamaker's department store in New York. This was because of the enterprise of its young Marconi man, a Russian Jewish immigrant named David Sarnoff (1891–1971). For a small but influential coterie of journalists, Wanamaker's became the disaster's nerve center—a 1912 version of "mission control." It also provided a launching pad for Sarnoff's unprecedented career in broadcast media.

CHAPTER 3

Sarnoff's Luck

Sarnoff began at Wanamaker's two years before the *Titanic* entered his life. It was nearly a short-lived assignment. In his previous wireless posting at Siasconset (Massachusetts), he had been instrumental in relaying the distress call and organizing a rescue when the airship *Vaniman* ran into trouble. A new *Vaniman* was launched shortly after Sarnoff started at Wanamaker's, and he volunteered to serve as a wireless operator for an early test flight. Several transportation snags between New York and Atlantic City prevented him from arriving before the *Vaniman* took off. She crashed and burned, killing all on board. This incident contributed to the legend of "Sarnoff's luck"—his ability to be in the right place at the right time—or, in this instance, perhaps we could say, "the wrong place at the right time."

Throughout his life Sarnoff had the prescient ability to turn unexpected challenges into opportunities. This would eventually lead him to an eminence in the field of electronic mass media that in many ways paralleled what Henry Ford achieved in the realm of the automobile. Entry into this domain began with one such challenge. In 1906 Sarnoff was an ambitious but nervous 15-year-old when he trekked into the *New York Herald* building determined to begin a career in the newspaper business. Unperturbed by the thought of starting at the bottom, he asked the man behind the window in the lobby for a job, any job. He soon found out he was in the outer office of the Commercial Cable Company, not the *New York Herald*. With telegraph keys clicking hypnotically in the background, he was offered a job as messenger boy for $5 a week. Intrigued by the opportunity and the unusual work environment, he duly accepted. Subsequently, and largely on his own, Sarnoff learned Morse code and acquired a practice telegraph. Within a year he had a job with the Marconi Wireless Telegraph Company of America, where his prowess at the key became legendary.

Before the Marconi Company offered Sarnoff the position of manager at its Wanamaker facilities, he was assigned to the shore stations of Siasconset and Sea Gate, New York. During this time he also had brief but significant experience as a shipboard operator. While serving these assignments, he read all the literature he could that dealt with the nature and application of wireless. Eventually, he had several meetings with the legendary Marconi himself, whom the young Sarnoff regarded with awe and respect. Although neither could realize it at the time, the next decade would see them become firm friends, with the younger man achieving his own renown.

Sarnoff's strategic moment at Wanamaker's, when he relayed news of the plight of the *Titanic* to a desperate public, became an oft-recalled aspect of his career. It was also an event he was prone to embellish or distort for the sake of self-promotion. How it began has never been completely clear. Most accounts say that he was at his post when he picked up the *Titanic*'s distress signal via relay from her sister ship, the *Olympic*. Sarnoff always insisted that this was the case, most notably in a statement about the incident that later provided the basis for an article in the *Saturday Evening Post*.

Two recent commentators see it differently. In a respectful but tempered biography, Carl Dreher argues that Sarnoff could not have been at Wanamaker's that night (Sunday) and, even if he was, that the wireless signals from the *Titanic* and *Olympic* would not have been strong enough to reach New York that night. Dreher's alternate scenario has Sarnoff somehow getting word of the event, perhaps through a newspaper extra, and then going to his station to see if he could be of help. A similar view is expressed by Tom Lewis in his book *Empire of the Air*, which became the basis for Ken Burn's evocative 1992 PBS documentary of the same name. What happened at Wanamaker's after Sarnoff donned the earphones, however, can be accounted for with more certainty.

The first conclusive signals Sarnoff received came from the *Olympic*. He made contact with her and notified the press. Reporters came. So did store employees, relatives and friends of the passengers, and a mélange of the curious. Eventually the police had to be called in to prevent chaos from happening at Wanamaker's, which was rapidly becoming a secondary news story as a result of reporters working for the Hearst papers. Fueled by coffee and donuts, Sarnoff remained at his post for three days and three nights, a performance that reminded many of young Jack Binns's role in the rescue of the *Republic* three years earlier. By Wednesday the 17th, the airwaves were plagued with interference from the plethora of transmissions. The Marconi Company decided to shut down most of its Northeast operations, and the Wanamaker apparatus had to cease in deference to several of the company's more primary stations, such as the head office on William Street.

The news that Sarnoff—and two assistants he fails to mention in later recollections—received was dismal: no details regarding the sinking, only the names of survivors, far fewer names than anyone expected, then slowly and inexorably the names of assumed casualties. After the shutdown of the Wanamaker station, and with the *Carpathia* approaching New York, Sarnoff's entourage dispersed. Many headed dockside to begin a vigil. Sarnoff took a short break for a Turkish rub at the Astor Hotel on Lower Broadway, compliments of Vincent Astor, who had been at Sarnoff's side when news confirmed that John Jacob Astor, Vincent's father, was not among the survivors. Sarnoff emerged from the hotel refreshed but still tired and made his way to the Sea Gate station to see if there was anything more he could do. Little remained. Wireless had done its job, and the press descended on the *Carpathia*. Mission accomplished, Sarnoff, who was emotionally as well as physically exhausted, went home and slept for 24 hours. He would later observe, "It seemed as if the whole anxious world was attached to those phones."

In ancient times, a messenger bearing the kind of unfortunate news that was Sarnoff's burden might have found himself in jeopardy. But since the dawn of the electric age and the accompanying rise of the mass media, almost any information about an event is preferable to uncertainty. Sarnoff became the exalted messenger for a company that rose in esteem and affluence as a result of the *Titanic* disaster. His fortunes did likewise. By the end of the year he became chief inspector for Marconi facilities throughout the country. After World War I, American Marconi was taken over by General Electric, which called its new subsidiary the Radio Corporation of America (RCA). Sarnoff thrived in the new order and became RCA's general manager in 1926, guiding that company's destiny over the next four decades. Throughout his rise he often noted how the *Titanic* disaster "brought radio to the front, and incidently, me."

Before leaving Marconi for RCA, Sarnoff wrote a prophetic memo. In November 1916, he proposed turning one of radio's greatest liabilities—access to private point-to-point messages by anyone with adequate equipment tuned into the wavelength in use—into a powerful asset. He proposed the "Radio Music Box," a radio receiver to be located in living rooms and parlors, which would employ loudspeakers rather than earphones to bring music and voice to a wide public. His superiors were uninterested. Perhaps their attitude reflected Marconi's persistent belief at this time that radio was, and should only be, a medium for telegraphic rather than vocal or musical communication—if people wanted music they had the phonograph, he is reputed to have said. Ten years later broadcast radio as an information and entertainment medium would be a reality. Although Sarnoff and RCA were not the first in this endeavor, they eventually became major players in a collective effort that involved several interest groups and companies.

CHAPTER 4
The Call for Change

The sinking of the *Titanic* demonstrated that nothing in the realm of transportation and communication could or should be taken for granted. Wireless was now deemed indispensable and in need of regulations appropriate to the role it played in the movement of information and people. Prior to the events of April 1912, attitudes about how to control the new medium had been ambivalent.

In the years leading up to the *Titanic* disaster, the general public regarded wireless with a mixture of awe and indifference. It was awesome when a heart-stopping event, such as the sinking of the *Republic*, thrust the technology and those associated with it into the spotlight. Apart from these highly visible media moments, in its normal day-to-day, year-to-year operations wireless was often taken for granted. Although Marconi was widely known, the profit margin of his commercial ventures—owing to relentless investment in their expansion—lagged behind the renown of his name. Not until 1910 would his empire be solidly in the black to stay.

During this period there was little call for regulation on the part of the press. Most newspapers seemed content to wait for the next wireless event or hero. While the sinking of the *Titanic* inherited this expectation, it did so with a difference, particularly when news broke about the inaction of the *Californian*. On one hand, the press regarded wireless as having performed up to all previous expectations; on the other, it suggested that with better monitoring the medium might have helped save more lives.

The attitude among those interest groups that were closest to and most dependent on wireless during its first decade—governments and shipping and insurance companies—favored increased regulation. It was their concerns that led to the Berlin international conferences dealing with the no-intercommunications policy of the Marconi company, the licensing of stations and operators, and the establishment of an international distress call and procedure. The fate of the *Titanic* showed that more sweeping aspects of wireless practice had to be regulated, among them the range of the apparatus, its power source, the hours a station should be operative, and the allocation of frequencies.

In the United States some of these concerns had already been raised in Congress, but pre-*Titanic* wireless regulation was minimal. The most important policy measure was the Wireless Ship Act of June 1910, which took effect in July a year later. It was a reaction to the increasing passenger volume on North Atlantic routes and an attempt to frame a U.S. response to the issues raised in the Berlin conferences. The bill stipulated that all oceangoing steamships using U.S. ports, carrying 50 or more passengers, and traveling to destinations 200 or more miles apart must carry an "efficient apparatus" for radiotelegraphic communication and a "skilled operator." It also required the equipment to have a daytime range of at least 100 miles and made intercommunication compulsory. No provisions were established regarding what constituted a "skilled operator," the frequencies to be used and by whom, or the amount of time a station was required to remain on the air.

The Wireless Ship Act pressed home to legislators lessons learned from the *Republic*, but her fate would have impressed them more had a major tragedy ensued. What if Jack Binns had been incapacitated, with no one else capable of sending a distress call, or suppose he had only been able to render his call for a few minutes and someone at the receiving end had dismissed it as another amateur hoax?

At least some farsighted legislators must have been thinking along these lines. A House of Representatives report from 1910 prophetically noted that without further and more specific wireless regulation a major disaster might be inadequately reported or not reported until it was too late for proper action to be taken. Thoughts such as this led to the circulation of six bills in 1910, and 13 in 1912 prior to the fateful events of April. But the Wireless Ship Act was as far as the government was willing to go, and even that policy was violated on numerous occasions when Marconi operators followed the old no-intercommunications rule and snubbed transmissions from American companies such as United Wireless and Lee De Forest.

Why was this call for further regulation not more emphatic or more fully supported? In part the answer is because this was still the age of classical capitalism. Antiregulatory lobbies were a fact of America political life. In the case of wireless policy, which began to be debated in the press in 1910, the opposition invoked such sacred tenets of American ideology as free enterprise, free speech, and property rights—rights to the airwaves above a transmitter that the sender either owned or leased.

The situation in Britain was similar. A bill proposing the mandatory use of wireless on oceangoing ships carrying 50 or more passengers was tabled in the House of Commons in 1910. It was prompted by concerns about safety and navigation and defeated on the grounds that it would be a further expense to shipping companies and thus hinder their international competitiveness. Doubtless the intense Anglo-German rivalry for maritime supremacy weighed on the minds of many legislators.

In the United States the antiregulatory position was occasionally vulnerable to challenge as a result of the actions of the amateur operators who were starting to become a nuisance to commercial and military interests. Marconi wanted to see them contained, but he preferred to put up with the situation rather than support regulatory policy that might result in the passage of bills so inclusive they might affect the way he managed his operations. In the pages of the *New York Times* he occasionally voiced his opposition to what worried legislators were conjuring.

In the aftermath of the *Titanic* disaster Marconi modified his position on wireless regulation, but his new outlook remained self-serving. His views appeared in an "Authorized Interview" in the June 2, 1912, issue of *World's Work*. There is no indication of the exact date of the interview or when it occurred with respect to the U.S. inquiry, which began on April 19, or the British, which commenced on May 2.

Marconi urged that a major lesson of the disaster was the necessity of having two operators on an oceangoing vessel. The *Carpathia*, he noted, picked up the *Titanic*'s distress signal by the "merest accident." He made no mention of the *Californian* incident. Either it had not been discussed in the press or at either inquiry at the time of the interview, or it is possible that he wanted to refrain from entering the controversy. In reaffirming his opposition to broad regulatory changes, he went on to consider the notorious no-intercommunications policy. He argued that it should only be waived in the case of urgent messages in the CQD or SOS category: "Beyond such regulations and those bearing on the loss of vessels and lives, I hardly think it feasible for international agreements to go." It is remarkable here, in light of the events surrounding the sinking of the *Titanic*, that he did not affirm the necessity of specific intercommunications relating to navigation—ice warnings, for example.

But what about those pesky amateurs? On this subject Marconi was much less committed to an antiregulatory position. He called for stringent policies whereby governments would tighten the licensing procedure for wireless operators, limit amateurs to specific wavelengths, and impose stiff fines for interference.

No one felt the need for wireless regulations following the *Titanic* disaster more acutely than Michigan senator William Alden Smith, who led the U.S. inquiry. Although Smith was a Republican, his populist leanings and frequent criticism of the monopolistic power of large trusts did not always endear him to his party's old and still powerful elite. He saw Marconi engaging in corporate practices that were not always in the public interest. Smith was irked by the failure of the *Carpathia*'s Marconi man, Harold Cottam, and the *Titanic*'s surviving operator, Harold Bride, to forward more information about the tragedy.

Marconi testimony at the inquiry deepened Smith's suspicions about the way the "big business" of wireless conducted its affairs. A Marconi operator's first loyalty seemed to be to the Marconi Company, not the ship's captain, the shipping line, or government officials. Smith kept implying the need for more comprehensive wireless regulations during his questioning of those involved with this aspect of the disaster. His closing summation contained an impassioned plea for legislation to help bring this about.

The initial public response to the role of wireless in the disaster was largely positive. Marconi, along with the *Titanic*'s deceased operator, Jack Phillips, was given heroic treatment in the press at a time when heroes were sorely needed. The sentiments expressed in a speech by the British postmaster general on April 18 summed up the attitude of many people on both sides of the Atlantic (with the likely exception of Senator Smith): "Those who had been saved had been saved by one man—Mr. Marconi." Among the American accolades was a telegram from Thomas Edison, who had publically endorsed Marconi's abilities a few years earlier.

To be celebrated this way was perhaps the high point of Marconi's career. The invention that for over a decade had been linked with his name was now synonymous with it. Unprecedented business opportunities followed. The question marks clouding his reputation, particularly the "all safe on the *Titanic*" wireless message and his later collusion with the *New York Times*, would soon be forgotten.

Because wireless had at least performed up to previous expectations, its practitioners were spared admonishment. Marconi was critiqued rather than criticized, and advised on how a good thing could be made better.

The call for wireless regulations by the press and at the two inquiries was more tempered than the one dealing with shipping and navigational practices. In the latter category, outrage was expressed over the frequent practice of large liners, with fewer lifeboat spaces than passengers, steaming rapidly at night through regions where ice was present. Here, the White Star Line was chastised for doing what was often being done by other companies.

In the wake of Senator Smith's inquiry, the U.S. government had no intention of waiting over a year for a new international wireless conference to make policy changes. In July, President Taft signed into law an amendment to the 1910 Wireless Ship Act. Vessels covered by the original act described earlier now had to have two operators on board so the station could function 24 hours a day; an auxiliary power source was also mandated. That month a new and sweeping bill, the Radio Act, was passed, which became law the following December. It required all operators to be licensed, with the secretary of labor and commerce in administrative charge. Stations now had to have a specific transmitter capacity and adhere to a given wavelength. The amateurs, who had been heroic figures a few years earlier, were now out of favor with government, the wireless companies, and, because of what allegedly happened with some of the *Titanic*'s transmissions, the press. They were still permitted to listen in—something that would be difficult to prevent in any case—but could only obtain a license to transmit for the shortwave part of the radio spectrum.

Susan Douglas, in her detailed history of the early years of American broadcasting, refers to these amateurs, now limited to shortwave transmission, as being "exiled to an ethereal reservation." And so it must have seemed at the time. Although Marconi's initial experiments had used shortwave, he thought it had limited potential for long-distance transmission. Long, low-frequency wavelengths seemed to work better, especially in following the curvature of the earth over saltwater; they also required an increase in power with respect to the distance to be covered. Going with what worked rather than reflecting on what might be theoretically possible, Marconi committed himself to the longwave/high-power strategy. Others followed his lead.

By 1920, however, he was forced to reevaluate this commitment. Amateurs were achieving extraordinary results communicating over great distances using shortwave and low power. Douglas's "ethereal reservation" was becoming a small-scale version of Marshall McLuhan's "global village." A theoretical explanation emerged when Arthur Kennelly in the United States and Oliver Heaviside in England explained the role of the ionosphere in reflecting radio waves back to earth. Short wavelengths are exceptionally efficient exploiters of this property, and after 1920, Marconi committed himself to using them to develop radio's potential for international communication on a global scale.

The American Radio Act also established new procedures for distress calls, in part to prevent the type of confusion that plagued some of the *Titanic*'s last transmissions. A distress frequency was established, and when it was being used all ships and shore stations unable to assist directly or relay the message were to cease signaling. In addition, shore stations had to monitor this frequency every 15 minutes for 2 minutes. SOS was deemed to be the official distress call—any reluctance to use it, instead of CQD, had by this time been erased by the notoriety given SOS by the *Titanic*. And, to keep amateur operators from interfering with or faking such transmissions, the right to impose heavy fines and suspend their licenses was made law.

Marconi was not unappreciative of the positive benefits to him of regulations deriving from the Radio Act. It would be easier for his large company to implement them than for smaller rivals. However, over the next several years, another legacy of Senator Smith would pursue him, as it would Western Union and the American Telephone and Telegraph Company: antitrust legislation.

The Radio Act also conceded more to the military than must have been to Marconi's liking. A wide part of the spectrum was reserved for the navy, and provisions were made for them to upgraded their (non-Marconi) equipment and extend their jurisdiction. Private stations could now be closed down or taken over should conditions warrant, which is what came to pass with the United States' entry into World War I in 1917. This set the stage for the postwar takeover of American Marconi by General Electric through its subsidiary, RCA.

The quick action on the part of American legislators following the *Titanic* disaster influenced the proceedings of the International Conference for the Safety of Life at Sea, held in London between November 12, 1913, and January 20, 1914. Policies were implemented affecting lifeboats, navigational procedures in hazardous conditions, the establishment of an international ice patrol, and communications.

To prevent a recurrence of what happened with the *Californian*, all rockets were deemed to be distress signals and had to be responded to accordingly. Although oceangoing ships had to carry a wireless with sufficient range and an auxiliary power source, the U.S. requirement of two operators was waived in the case of certain freighters, where a member of the crew competent enough to decipher an emergency transmission could substitute for the second operator.

A total of 74 articles were signed into agreement by the 13 nations who participated in the London conference. The measures pertaining to wireless did not go as far as the American Radio Act, but the desired results were achieved. Since the *Titanic* perished in 1912, no oceangoing vessel using the Atlantic shipping lanes has been lost because of a collision with ice. The London conference unequivocally showed that maritime communication had come a long way from the incident that befell the Collins liner *Pacific* in 1856: months after she disappeared without a trace, a message in a bottle drifted to the Hebrides. It described the ship going down surrounded by icebergs.

PART TWO

Story of the Century

Journalism is the first draft of history.

—Philip Graham, *Washington Post* publisher

CHAPTER 5

The Battle for New York

What makes the sinking of the *Titanic* such an impressive episode in the history of twentieth-century journalism is not just its intensity but its duration. Like the Kennedy assassination, the *Titanic* disaster was front-page news for almost a month throughout North America and parts of Europe, and it lingered for several days to over a week in the rest of the world's papers. Using this measure, the story that stands just behind it in longevity (if we factor out war-related coverage) is the Lindbergh baby kidnapping, not the epoch-making flight. It held the front page longer and, unlike the flight, was an important item in the newspapers of countries not favorably disposed toward the United States.

News about the plight of the *Titanic* circulated with a rapidity unmatched by any previous event. It set a journalistic precedent, one that would be redeployed during the great upheaval of World War I. Seventy-five years of instantaneous electric communication came to the fore and demonstrated that global communication need never again be dependent on the available means of transport. Information moved to and from news agencies via the wireless (barely a decade old), transoceanic cable (widely established in the third quarter of the previous century), and the overland telegraph (a mid–nineteenth century innovation). In terms of news dissemination, the *Titanic* disaster can be seen as the beginning of what media guru Marshall McLuhan called the "global village," though he coined that term with 1960s satellite communication in mind.

Nowhere was the reach of this new communication network more evident than in the news reports that reached the country farthest away from where the sinking occurred: Australia. Being so far away from the source of the story, Australian press coverage was limited to major updates accompanied by the occasional cautious interpretation. It lacked the rampant speculation that characterized the North American news media.

Perhaps the "tyranny of distance," as they say down under, was in this instance a blessing. And what a distance late-breaking information about the *Titanic* had to travel: early wireless reports reaching North America were relayed to England via cable, then eastward across Europe, the Middle East, and Asia using overland and submarine lines; after arriving at Darwin in the north of Australia, the dispatches went south along the great overland telegraph to Adelaide and thence to major centers east and west.

Newspapers in other countries used some of the same means to access what at the time was called the "story of the century." Nevertheless, most of the information that went global did so after arriving first in New York, where it was processed and interpreted by the most innovative assemblage of newspapers that graced any city. New York press coverage of the sinking attracted worldwide attention and ultimately resulted in journalistic accomplishment being added to the city's list of internationally renowned achievements.

New York in 1912, diverse, lively, and not without its dangers, had become the emerging metropolis of the new century. The *Titanic*'s planned maiden voyage from Great Britain to that city can be symbolically construed, along with numerous other events at the time, as symptomatic of an inexorable passing of the torch of industrial and cultural leadership to New York from London, the urban monarch of the previous 100 years.

A less symbolic and more concrete indicator of the shift resides in the fact that the *Titanic*, the pride of British mercantile shipping, was ultimately owned by a trust headed by New York's, the United States', and the world's reigning doyen of the dollars, J. P. Morgan. From his Fifth Avenue mansion he controlled a plethora of industries. Aging and too ill to occupy his personal suite on the *Titanic*, Morgan's physical demise followed the legendary ship's by a year; 1913 would also see the power of trusts such as his challenged by new federal legislation.

As the terminus to which nearly all information roads led regarding the plight of the *Titanic*, New York, with its burgeoning population, had more news-gathering resources than any other city. At least a dozen of the city's dailies took up the challenge of chasing the story. This tradition of a comprehensive popular press had been over three-quarters of a century in the making. Its starting point can be traced to the birth of the *New York Sun* in 1833.

Founded by Benjamin Day and reinvigorated by Charles Dana in 1868, the *Sun* was the first of the "penny papers." This epithet referred not just to price but also to a new, implied journalistic philosophy. Social issues, crime, scandal, and human-interest stories, along with sports and entertainment, were given regular coverage. As in the past, politics often guided editorial policy, but the views expressed now tended to be issue oriented rather than following the platform of any particular political party. They also anticipated the populist position that would make the papers of Joseph Pulitzer and William Randolph Hearst so successful by century's end.

The penny press featured more rapid news coverage than its predecessors. Born in an age when the railway and steamship were just beginning to make transportation, and with it communication, faster, the new journalism's addiction to rapid information gathering was further fueled by the advent of the telegraph in the 1840s. Telegraphy provided a definitive separation of communication from transportation and ushered in the electric age—by the late 1860s the transatlantic cable enabled London news to appear in New York papers the next day.

Following on the heels of Day's successful venture with the *Sun* came James Gordon Bennett's *New York Herald* in 1835, and Horace "Go West Young Man" Greeley's *New York Tribune* in 1841. This first wave of the penny press would eventually be challenged by the more sedate and information-oriented *New York Times*, founded in 1851 by Henry Raymond. In 1912, reporting the story of the *Titanic* would involve all three representatives of the original penny press and a *Times* that had been reborn in 1896 when Adolph Ochs took over. They would all have to battle with the two papers that actually led the city in circulation in 1912, Pulitzer's *New York World* and Hearst's *New York Evening Journal*.

Pulitzer, a Hungarian immigrant, took over the *World* in 1883 after having performed a minor miracle the previous decade by reviving the ailing *St. Louis Post-Dispatch*. He increased the *World*'s human interest stories and conjured publicity stunts to boost circulation, such as sending Nellie Bly on a record-breaking 72-day trip around the world in 1888 and 1889—the feat being inspired by Jules Verne's popular novel *Around the World in Eighty Days*. The paper also outdid its competitors in the use of illustrations while maintaining quality editorials and adopting a distinctly populist and often pro-union position. By the mid-1880s the *World* had pulled even with the leading *Sun* and

Herald. At the outset of the 1890s it became the paper of choice for the majority of New Yorkers.

A serious rival to the *World*'s supremacy emerged in 1895, when Hearst took over the marginal *New York Morning Journal*, turning it into the *New York Evening Journal* in 1896. The *Morning Journal*, ironically, started out as the brainchild of Pulitzer's brother, Albert. The battle between Pulitzer and Hearst yielded "yellow journalism," with Hearst taking some of the conventions of this tradition—scandal mongering, screaming headlines, and support for the underdog—to often ludicrous extremes.

Hearst also gained a reputation for news making when news reporting would not suffice. His most notorious foray in this direction occurred in 1898, when he drummed up sentiment for the United States to initiate the Spanish-American War. This episode, along with a famous quip to his correspondent Frederick Remington, "I'll furnish the war, you furnish the pictures," is humorously recreated in the first part of Orson Welles' cinematic masterpiece, *Citizen Kane* (1941). The film goes on to elaborate several aspects of the rivalry between the *Journal* (called the *New York Inquirer*) and the *World* (dubbed the *New York Chronicle*). As we shall see, when confronted with having to cover the enormously difficult and important story of the *Titanic* in head-to-head competition with other New York dailies, Hearst's paper, with its misguided speculation, yielded coverage that was nothing short of a journalistic disaster.

MONDAY, APRIL 15

On this day the world learned that something was amiss with the *Titanic*. Eerily, New York press coverage of the story can be seen as having commenced the previous day. The Sunday edition of the *Times* ran an article on page 6 describing the massiveness of the new ship and included a small photograph, which wound up enlarged and moved to the front page the next day. Thus from the outset, as well as throughout the coming weeks, the *Times* managed to be one step ahead of its rivals.

The first wireless reports stating that the *Titanic* had struck an iceberg, was sinking by the bow, and was putting women into lifeboats reached newsrooms in the early morning hours of April 15. Available information also indicated that several ships were rapidly steaming to her aid. Around these "facts," and a number of additional sketchy and sometimes conflicting bits of information, stories had to be written. With so few details, interpretation had to substitute for eye-witness reporting. That these interpretations varied considerably was due to the question marks surrounding the information. How fatal was the Titanic's wound? Would she sink rapidly, slowly, or merely remain incapacitated at the surface? How quickly could potential rescue ships arrive, which even cautious papers such as the *Tribune* implied constituted an armada?

The varying responses to these questions must have caused considerable consternation among readers perusing the newsstands. The tenor of the coverage ranged from the *Times*' somber assemblage of evidence suggesting the worst to the imprudently optimistic exhortations of the *Evening Journal*.

The *Times*' account listed the known facts in an extended headline: "NEW LINER TITANIC HITS ICEBERG; SINKING BY THE BOW AT MIDNIGHT; WOMEN PUT OFF IN LIFEBOATS; LAST WIRELESS AT 12:27 A.M. BLURRED." The ominous follow-up text noted how the wireless transmission ended abruptly and that the *Virginian* and *Baltic* were attempting to go to the *Titanic*'s position. It also mentioned the near miss the *Titanic* had with the *New York* when leaving Southampton and cited the *Niagara*'s earlier mishap with ice as evidence of the attendant dangers in the North Atlantic at that time of year. No other paper seemed to offer so little hope that all would be well.

The *Tribune* ran most of the same information on its front page but emphasized the "reassuring feature" that considerable assistance was on the way. The *Herald* did likewise, with part of its headline reading "VESSELS RUSH TO HER SIDE." This must have strongly suggested to 1912 readers that a concerted rescue operation was underway. The *Herald* added another glimmer of hope by running an article on the front page, below its *Titanic* commentary, that mentioned how the *Niagara* had hit ice in the same region as the *Titanic* and was nonetheless able to make her way to port.

The *Niagara* incident was elaborated at greater length in the *World*, where it served to temper a more ominous lead article that paralleled the *Times* assessment. The paper noted that the *Niagara* was punctured twice by ice, and although she summoned help, would-be rescuers were eventually waved off. For readers who were clinging to a vestige of hope, the connotations must have seemed obvious: if the puny *Niagara* could survive such a mishap, why not the mighty *Titanic*?

The hint of hope became a virtual promise in the *Sun* and *Evening Journal*. Although the morning *Sun* merely reported that the *Titanic* had hit an iceberg, the headline of the evening edition read, "TITANIC'S PASSENGERS ARE TRANSHIPPED." The subheadline claimed a rescue by the *Carpathia* and *Parisian*, with the *Titanic* being towed to Halifax by the *Virginian* (no doubt a result of the wireless confusion discussed in Chapter 2). The headline of the final edition read, "ALL SAVED FROM TITANIC AFTER COLLISION."

The accompanying article attributed this information to Captain Haddock of the *Olympic*. He later denied making such a statement. It probably resulted from wireless misinterpretation, whereby a transmission noting that the *Parisian* and *Carpathia* were headed to the site of the collision was construed as affirmation of immediate rescue, with the information somehow linked to a transmission of some kind from the *Olympic*'s captain. The *Sun*'s copywriters embellished this false story with their own description of the *Titanic*, still afloat with pumps laboring while her lifeboats were being rowed to the *Carpathia*. A contributing element to the elaboration of this scenario could have been the widely known and cited fact that weather at the scene of the mishap was exceptionally calm and clear.

Hearst's *Evening Journal*, using the boldest headline of any paper, was even more optimistic: "ALL SAFE ON TITANIC." A box to the left contained a subheading claiming the liner was in tow, along with a picture of the ship and her captain. Subsequent commentary posited that four vessels were involved in the rescue, which was facilitated by calm seas. More specific pronouncements soon followed. One statement had 20 lifeboats (which probably unbeknown to the paper was the ship's actual complement) going to the *Carpathia*. It was also noted that survivors had been picked up by the *Baltic* and *Virginian* and that a wireless message stated that there were no casualties. Sources are not cited for any of this information; one suspects the paper's penchant for creating reader-friendly copy when information was not forthcoming. This is evidenced on page 2, with the alleged towing of the *Titanic* by the *Virginian* described in the manner in which it might have taken place.

Several papers outside New York also elected to print the "all safe. *Titanic* in tow" story in their April 15 editions despite the sketchiness of the information. They include the *Springfield Evening Union*, *Columbus Evening Dispatch*, and *Montreal Star*. Although some of this information was routed through Montreal from North Atlantic wireless messages, that city's other English-language daily, the *Gazette*, took a more cautious approach and did not go with the rescue story. The *Star*, in deciding to run it, put out three extras. The first described the ship still afloat; the second cited White Star's assurance that the ship was safe; however, by the third edition the headline read, "SS TITANIC IN BAD SHAPE." Montreal's weekly newspaper, the *Witness*, which came out on April 16, refused to abandon the hopeful news and ran a story to that effect at a time when most other sources had concede that the ship was lost.

TUESDAY, APRIL 16

Building on it previous guess of the disaster's magnitude, the *Times* ran a headline that put the death toll at 1,250, with 866 assumed survivors. Among those saved, the paper listed as definite the director of the White Star Line and president of International Mercantile Marine, Bruce Ismay, and as a maybe the young Mrs. Astor. Subsequent front-page commentary served to remind readers of the paper's prescience the previous day, noting that While Star did not concede that the liner was lost until 8:20 the previous evening and that the widely circulated reports in other papers about the *Titanic* being towed by the *Virginian* had no foundation. A large photograph (normally not the *Times*' style) of the ship being towed out of Belfast, perhaps for her trials, accompanied the headline. The *Times* also contended that there were too few lifeboats to accommodate all the passengers, information the White Star office in New York could or would not verify.

For its part, White Star seemed to labor under the delusion that, as their advertising hype had put it, the ship was "practically unsinkable." The person in charge of the New York office was Phillip Franklin, vice president and general manager of International Mercantile Marine. For almost a full day after the first reports of trouble came in he insisted that the ship had not foundered. He would later be accused of knowing the worst while refusing to acknowledge it publically. Perhaps no one was as chastised during this stage of reporting, especially by newspapers that had run stories consistent with his denials. Fortunately for him, public animosity eventually went up the chain of command and was transferred to his boss, Bruce Ismay, soon after the *Carpathia* docked on the evening of April 18.

Did Franklin really not know how many lifeboats the *Titanic* carried? If so, the *Times* did not make an issue of it. Their research had already uncovered the number on the sister ship, the *Olympic*: 16 plus 4 collapsibles. Readers were left to ponder the unlikely possibility that the *Titanic* carried more.

Confident that the important and decisive factors pertaining to the disaster were now established with certainty, the April 16 *Times* then engaged in some speculative filling in of details. Several paragraphs described the rescue while others focused on the circumstances of the collision. This strategy was tempered by using the words "must have." The paper suggested that the shock of the impact perhaps destroyed the operation of the electrically operated watertight doors (not the case) and that the iceberg could have opened gaps further along the hull (an accurate guess). In support of its assessment of the collision scenario, the paper mentioned the *Olympic*'s encounter with the *Hawk* as an indicator of the poor maneuverability and vulnerability of this new class of giant liners. Several maritime experts were interviewed who supported these contentions, and they in turn added insights pertaining to the dangers of ice in the North Atlantic at that time of year.

The remainder of the coverage monitored reactions around the world as well as in different parts of New York. It also presented a gallery of some of the most notable passengers on the voyage, gave a summary of Captain Smith's career, and provided an annotated list of previous maritime disasters. In all, there were eight pages of meticulous, well-organized copy, setting a standard for other papers to match. None could. The strategy behind this remarkable coverage will be discussed in the next chapter.

The *Tribune* estimated that there were 1,350 casualties and 866 survivors, most of the latter being women and children. What no one at the time could have realized was that, given the presence of crewmen in many of the lifeboats, one-third of the survivors turned out to be men. Covering some of the same ground as the *Times* but with less detail, the *Tribune* also discussed the new giant liners, the dangers of ice, and the career of Captain Smith. As befitted its business orientation, the paper contained an article on the probable insurance loss entailed by the disaster.

The *Herald*, which in reporting the disaster on April 15 had broken with its regular format of putting classified advertisements on the front page, now went to a greater extreme in its consideration of casualties. A bold slanted headline declared the death toll at 1,800 with 675 survivors. It was accompanied by a spectacular drawing of the collision, creating the most eye-catching front-page report of the tragedy that my research has unearthed. Whoever did the artwork is not credited—to cite the person would of course detract from the realism implied in the illustration—but the style is evident in other issues of the paper throughout that week.

In going over ground also covered by the *Times* and *Tribune*, the *Herald* included more commentary on the false reports of rescue, noting in a subheadline that after the collision the "WHOLE WORLD THOUGHT TITANIC SAFE." Whoever wrote this seemed not to have had in mind devoted *Times* readers.

The headline of the *World* listed 1,500 lost (the most accurate estimate) and 866 survivors. Consistent with the paper's tradition of journalist exposés, it made White Star's early denial of the sinking into a topic for critical commentary. Without accusing Phillip Franklin of deceit, his professed ignorance of the number of lifeboats on the *Titanic* was implied to be the next worst thing, along with reassurances he gave that the ship's unsinkable status would enable her to float after any collision with ice. With only five pages of coverage in its April 16 issue, the *World* might have said all that had to be said. However, the paper may have lacked the resources to handle the story more fully.

The newspapers that had the most difficult decision regarding what to print on April 16 were the *Sun* and *Evening Journal*. The previous day both had elected to go with stories affirming a complete rescue. Now, knowing the worst, they had to backpedal to save face.

The morning edition of the *Sun*, rather than conceding that 1,500 were lost, used the phrase "1500 MISSING" in its headline. The ice thus broken, to use an unforgivable pun, the evening edition could then state that 1,400 perished, 800 were saved, and that only one ship, the *Carpathia*, was involved in the rescue; however, the final edition did hint that the *Virginian* "might" have more survivors. The earlier false reports were blamed on White Star, which, it was alleged, gave forth inaccurate information in the face of the pandemonium engulfing its New York office. What the paper failed to note was that White Star only issued denials of the worst, not details on the alleged rescue and towing scenario. Responsibility for this information resided with those papers that reported it on the basis of meager evidence. Having thus attempted to make peace with its readers, the *Sun* settled down to the business of discussing what was known about the sinking, the conditions surrounding it, and personalities involved.

Hearst's *Evening Journal* faced its readers on April 16 with a bit of deceit. The same screaming headlines that had announced "ALL SAFE" the previous day now declared "866 SAVED," with "VIRGINIAN TOO LATE" just below in muted gray characters one-quarter the size. For the paper to preface the initial headline with "only" would have been a concession to journalistic honesty it was not prepared to make. How many people actually perished? To find the estimates, readers had to consult the text of subsequent pages.

To further encourage amnesia among its readers regarding the previous issue, the paper raised the question of initial culpability for the loss of life. White Star was targeted. Several articles, including the editorial, dealt with the "titanic crime" of the ship not having an adequate complement of lifeboats. Other coverage, amply illustrated, stressed the dangers of ice along North Atlantic shipping routes.

Another kind of danger implied in the *Evening Journal*'s coverage—in the eyes of some moralistic beholders—derived from the lovely young Madeleine Astor, who had survived the sinking. Several siren-like portraits of her appeared, along with a statement announcing that her husband's body had just been found close to the site where the ship went down. Astor's divorce and eventual marriage to this 19-year-old just before the voyage had created an international scandal, and the paper could not resist reminding readers of the liaison. Ironically, Hearst himself would later raise eyebrows by having an extended affair with the young actress Marion Davies, a relationship parodied in *Citizen Kane*.

WEDNESDAY, APRIL 1₇

As anxious readers sought their paper of choice, few held out any hope that the tragedy would be of a lesser magnitude than reported the previous day. What they did hope for were more details and a possible explanation for why, on the clearest of evenings, an experienced captain commanding a state-of-the-art ship allowed it to collide with an iceberg and founder. For anyone following the story it was obvious from earlier coverage, as well as expert testimony, that the collision could not have been the iceberg's fault; in other words, it was in the region where it was supposed to be, given the time of year and earlier navigational reports. Why then was the *Titanic*, whose role was that of a speeding interloper into a known colony of natural hazards, so rudely oblivious to the residents?

Answers could only be hinted at, and carefully at best. Without doubt most papers were conscious of possible embarrassment in reporting something that might later turn out to be otherwise—most papers, that is, except Hearst's *Evening Journal*, which took one more stab at chronicling an important turn of events overlooked by rivals. As we shall see, the result was another news-guessing error that further diminished the paper's credibility. In following a more cautious strategy, the rest of the New York press corps subordinated conclusive statements about what might have happened to an elaboration of the context surrounding the voyage and sinking. Archival sources and expert commentary aided the task.

Once again, the *Times* took the lead in providing detailed, comprehensive coverage. Its efforts the previous two days had probably succeeded in attracting readers who normally subscribed to rival papers. Circulation figures certainly suggest this, for although the number of copies sold for all papers increased, the rise was most pronounced in the case of the *Times*.

What was known with certainty was the passenger manifest, which the *Times* printed. Readers could then compare it to a subsequent list containing the names of 400 known survivors that had come in via the *Carpathia*'s meager wireless reports. What made many of the names that appeared on the first list but not the second so interesting was their social status. Reliable reports had already put John Jacob Astor among the deceased, which led to an awareness that wealth and privilege was no assurance against this nautical Armageddon. When other famous names did not appear on the initial survivor lists or were listed as missing, their possible demise piqued the interest of many.

The *Times*' response to this fascination with the rich and famous was to devote most of the April 17 front page to photographs, drawings, and biographical profiles of some of the notables who made the nightmare voyage. In a number of instances their understandably distraught family members provided statements.

By page 3, technical and regulatory details earned consideration. The features of the ship were described, along with reactions to the disaster voiced by authorities in London, most notably Lloyd's, which faced a phenomenal insurance loss. The paper's investigation of Lloyd's role in the tragedy was one of the few areas in which it had not been first, since the *Tribune* had already broached the issue the day before. What the *Times* added was a citation of the British Board of Trade regulations governing the number of lifeboats on a ship: vessels of 10,000 tons or more must carry a minimum of 16 boats. The *Titanic*, at almost five times that tonnage, carried but 20—wholly inadequate, but more than the letter of the rules stipulated. The paper then joined the growing chorus that demanded the rule be changed. In doing likewise, the rival *Herald* noted that United States regulations required lifeboats to accommodate *all* on board. Nevertheless, we must note that the country was not endowed with Olympic-class liners carrying 3,000-plus passengers. A full complement of lifeboats would have limited valuable deck space, or so Bruce Ismay and White Star had earlier decided.

In subsequent pages, the *Times* discussed again the dangers of ice. There were photographs of icebergs, and one of the crushed bow of the *Arizona* taken after her spectacular but benign collision with such a hazard in 1879. An article on the *Niagara* was included, along with a statement from Captain Inman Selby of the *Republic* that echoed the previous day's speculation that the *Titanic*'s collision was probably along the lines of a glancing blow that sliced open a considerable portion of the ship's hull. The day's coverage concluded with a chart of the ocean's depth where the sinking took place and a final query as to whether such massive and luxurious vessels are desirable.

One final point should be noted with respect to the April 17 *Times*. The paper could not resist suggesting to readers that its coverage was widely regarded as the most complete and up-to-date. Page 5 contained a self-congratulatory article describing how crowds were being attracted to the *New York Times* building by the regularly posted bulletins, which in turn were being sent "far and wide" to places such as hotels and Pennsylvania station.

The *Tribune* devoted the bulk of its commentary, as did many papers, to the notables who might have gone down with the ship. The *Herald*, using the work of the unnamed illustrator mentioned previously, went with a headline story that claimed the ship was "torn asunder" while traveling at 18 knots. At the time this may have seemed to readers to be an impressive and reckless speed, but the actual rate surpassed the conjecture. At the U.S. inquiry it would later be learned that something in the vicinity of 22 knots was the actual speed—not quite the maximum 24 knots of which the *Titanic* might have been capable, but close.

The *Herald*'s coverage exceeded the *Tribune*'s in length and was only slightly less than that of the *Times*. Going over some of the same ground as the latter, the *Arizona* incident was discussed and illustrated with a drawing (the *Times* used a photograph) of her wrecked bow. Comparative interest in the two collisions was then piqued by an eyewitness description from an *Arizona* passenger who had observed events 32 years earlier. Speculation on how the damage may have differed was offered by a naval architect, W. A. Dobson. He accurately suggested that the *Titanic*, in try to avoid hitting the iceberg, inadvertently sideswiped it, resulting in a gash along the ship's hull. The paper ended its coverage by proposing the establishment of a government patrol to warn of ice, an idea that eventually came to pass with the establishment of the International Ice Patrol.

Speculation about the nature of the collision, along with comments on the physical features of the ship and an updated survivor list, were featured in the *World*. Consistent with the celebrity watching no paper was immune from, the coverage included an article on Vincent Astor. Now aware of his father's death, he was described as being in the throes of preparing to send for the recovered body. The issue of who died and why was further elaborated in a discussion of the wisdom and history of the edict "women and children first." In the coming weeks it would emerge as a source of debate in many quarters.

The *Sun*, still retreating from its overly optimistic pronouncements two days earlier, provided coverage that was surprisingly brief and cautious. However, one area that received extended commentary, given the paper's business orientation, was an assessment of the financial wherewithal aboard the ship and the ensuing loss.

Unlike the *Sun*, the *Evening Journal* failed to heed the earlier lesson of not proclaiming sketchy information to be unequivocal fact. The April 17 headline blared, "EVERY WOMAN SAVED." The paper's reasons for this pronouncement are unfathomable. The headline must have been just as much an affront to common sense then as now. How could a chaotic accident at sea, which claimed 1,500 lives (as clearly established by April 17), with an estimated 600 to 800 survivors, not result in the loss of life of at least a handful of women? Despite the call for women and children first, the ship's condition and the ensuing evacuation posed obvious hazards for anyone attempting to leave, female or male.

We should also wonder why Hearst reporters, who were attending David Sarnoff in the wireless room at Wanamaker's department store, did not pick up on the fact that the names of survivors coming in included a disproportionately high number of men, especially given the way the evacuation was *supposed* to have taken place. Perhaps the editors were bedazzled into thinking that the fate of Madeleine Astor, who appeared in yet another large and ravishing portrait, was representative of all women on board.

THURSDAY, APRIL 18

What every paper reported was that the *Carpathia* would be landing in New York by early evening. The names of those who survived, as well as the casualties, would then be known with cold certainty. Most readers were also expecting the ship's arrival to clear up the mystery of how and why the sinking had occurred. Alas, the initial answers would only raise more questions—some of them would linger for the next 100 years. It would take the better part of another week for the U.S. inquiry to present a series of solid, if not always satisfying, findings.

One fact of which all New York newspapers were certain on April 18 was that with the arrival of the *Carpathia* they would not be the only press corps having access to eyewitness testimony regarding the disaster. Reporters from many parts of the United States and Canada were descending on the city for what promised to be the most massive journalistic scrum in history.

The *Times* was well prepared for the challenge, and confident enough, as we shall see in the next chapter, to declare that their next day's edition would mark a turning point in our knowledge of the tragedy. On April 18 it mostly discussed the false reports of complete rescue and the issues at stake in the forthcoming inquiry. The *Tribune* did likewise but included an article in which Phillip Franklin was allowed to present his claim that White Star did not withhold information from the public. The *Herald* also mentioned the Senate inquiry and went on to note that one would also be convened in London at a later, unspecified date. Consistent with the exciting visuals it had been presenting throughout the week was a front-page illustration of the *Titanic* going down with lifeboats beside her and the iceberg in the background. Page 3 included a photograph of an iceberg with a cleverly drawn-in likeness of the *Titanic* behind it.

Going over previous coverage was also a strategy the *World* employed. The paper marshaled available evidence to present a summary account of what might have happened, knowing that the next day this would be measured against the words of those who were there. That these words would themselves be contradictory probably helped soften later criticism directed at the interpretive license taken by the press as a whole. One final point worth noting regarding the *World*'s coverage is that in each day's paper it presented a news cartoon critically commenting on some aspect of the disaster. This practice became widespread, but the *World* did it with more poignancy than any other paper I have surveyed, American or otherwise.

The *Sun*, after gradually having gradually recovering credibility from its inaccurately optimistic headline of the 15th, used the edition of the 18th to summarize events to date. One that it amplified, which had only been mentioned by rival papers, was the preparations being made for the survivors. Several articles were given over to describing the lodging and support that would be provided. In most instances the individuals and groups responsible were mentioned by name.

Not surprisingly, the strangest lead story of the day came from the *Evening Journal*. On the basis of what must have been meager evidence—but probably a reasonable deduction—the paper discussed how a number of survivors had been rendered ill by their ordeal. The remainder of the coverage dealt with reactions to the disaster, the known facts pertaining to it, and the upcoming inquiry. However, one area where the paper did something unique and interesting had to do with events slated to transpire that evening. On page 3 there was a large photograph of Pier 54, where the *Carpathia* would land, and an explanation of how the passenger would probably disembark.

The *Carpathia*'s arrival would initiate a new dimension in reporting what was already being called "the story of the century." So far the press battle for New York had not resulted in a decisive victory for any of the participants, although the *Times* had perhaps surprised many by taking the initial lead; today it is the first paper mentioned when *Titanic* aficionados discuss press responses to the tragedy. Their reactions are usually influenced by the April 19 edition. It gained worldwide recognition and bestowed a prominence on the paper during the coming weeks that no rival could match.

Nevertheless, honorable mention for coverage during those crucial first four days should go to the *Herald*. The paper used exciting visuals and thoughtful articles to cover a salient range of topics. At the other end of the press continuum, it might be appropriate to award a booby prize to Hearst's *Evening Journal* for its misguided sensationalism.

CHAPTER 6

Carr Van Anda and the New York Times

The success in the battle for New York that the *Times* attained with its coverage attracted worldwide notoriety. Fourteen years earlier, when Adolph Ochs took over the paper, the circulation was 9,000 and dropping; out of 15 dailies in the city, the *Times* stood 13th.

To the rest of the world the *Times'* rise following the disaster may have given the impression of a sudden transition from obscurity to prominence, but it had been over a decade in the making. During those years three elements converged, and any assessment of the *Times'* *Titanic* coverage should acknowledge them: the paper's historical commitment to leading-edge investigative reporting; Ochs' plan to extend this mandate in a more efficient and comprehensive manner; and the innovative field generalship of managing editor Carr Van Anda, who was hired in 1904.

The paper first came into existence on September 18, 1851, as the *New-York Daily Times*—the word "daily" was dropped in 1857 and the hyphen in 1896. It was founded by Henry Raymond, whose name would be eventually added to a pantheon of nineteenth-century press pioneers based in New York that includes Benjamin Day of the *Sun*, James Gordon Bennett of the *Herald*, and Horace Greeley of the *Tribune*. The *Times'* early commitment to rapid news gathering rather than editorializing was demonstrated in its coverage of the Civil War. In those early years Raymond also deemed that news is a phenomenon that includes what goes on in the literary and cultural world. To that end a Sunday edition was launched in 1861. One of Ochs' first decisions when taking over in 1896 was to revamp and expand it, thereby creating a ritual for people that still thrives.

Up until 1884, the *Times* was Republican in affiliation—"the party of Lincoln," as it was often called by supporters—but the paper maintained an independence that was not pleasing to party extremists. With Raymond's death in 1869, his trusted lieutenant, George Jones, took over. He led the *Times* into the 1870s with one of the major U.S. news stories of the century: the exposure of Boss Tweed and his ring of New York municipal corruption.

The 1880s saw the rise of Joseph Pulitzer's *New York World*. Increased sensationalism also began to typify several other metropolitan dailies. It would lead to the yellow journalism of the 1890s when William Randolph Hearst took over the *New York Evening Journal*. The *Times'* leadership was uncertain as to how to respond, and circulation declined. The beginning of the paper's slide, however, was marked by a spectacular scoop, the last one under the regime of Jones, who would die in 1891. The story involved a mishap at sea and prefigured the paper's coverage of events in 1912.

On Sunday, May 14, 1886 (the same day and day of the month as the *Titanic* disaster), a rumor circulated on the waterfront that the Cunarder *Oregon* had been involved in a collision off Fire Island and that most or all of the 1,000 on board had been picked up by the German liner *Fulda*. City editor William J. Kennedy gathered his staff, much as Carr Van Anda would do a generation later, and got down to maritime basics. From tide tables and ship data they knew that the *Fulda* could not cross Sandy Hook before high tide at midnight; therefore it would be 3:00 a.m. before she reached quarantine, where boarding and information gathering could be effected. This would preclude coverage of the story in the Monday edition.

According to Meyer Berger in his partisan history of the *Times*, Kenny and staff braved a severe storm to charter a tugboat to take them to the *Fulda*. The agreement with the tug's captain, who was understandably hesitant to leave port given the conditions, called for the newspapermen to double as crew. En route they encountered a smaller tug in distress and took her in tow, only to find out that one of her passengers was a *Sun* reporter. Kenny persuaded the captain not to allow the reporter onboard, and, after safely depositing the smaller vessel in a quiet cove, the larger one continued on her mission.

Under the pretext of being health officers, the *Times'* men boarded the *Fulda*. When her captain discovered the ruse a mêlée ensued. The *Times* men scattered, found the *Oregon*'s master with some of her survivors, and gleaned the story of the shipwreck and miraculous survival of all involved. Wrapping their notes around heavy cutlery,

Kenny and his press commandos then bolted for the top deck. Another confrontation arose. One reporter made a spectacular leap to the waiting tug; the others threw all their weighted copy onto her deck before being arrested. The May 15 edition recounted the complete saga of the *Oregon* while not a word of it appeared in rival papers.

The *Times*' astute coverage of maritime incidents would again be demonstrated in 1908 with an exclusive account of the *Cymric*'s rescue of most of the crew from the fire-ravaged *St. Cuthbert*. Another such event occurred in 1909 with the paper's detailed account of how Jack Binns's wireless heroics enabled the *Baltic* to rescue those onboard the *Republic* and *Florida* following their collision (both incidents are discussed more fully in Chapter 2). By 1912 no paper had a better track record in covering maritime mishaps, and none were more prepared to handle the kind of scenario that would befall the *Titanic*.

Unfortunately, in the years leading up to 1896, the *Times* itself became a sinking vessel. New leadership seemed the only possible rescue strategy. It came from an unlikely source in the person of Adolph Ochs. He was a southerner with a background as a printer rather than as a news writer, but he had been modestly successful in guiding the *Chattanooga Times* to solvency. Born of German-Jewish parents in 1858, Ochs had an entrepreneurial spirit tempered by a willingness to proceed cautiously and meticulously toward his goals. In taking over the *Times*, he sought to return the paper to the spirit of Henry Raymond—minus the Republican Party politics, although critics of his early years at the helm accused the paper of favoring big business.

On August 19, 1896, a reborn *Times* hit the street bearing Ochs' declaration of principles. The famous slogan, "All the News That's Fit to Print," made its first appearance on the masthead on February 10, 1897. The maxim was the work of the paper's staff and just as contentious then as now, with its suggestion of a kind of censorship. A contest was held to find a better phrase. A winner was chosen and duly awarded the $100 prize for "All the World's News, but Not a School for Scandal." Wisely, the staff decided that their original effort was superior and retained it.

Ochs streamlined and expanded the paper. He also tried various new ways to attract subscribers, such as telephone solicitation. Circulation increased, as did the esteem of the paper. Then, in 1904, Ochs made a decision that would give the *Times* national and ultimately international stature: he hired Carr Van Anda as managing editor.

Van Anda, a.k.a. "V.A." or "Boss" in the newsroom, was born in 1864 in Georgetown, Ohio, and came to the *Times* after 16 years on the rival *Sun*. Histories of U.S. journalism describe him as one of the most eminent managing editors ever to work on a U.S. daily. A supreme tactician of news gathering, he also had an exceptional knowledge of science and history. Two incidents dramatized to colleagues his knowledge in these areas: the discovery of a mistake in the translation of a paper by Einstein, which duly impressed the great scientist; and when Van Anda's ability to read Egyptian hieroglyphics led him to spot inaccuracies in the genealogy of Tut-Ankh-Amen, which the British museum promptly corrected. He was also a gifted lecturer and excellent writer on a variety of topics, but he rarely allowed his name to appear in conjunction with something he had written, nor did he grant interviews.

Ochs, in contrast, was neither an intellectual nor a practicing journalist. Nevertheless his vision of what the *Times* could and should be powerfully complemented Van Anda's sense of strategy and detail, thereby creating an extraordinary partnership.

Much of the promise of the new century the *Times* was entering involved applied scientific research leading to improvements in transportation and communication. Perusal of the paper from 1904 to 1912 reveals numerous articles on these topics, many commissioned and some written by Van Anda.

In 1907 it was Van Anda who proposed a transatlantic news service using wireless. Marconi doubted that all the elements necessary were sufficiently developed. Van Anda convinced him otherwise and took the initiative in organizing the setup. The transmission sequence began in London, with information traveling by telegraph to Clifton, where it would be held until noon (7:00 a.m. Eastern Standard Time), then sent by wireless to Glace Bay, Nova Scotia. From there it would go via telegraph to New York, Van Anda having arranged to lease the Glace Bay–New York line each day at the same time. The plan was met with opposition and skepticism, but it worked. The total cost was half of what would have had to be paid if the transatlantic cable were to be used for the same messages. Over the years Van Anda expanded the network and, in 1919, had a wireless station set up in the *Times* building.

In the years leading up to the *Titanic* tragedy, Van Anda helped coordinate a series of major stories that gradually raised the fortunes of the paper: the Russian-Japanese War in 1904–1905; Peary reaching the North Pole in 1909 (a *Times* exclusive); and the Jim Jeffries–Jack Johnson heavyweight fight in 1910 (with commentary to the *Times* provided by former champion John L. Sullivan). As impressive as these accomplishments were, they would pale in comparison to coverage of the chain of events that began shortly before midnight on April 14, 1912.

According to *Times* historian Meyer Berger, in the early morning hours of the 15th Van Anda was talking to the telegraph editor when a dispatch came through stating that the *Titanic* had struck an iceberg and was sending out a CQD for assistance. Just as his precursor, William J. Kenny, did in 1886 when information came in about the *Oregon*, Van Anda assembled his troops and drafted a campaign plan. He sent one man to the morgue (the papers archives) to gather all known facts about the ship, another to search for information about who the passengers were, and a third to secure the last description of the *Titanic* and to find out about hazards in the North Atlantic at that time of year.

Activity in the newsroom at this time, according to Van Anda biographer Barnett Fine, was intense: the telegraph clicked, phones rang, and typewriters pounded. When no further information on the ship's plight came over the wire, Van Anda suspected the worst. With the press already rolling for the mail edition, he ordered the lead story to be replaced by the headline, "TITANIC SINKING IN MID-OCEAN; HIT GREAT ICEBERG." Several hours later the city edition also voiced a worst-case scenario and supplemented the contention with information that had been gathered by the staff during those hectic early morning hours. During the excitement none of the staff noticed that an advertisement for the return voyage appeared on page 11.

No other paper had as much coverage, and none seemed as convinced that the ship was doomed. Van Anda had taken a great risk, but a well-informed one. Within 24 hours the magnitude of the tragedy was acknowledged by White Star's New York office; they had earlier denied the seriousness of the situation to Van Anda when he had inquired by telephone. The *Times* earned national and international attention for its astute coverage, as well as through its sale of some of its stories to other papers over the next several days. But the saga of the disaster was far from over, and the *Times*' campaign to cover it had only just begun.

With the *Carpathia* slated to arrive in New York on Thursday night, April 18, Van Anda booked a floor of the Strand Hotel on 11th Avenue and 14th Street, just a few hundred yards from where the ship would dock. He arranged for the suites to be connected directly to the *Times* office by telegraph and telephone. Since no reporters would be allowed onboard the *Carpathia*, it seemed the paper would have to scramble for stories on a level playing field with its rivals. If this was to be the case, the initial assault would have to be well coordinated. Van Anda's lieutenant, Arthur Greaves, sent 16 reporters to the scene, although press passes to the pier were limited to only four per newspaper. He also plotted their itineraries and provided advice. Meanwhile, Van Anda worked out a plan that would give the *Times'* coverage a decisive edge on all it rivals.

He sent reporter Jim Speers to Marconi, who at the time was dining with his New York manager, John Bottomley. Van Anda then contacted the inventor by telephone to persuade him to board the ship with Speers. Marconi indicated that he was indeed planning to board later that evening in order to talk to his two wireless men: Harold Bride, who had survived the sinking, and Harold Cottam of the *Carpathia*. Van Anda's sense of the urgency of the situation led Marconi and Bottomley to interrupt their dinner and head for the ship with Speers. The routes and transportation were suggested by Van Anda, who had worked out a strategy to enable the men to circumnavigate the growing congestion of people and vehicles.

Although things *might* have happened this way, the spontaneity suggested by the scenario seems odd given earlier wireless transmissions to the *Carpathia* sent by Marconi's chief engineer in New York, Frederick Sammis. The messages had urged Marconi operators on board to withhold information in anticipation of an arranged exclusive. They were intercepted by the navy and brought to light by Senator Smith at the U.S. inquiry. Marconi's subsequent denial of any knowledge regarding these dispatches has few believers among those who have assessed the incident, the present writer included.

As police barricades held back a throng of between 30,000 and 50,000 people, Marconi, Bottomley, and Speers made their way to the ship at approximately 9:30 p.m. When stopped by police they pleaded their case. According to Berger, the status of all three was declared, whereupon the officer in question said something about no reporters being allowed on board and then, mistaking Bottomley for Speers, held him back and let the other two up the gangplank. One suspects a more deliberate ruse given the wireless messages from Sammis and Marconi's liaison with the *Times*.

Speers took down Bride's account as quickly as possible and then rushed back to the *Times* office to get his notes rendered into copy. The interview became the lead story on the front page of the morning edition. The rapidity with which all this transpired—the edition went press at 12:30 a.m., April 19—would be impressive even in this era of electronic news gathering and mobile communications.

The interview was somewhat stream of consciousness and contained several "facts" that would later be changed and in some cases were absent from Bride's testimony at the U.S. inquiry. Under the circumstances, some misquotation or misinterpretation on the part of Speers is understandable, and even the slight shift in Bride's recall is not unusual for survivors of a chaotic trauma.

Bride began by defending the limited wireless communication from the *Carpathia*. He contended that he and Cottam had their hands full sending out messages pertaining to the survivors. He also claimed that the ship best able to receive and relay their transmissions, the U.S. Navy's *Chester*, had "wretched operators" who were "as slow as Christmas coming." He added that although they knew American Morse code, the navy men were not well versed in its Continental equivalent. Whether or not this was true, the emphasis Bride gave to it indicates that he probably felt his actions might be subject to later scrutiny, as indeed they were at the inquiry. However, rather than pursuing Bride's points further, Senator Smith preferred to explore the issue of wireless practice during the disaster by concentrating on Marconi.

Bride went on to recount the circumstances of that fatal night, noting how he barely felt the collision. Shortly after the *Titanic* hit the iceberg, Captain Smith showed up in the Marconi cabin and asked the two operators to send the regulation international call for help and to stand by. They sent CQD. When Smith returned with the grave news, the Marconi men maintained their composure and sense of humor. Bride admitted suggesting that Phillips send the new call, SOS, pointing out that another opportunity to do so might not occur. In a more somber vein, he also described the incident whereby he had to knock out the stoker trying to steal Phillips's lifebelt.

During the ship's last moments, Bride told of his helping to disengage a collapsible lifeboat and then being washed overboard. While struggling in the freezing water, he kept hearing the band. Three times during the interview he indicated that the last tune played was "Autumn," although he failed to indicate whether the piece was the Episcopal hymn or the popular song, "Songe d'Automme." Little did anyone at the time realize how the question of what the band played would live on for over 100 years as an enduring aspect of the history of those terrifying final moments.

Subsequent events from that night were elaborated in stark detail. Bride described how he was pulled aboard the overturned collapsible, then transferred to one of the partly filled lifeboats, where he noticed the body of Phillips; at the inquiry he would credit this observation to another unnamed person. Plagued by injured legs throughout his sojourn on the *Carpathia*, Bride nonetheless told the captain of his willingness to assist Cottam in the Marconi cabin. And again, this time in conclusion, he restated reasons for his retentive communication, decrying the *Chester*'s operators for a third time.

The article is riveting. Of all the eyewitness accounts to appear in the press, Bride's became the most cited. It established for posterity the courageous actions of Phillips. This must have pleased Marconi, for with Phillips not around to receive the accolades, some of them were directed his way. The public ceded more heroism to the inventor than was his due, even after Senator Smith's exposé of his collusion with Van Anda. Finally, Bride's "earwitness" account of the band playing until the bitter end added to a growing legend. However, at the time the public wanted the last song to be the more memorable, "Nearer My God to Thee," which less credible witnesses claimed they heard, and so it became the one immortalized in most representations.

At the time Speers was interviewing Bride, the *Carpathia*'s Marconi man, Cottam, left the ship and headed for the *Times* office to add his observations to what would appear in the morning edition. That this was prearranged, as was the interview with Bride, seems certain; that both men were paid is established fact. Van Anda biographer Barnett Fine even has Cottam wandering by accident into the *New York Herald* building in his quest for the *Times* office; needless to say Cottam recounted nothing until he reached his chosen destination. His interview appeared on page 2, making the paper's coverage all the more impressive.

Neither Fine, nor Berger or Elmer Davies in their histories of the *New York Times*, question the ethics involved in the gathering of these stories. Senator Smith did, and his views were amplified by other newspapers, most notably those of Pulitzer and Hearst, which the above-mentioned *Times* chroniclers seem not to have consulted.

Around these two spectacular scoops, the *Times* deployed numerous observations and accounts gleaned from whomever their platoon of reporters could elicit commentary. The issue contained 13 pages of coverage, with pages 12 and 13 given over to the names of those known to be missing. It was an astounding piece of rapid news gathering. Understandably, the stories could not always be checked for accuracy. The urgency to take down as much information as rapidly as possible led to some verbose and occasionally silly statements. The paper's own copywriters were not immune to such lapses. Witness the following example taken from the front-page article next to the Bride interview:

> In a clear starlit night that showed a clear deep blue sea for miles and miles, the *Titanic*, an hour after she had struck a submerged iceberg at full speed and head on, sank slowly to her ocean grave.

With "clear" repeated twice, the use of the phrase "miles and miles," plus the length of the sentence, it would have a hard time passing muster in English 101 or the scrutiny of Joseph Pulitzer. Less forgivable is the assumption that the ship struck the iceberg "head on." Perhaps this copy was composed before the scramble for stories dockside since comments that appear later in the paper refer to the ship as only having grazed the iceberg—almost everyone interviewed who was aware of the impact noted how minimal it was.

Getting the stories typeset as soon as they were available also created an order of priority that did not always reflect what we would now deem to be the importance of the information in question. For example, the two front-page articles on either side of Bride's story contained a series of statements that the *Times* conceded would in some instances be "hearsay" or "rumor." Then, tucked away in the middle of page 3, we find Lawrence Beesley's keen-eyed and thoughtfully worded account. He would go on to write a book about the disaster, which appeared later that year: *The Loss of SS Titanic: Its Story and Its Lessons*.

In the hearsay and rumor category, we find frequent commentary regarding the *Titanic*'s most notorious survivor, Bruce Ismay, the managing director of White Star. One interviewee claimed Ismay paid the crew of a lifeboat; another stated that a group of women in a partially filled boat beseeched him to enter. Ismay did not get his say until page 7. He denied the ship was either trying to set a record or traveling at full speed. When confronted with the issue of his survival, he claimed that he had gotten off on the last boat and then declined further questions. In a subsequent statement at the U.S. inquiry, he said he boarded a lifeboat (not the last one) of his own volition since the boat was being lowered and there was no one else in the vicinity.

Another popular source of speculation was Captain Smith. One passenger insisted the captain and several officers shot themselves as the end neared. According to fireman Harry Senior, who provided a *Times* reporter with several observations, most of them suspect, the captain swam to a lifeboat with a child in his arms. After depositing the infant, he took off his lifebelt and said, "I will follow the ship." In fairness to Mr. Senior, he was not the only one who professed to have witnessed something along these lines. The incident, real or imagined, was what many people wanted to believe. It became duly immortalized in a cartoon that ran in some of the more sensational papers. No evidence that this heroic act actually took place, or that the captain shot himself, emerged at either inquiry.

The *Times'* coverage also abounded with survivor comments about the fate of the famous passengers: how Isidor Straus, owner of Macy's, and wife Ida went down hand-in-hand, and the scenario of John Jacob Astor gallantly escorting his new 19-year-old bride, Madeleine, to a lifeboat. The paper's own description of events at the pier included a serene portrait of the young widow Astor.

Those of lesser social standing tended not to fare well in the recollections gathered. One unnamed passenger's observation that Chinese stokers jumped into lifeboats ahead of the women was uncritically cited. Although we do know that several Chinese in steerage did survive, the crew list clearly shows that no Chinese were in the employ of White Star. The detailed research Van Anda used to plan the coverage was not always in evidence when it came to verifying statements gathered by his reporters.

Amid these numerous claimed observations that strain credibility, we find the measured impressions of Lawrence Beesley. That his statement resides in the middle of page 3 may be the result of how the presses rolled when all the stories were gleaned or a deliberate decision not to let his account appear too prominent lest it diminish reader interest in the more sensational descriptions recounted by others. In any case, the *Times* sensed the credibility of Beesley's words and allowed them to fill four columns. Only the Bride account was longer.

Beesley presented his view of the sequence of events from collision to rescue. He noted the irony of his being able to get into lifeboat 13, which had sufficient room and, unlike the others, was not limited to women and children (crewman were permitted to man those boats, in any case). Two points in his account are particularly haunting: the way the ship remained motionless before the final plunge—five minutes by his estimate—and the horrifying scene of those crying out in the freezing water. The same incidents were noted by other survivors, but the understated tenor of Beesley's account gave his description of such moments an unmatched power. His portrait of dawn aboard the lifeboats is particularly evocative, with the distant icebergs that appeared through the mist likened to schooners.

The *Times* was obviously aware that this April 19 issue was a journalistic tour de force. At some point they must have also sensed that their news-gathering methods might draw criticism. This was evidenced on pages 7 and 10 in two statements by Marconi. The first contained an admission that both he and Bottomley received assistance from the *Times* in getting to the *Carpathia*. He added that the reporter accompanying them had not planned to board the ship, a statement that must have left the paper's rivals incredulous. Marconi did not, however, state how the reporter managed to board or why it was Bottomley rather than the *Times*' Speers who was held back.

In the page 10 article, Marconi began by decrying the lack of lifeboats. He then went on to explain the *Carpathia*'s minimal communication on the grounds that she had an old, small wireless and only one operator who had his hands full transmitting the names of survivors. Under such circumstances, he noted, the press had to come in second. He did not mention that the aging wireless set belonged to his company, as did the policy to allow single-operator stations. An inkling that both he and the *Times* would have to further explain themselves is suggested in an announcement that appeared on the following page. It noted the arrival in New York of Senator Smith, who was said to be heading for the *Carpathia*, and mentioned the soon-to-be-convened inquiry.

Despite the controversy surrounding the creation of the April 19, 1912, *New York Times*—a controversy of more concern to rival papers and Senator Smith than to the public at large—the issue has become a classic. Not since the exposure of Boss Tweed had the paper had such a high profile, and this time the visibility was international. When Van Anda went to London and visited the offices of Lord Northcliffe's *Daily Mail*, the editor on duty produced a copy of the renowned April 19 issue of the *Times* and said, "We keep this as an example of the greatest accomplishment in news reporting." Even today, it remains the single most important issue contributing to the establishment of the *Times* as a global voice.

CHAPTER 7

Canadian Journalists in New York

Michael Dupuis

Once it was known that the rescue ship *Carpathia* would arrive in New York during the evening of April 18, over 500 news personnel from across North America began to converge on the city. Among those seeking details of the disaster and exclusive stories from survivors were at least 20 Canadian reporters. Most were in their mid-20s to early 30s, and all but two were men. Though several would go on to distinguished careers in journalism, few would again participate in an event of such interest and magnitude.

When the *Titanic* story broke, *Toronto Evening Telegram* editor John "Black Jack" Robinson sent reporter Mary Snider, exchange editor J. G. Muir, and a staff artist to New York to cover the story. Told to meet *Titanic* survivors, especially Canadians, the correspondents were given letters for several first-class passengers from Toronto, Montreal, and Winnipeg. On the morning of April 18, forty-two-year-old Mary Snider and fellow reporters arrived at Grand Central Station. Their immediate task was to obtain press passes ensuring access to the White Star Line's docking sheds at Chelsea Pier 54, where after 9:00 p.m. *Carpathia* was expected to land with over 700 survivors. By 2:00 p.m. however, New York municipal authorities and White Star representatives posted an official bulletin at the Battery Park Customs House announcing their allotment press passes, a decision that effectively excluded all but New York City press from Pier 54. Police and security soon gathered on West 14th Street and 12th Avenue and endeavored to hold back an anticipated crowd of 30,000. Their instructions were to allow no one beyond the blockade without a special pass.

By 3:00 p.m. Snider had left her colleagues and reached the police barricade minutes before *Carpathia*'s arrival. In an April 22 front-page story headlined "Through the Needle's Eye: How Woman Writer Went," Snider explained how she breached the blockade and obtained the scoop of her career. "Take me to that corner and tell me when an ambulance is coming," she told a companion. Almost immediately one swung into West Street, and as it slowed to show police credentials, Snider pleaded with a young intern. "Take me on the pier, doctor?" "You will have to ask Dr. Spier," he replied. "Dr. Spier," she beseeched, "will you take me? I've been at the Customs House all day. I cannot get a pass." "Get in with Miss Smith," the doctor said, "and mind, you're a nurse."

Minutes later Snider stood in the pouring rain and watched the black-hulled *Carpathia* dock as "flashlight flares from the tugs alongside showed the passengers crowded on deck." She then joined anxious watchers near the liner's forward gangplank, waiting with letters for wealthy Toronto business and military man Major Arthur Godfrey Peuchen; Grand Trunk Railway president Charles M. Hays; his broker son-in-law, Thornton Davidson of Montreal; and George Graham, a chinaware buyer for Eaton's department store.

According to Snider, Peuchen "came down the plank with the orphaned boy [Trevor] Allison in his arms. A brief greeting, and a promise of the full story at leisure—a promise faithfully kept." A few minutes later she saw the official list of survivors and learned that "Messrs. Hays, Davidson, Graham and others . . . had gone down with the monster of the deep." Finally, Snider assisted third-class women and children, a task she implied would have been unlikely had she not been female.

Before returning to Toronto, Snider sent three more dispatches. One was based on a lengthy April 20 interview with 52-year-old Peuchen, in which he furnished a complete account of *Titanic*'s wreck and rescue as well as an explanation for his survival. Another explained how Calgary businessman Albert Dick was saved by his young bride Vera. All of Snider's stories were bylined, and she was given front-page recognition for her *Carpathia* scoop. "One of the few Canadian newspaper writers to secure admission to the pier when the *Carpathia* docked," trumpeted the paper's editor in a sidebar to her first report.

After the announcement concerning restrictions for out-of-town press, *Toronto Telegram* reporter James Muir and the paper's third representative attempted to charter a tugboat to shadow *Carpathia* as it navigated the Hudson River, but missed the last tug and so returned to the Cunard office. Fortunately Muir was able to acquire one of the prized permits to Pier 54 from the port surveyor.

Once on Pier 54, Muir witnessed scenes of joy and despair. Like Snider, he sought Canadian survivors. One was 27-year-old Montrealer Mary Douglas, who added to the controversy of whether shots were fired during the loading of lifeboats. On April 19, he quoted Douglas: "We could hear revolver shots all over and the confusion was terrible. . . . We heard that several people had been shot, but we did not know the details. I know that one man jumped into a boat, crushing a woman's foot as he fell. The officer in charge, jumped up, pointed a revolver right at his temple and was about to shoot, when the woman whom the man had hurt pleaded for his life, so he was saved." Another survivor with a Canadian connection was third-class passenger May Howard, a 27-year-old English nanny on her way to join her brother in Toronto. In the April 20 edition she provided an eyewitness account of how "foreigners" and officers behaved: "The foreign men, and there were a lot of them, behaved finely," Howard told Muir. "The officers behaved splendidly, as well as the men, and the people were put into the boats without any trouble. . . . "

On April 20 the *Toronto Daily Star* ran a sidebar to its front-page *Titanic* coverage stating that when *Carpathia* arrived in New York seven staff members were set to cover the story. Furthermore, these correspondents "remained on duty from the time the boat docked . . . until after the regular editions of The Star went to press yesterday afternoon with the result that 24 columns of matter dealing with the disaster came 'from staff reporters' alone."

In *Ink On My Fingers*, long-time *Star* editor J. H. Cranston recalled how sports writer Lou Marsh was sent to New York along with other reporters to find Toronto survivors and gather their accounts. He took along his friend Harry Rosenthal, a member of the Ottawa Senators hockey team. Outside Pier 54 they had trouble identifying Toronto people, so Marsh had Rosenthal stand on a pile of ropes and yell. According to Cranston this worked, and Marsh was able to secure a dozen names and interviews, scoring a major scoop for the *Star*.

According to Ross Harkness in *J. E. Atkinson of the Star*, the major *Titanic* story published on April 19 was written by 25-year-old Harry Hindmarsh. After interviewing many survivors, he wrote a dispatch stating that stories in newspapers alleging panicking male passengers had pushed women and children out of the way to clamber into lifeboats and save themselves were untrue. In fact male passengers, wrote Hindmarsh, had been ordered to get into lifeboats to row and to prevent them from swamping. As proof, he cited Major Peuchen's view that every woman who desired to leave was able to. When Hindmarsh returned to Toronto, the paper's owner and publisher, Joseph Atkinson, though impressed by his future son-in-law's account, wanted proof. Hindmarsh was able to produce written statements from the ship's officers verifying they had ordered men into the lifeboats as well as copies of written orders demanded by male passengers.

Betty Thornley was the second Canadian newspaperwoman in New York on the *Titanic* story. She wrote three dispatches for the paper's news pages—the first two appeared on April 19, and the third on April 20—signed "By A Member of The Star's Women's Department." She also wrote a column in the women's page under "Betty." In her first dispatch, Thornley admitted to being unable to gain access to the White Star's docking shed because she lacked the " 'magic endorsement' [police pass] supplied by the Surveyor General of Customs." Nevertheless, she conveyed the tragedy of a "grey-haired woman" who went from New York a wife and returned a widow, and "an unknowing babe [perhaps Trevor Allison] carried in the nurse's arms" who lost both parents. Her second dispatch described an interview by fellow *Star* representative Harry Hindmarsh with Major Peuchen in his Waldorf-Astoria hotel room. Surrounded by family members, Peuchen provided a detailed account of the disaster. Thornley's third report was given an eight-column, 18-point spreader headline, "BETTY, OF THE STAR WOMEN'S DEPARTMENT, TALKS WITH TITANIC SURVIVORS AT BELLEVUE."

The *Toronto Globe* sent a single reporter, Harry Willmott, to cover *Carpathia*'s landing. Accompanying his April 19 front-page dispatch, a sidebar stated: "The following story was telegraphed by Mr. Harry Willmott of The Globe staff, the only Toronto newspaperman on the dock when the *Carpathia* arrived." Although Pier 54 dispatches by other Canadian reporters would disprove the *Globe*'s claim of exclusivity, Willmott's story, "Gross Carelessness, Says Major Peuchen," was indeed a tour de force because it provided answers from a credible eyewitness to vital questions: Why had the disaster occurred? Who was to blame? Why were more people not saved?

Willmott greeted Peuchen as he disembarked from *Carpathia*. As an expert yachtsman on his 40th transatlantic sea voyage, he was the ideal person to ask about the tragedy. Peuchen quickly provided the story's headline: "I say it was carelessness, gross carelessness. Why, the captain [Edward Smith] knew we were going into an ice field, and why should he remain dining in the salon when such danger was about?" Peuchen also commented on the handling of the lifeboats. Stating "no women should have been drowned" because "there was plenty of room for them in the boats, and many of the boats were not filled," he criticized "the management for not providing sufficient raft capacity for passengers and crew." Furthermore, he insisted "the passengers were not instructed into how to file into the boats, and some of the crew didn't know how to handle them."

After taking a few moments to reunite with his family, Peuchen explained to Willmott how he survived. "It was my training as a yachtsman that saved me," he remarked, then described that there was only one man in Lifeboat No. 6 as it was being lowered, and Second Officer Lightholler cried out, "I must have somebody else to help manage this boat." According to Peuchen, "the officer turned to me and told me to get in. He said I would have to go below and break a port hole glass and crawl out. I told him I was a yachtsman, and if a line was thrown out I could go over the side of the ship. A 'yachtsman', said he, 'by all means get in, you should go before any of the crew.'" Peuchen later produced a written statement from Lightholler supporting his account. Although Peuchen is not mentioned by name, this incident is depicted in the 1958 film *A Night to Remember*.

The *Ottawa Journal* gave the *Titanic* story to 23-year-old parliamentary press gallery reporter Grattan O'Leary. In his memoirs, *Recollections of People, Press and Politics*, O'Leary recalls the assignment was handed him not because of his reporting ability but because he had spent several years at sea. Arriving in New York on the evening of April 18, he almost missed *Carpathia*'s arrival due to misinformation in an extra of one of the New York dailies. However, with help from an Associated Press night editor, he obtained a pass to Pier 54. A taxicab took him to the dock, and he began to interview survivors. On April 19, his front-page, bylined report was given two banner headlines: "Thrilling Narrative By Grattan O'Leary Of The Journal Staff" and "Titanic's Officers Shot Cowards Who Tried to Rush the Life-Boats." Featuring O'Leary's picture, the dispatch filled the entire front page. In an extra edition the same day, a sidebar applauded his journalistic feat.

Before his return to Ottawa, O'Leary wrote one more dispatch. On April 19 the U.S. Senate inquiry into the *Titanic* disaster commenced at the Waldorf-Astoria Hotel with J. Bruce Ismay, White Star's

managing director, as the committee's first witness. Through the auspices of several New York newsmen, O'Leary was invited to attend the
afternoon session (thus missing Ismay's testimony) and did so as one
of a handful of Canadian reporters. The next day, on April 20, in a
front-page story given the spreader headline, "EYES OF THE
WORLD ARE NOW TURNED ON NEW YORK TITANIC
INVESTIGATION," the *Journal* printed O'Leary's account of the
dramatic story recounted by *Carpathia*'s captain Arthur Rostron and
later accounts of death and heroism narrated by some of the passengers and crew.

The *Ottawa Citizen* assigned the *Titanic* story to 26-year-old junior
reporter and sports writer Tommy Gorman. Fortunate enough to
secure a press pass, Gorman could only join the scrum with other
reporters and wait as survivors streamed through the iron entryway
and headed to the street exit. Perhaps because of this limited access to
passengers and crew, Gorman's only known dispatch did not appear in
the *Citizen* until April 22. It was given the main headline "How Titanic
Wreck Story Was Handled For The Newspapers" and subheadlines
"Citizen's Staff Reporter's Reminiscences of Last Week in New York,"
"Details Of the Way In Which the World Got the Greatest Newspaper
Story Ever Told," and "Its Costs, Difficulties and How All the 'Special
Reporters' Were Scooped by The Associated Press." His story ran over
5,000 words and was the best description by a Canadian reporter of how
the North American press secured coverage.

His narrative begins by disclosing how *Montreal Gazette* reporter
Edward Stranger broke the story shortly after *Titanic* foundered by relaying the information to New York via the Associated Press. Then,
after tracing the efforts of five Montreal newspapermen to reach the
East Coast city, Gorman's story shifted to the Lower Manhattan headquarters of White Star, where he and other reporters had made several
unsuccessful attempts to obtain details about *Titanic* survivors from
company vice president Philip Franklin and his assistants. Gorman
focused next on the press coverage of *Carpathia*'s arrival by the *New
York Times*, *World*, *Herald*, and Associated Press. He praised the Associated Press, which had almost 50 men covering the story and had relayed
15,000 words by Thursday night, April 18, to major cities in Canada
and the United States. Finally, Gorman indicated how much money
newspapers were willing to spend on an exclusive article. One Canadian
reporter, he claimed, offered a seaman $200 when the boat arrived but
was turned down.

Although Gorman wrote that five reporters were sent to New York by Montreal newspapers, little is known about them. On April 18 the *Montreal Star* announced in a sidebar that it had a number of its staff in New York and had made arrangements to report the landing of *Carpathia* and the story of the *Titanic* disaster in all its details. In a follow up story on April 19, the paper published an account by a *Star* reporter who secured the services of a speedy seagoing tug. According to the dispatch the tug was able to come within hailing distance of *Carpathia*, allowing the unnamed *Star* reporter to learn about the deaths of Montreal-bound first-class passengers Markland Molson, Hudson Allison, Thornton Davidson, and Quigg Baxter.

From the initials H. P. F. under an April 19 story, "Passengers Picked up In Pitiable Condition," it is likely that the *Montreal Herald* had reporter Peter Feeney in New York. Feeney interviewed *Carpathia* passenger Simon Senecal of Montreal, who described the rescue of *Titanic* survivors, including French sculptor Paul Chevre. On the same day, and also possibly by Feeney, was another *Herald* story about Chevre. Under the front-page spreader headline "Montreal Survivor Tells Herald Tragic Story Of Big Liner's Wreck, Cowardly Men Were Shot To Death," was a sensational description of the loading of the lifeboats furnished by the "still dazed and terribly shocked" 46-year-old Frenchman who was en route to Canada. According to the story, Chevre stated that "fifteen hundred frenzied men and women fought for their lives when the lights on the Titanic went out. . . . Captain Smith . . . drew a revolver and blew out his brains . . . and Archibald Butt, President Taft's personal aide, stood at a gangplank and shot dead seven men who tried to push a frightened crowd of women away from a boat." However, when Chevre arrived in Montreal on April 22, he stormed into the French-language daily *La Presse* and denounced the *Herald*'s story as a complete fabrication, leaving one to wonder whether the *Herald* reporter who interviewed Chevre did not understand French or simply invented the entire account.

In 1912, 31-year-old Canadian Press Limited reporter George MacDonald was the wire service's resident correspondent in Montreal covering Quebec, the Maritimes, and the eastern United States. When the Canadian Press headquarters in Toronto learned of *Titanic*'s sinking, the fledgling agency sent MacDonald to New York to provide news to Canadian newspapers. Although he did little reporting on his own, as the New York Associated Press office was accessible to Canadian Press employees between April 17 and 23, MacDonald edited and relayed dozens of AP dispatches to Toronto, where they were distributed to papers across the country.

When the *Titanic* story broke, both Arthur Ford and Herbert Chisholm were parliamentary reporters in Ottawa. Twenty-six-year-old Ford was with the *Winnipeg Telegram* and 30-year-old Chisholm with the *Manitoba Free Press*. Since several prominent Winnipeg citizens, including millionaire realtor Mark Fortune (together with his wife, son, and three daughters), were first-class passengers on *Titanic*, Ford and Chisholm were sent to New York to learn their fate. Late on April 18, Ford learned from a fellow press gallery reporter that Chisholm had secretly left Ottawa at 5:00 for New York to meet the *Carpathia*. Ford quickly contacted *Telegram* editor Mark Nichols in Winnipeg asking for funds to be wired ahead to New York, and after borrowing money from colleagues in the Press Gallery he caught the train to Montreal and then connected to a New York–bound express. However, he arrived too late to cover *Carpathia*'s landing and went to the Murray Hotel where "$100 had been wired me for expenses." As earlier in his career he had worked for a New York financial daily, Ford was quite familiar with the city and made his way to the *New York Times*. With the help of the paper's managing editor, Carr Van Anda, Ford was able to locate members of the Fortune family at the Belmont Hotel.

Meanwhile, Chisholm had already wired a story to the *Manitoba Free Press* before *Carpathia* docked. Headlined "New Yorkers Awaited In Great Suspense," his April 19 lead summarized the general feeling in the city about the rescue liner's impending arrival. Even though Chisholm was subsequently present at Pier 54, he was unable to learn about the fate of Winnipeg passengers other than Mrs. Fortune and her three daughters. What happened next was serendipitous for both newspapermen. The two rivals ran into one another and agreed to work together rather than to try and out-scoop one another, thereby putting the interests and concerns of Winnipeg ahead of journalistic one-upmanship.

Ford interviewed insurance broker Charles Allen, fiancé of Alice, one of the three "Misses Fortune." In this April 19 *Winnipeg Telegram* interview, Allen, perhaps unwittingly, contributed to *Titanic*'s mythology. First he mentioned the Fortune women praising the sinking ship's bandsmen who were heroic and played until the end, concluding with "Nearer My God to Thee." Allen also provided details from the Fortune women about what would later become the "man dressed as a woman" legend. He told Ford that "Among the hundreds of cases of heroism, one story of a dastardly coward is told by the Misses Fortune. A man put on a woman's coat and donned a veil, and in this way succeeded in getting into their boat. They did not know his name."

Ford also interviewed Toronto native Wesley Allison, uncle of Montreal financial broker Hudson Allison, and the results appeared in the April 20 *Winnipeg Telegram*. Hudson, wife Bessie, two-year-old daughter Lorraine, 11-month-old son Trevor, and the baby's nursemaid Alice Cleaver were returning from England. The Winnipeg connection to Ford's story was that Hudson Allison had worked for two years in the Manitoba capital and knew realtors Mark Fortune and Thompson Beattie. Wesley narrated how after passengers were told to go to the lifeboats, Alice took Trevor on deck, and they were soon lowered in a lifeboat to safety away from the ship. Unaware of this development, Hudson grabbed Lorraine and went to find baby Trevor while Bessie searched the other side of the ship. According to Wesley they were unable to find each other before the last boat was launched. The fate of the Allison family would later emerge as a major storyline in the 1996 television miniseries *Titanic* (discussed in Chapter 10).

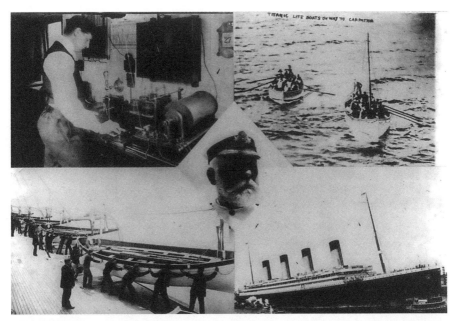

Photo montage with the *Titanic*'s captain, E. J. Smith, at the center.
Clockwise from the top left: a wireless operator receiving information
about the sinking ship; two *Titanic* lifeboats approaching the Carpathia;
starboard bow shot of the *Titanic* leaving Southampton; a lifeboat drill
(not from the *Titanic*). (Library of Congress)

The *Titanic* (left) and her sister ship the *Olympic* under construction.
(Library of Congress)

Under the *Titanic*'s stern just prior to her launch. (Library of Congress)

Titanic survivors on the deck of the *Carpathia*. (Library of Congress)

Photographed from the *Carpathia*, was this the iceberg that sank the *Titanic*, as has been claimed? Perhaps, but note others in the background, which represent the ice field into which the *Titanic* was steaming. (Library of Congress)

FIRST WIRELESS PRESS MESSAGE ACROSS THE ATLANTIC

Signalizing the Opening of the Marconi Service to the Public, and Conveying a Message of Congratulation from Privy Councillor Baron Avebury, Formerly Sir John Lubbock.

Form 103

THE WESTERN UNION TELEGRAPH COMPANY.

INCORPORATED

24,000 OFFICES IN AMERICA. CABLE SERVICE TO ALL THE WORLD.

This Company TRANSMITS and DELIVERS messages only on conditions limiting its liability, which have been assented to by the sender of the following message. Errors can be guarded against only by repeating a message back to the sending station for comparison, and the Company will not hold itself liable for errors or delays in transmission or delivery of Unrepeated Messages, beyond the amount of tolls paid thereon, nor in any case where the claim is not presented in writing within sixty days after the message is filed with the Company for transmission.

This is an UNREPEATED MESSAGE, and is delivered by request of the sender, under the conditions named above.

ROBERT C. CLOWRY, President and General Manager.

RECEIVED at 313 Sixth Ave. Corner 46th St.

TELEPHONE: 3907 BRYANT.

1B Lr Sn   Dh & 53 Collect   D, P R, Land lines,

London Via Marconi Wireless Glace Bay N S Oct 17th,

Times, New York.

This message marks opening transatlantic wireless handed
Marconi company for transmission Ireland Breton limited 50 words
only send one many messages received Times signalize event
quote trust introduction wireless more closely unite people states
Great Britian who seem form one Nation though under two Governments
and whose interests are really identical.

Avebury Marshall .... 1210 Am Oct 17th

ALWAYS OPEN.   MONEY TRANSFERRED BY TELEGRAPH.   CABLE OFFICE.

The above message was immediately followed by others which appear in
another column of The Times this morning.

MARCONI CONGRATULATES THE NEW YORK TIMES

GLACE BAY, NOVA SCOTIA, Oct. 17.—Mr. Marconi says: "Congratulate New York Times on having received first westward press message."

FROM THE PRIME MINISTER OF FRANCE.

WEST STRAND, London, Oct. 17, via Marconi Wireless Telegraph to Glace Bay, N. S.—THE NEW YORK TIMES' Paris correspondent forwards to me the following message for transmission across the Atlantic by Marconi wireless telegraph:

"Dans l'inauguration du prodigieux mode de communication mis désormais à leur disposition, les deux grandes républiques ne peuvent que trouver une heureuse occasion de se féliciter et de formuler les voeux les plus cordiaux pour le mantien de la paix dans le travail pour le bonheur des peuples dans la solidarité."

"CLEMENCEAU."

[Translation.]

In the inauguration of the marvelous means of communication put at their disposition from this time forward, the two great Republics could not but find it a happy occasion to congratulate themselves and to express the most cordial wishes for the maintenance of peace in the work for the happiness of the people in the joint responsibility.

CLEMENCEAU.

The New York Times
Published: October 18, 1907
Copyright © The New York Times

The October 18, 1907, *New York Times* proudly announces its business liaison with Marconi for transatlantic wireless news.

"All the News That's Fit to Print."

The New York Times.

THE WEATHER.

VOL. LXI...NO. 19,586.

NEW YORK, TUESDAY, APRIL 16, 1912.—TWENTY-FOUR PAGES.

ONE CENT

TITANIC SINKS FOUR HOURS AFTER HITTING ICEBERG; 866 RESCUED BY CARPATHIA, PROBABLY 1250 PERISH; ISMAY SAFE, MRS. ASTOR MAYBE, NOTED NAMES MISSING

Col. Astor and Bride, Isidor Straus and Wife, and Maj. Butt Aboard.

"RULE OF SEA" FOLLOWED

Women and Children Put Over in Lifeboats and Are Supposed to be Safe on Carpathia.

PICKED UP AFTER 8 HOURS

Vincent Astor Calls at White Star Office for News of His Father and Leaves Weeping.

FRANKLIN HOPEFUL ALL DAY

Manager of the Line Insisted Titanic Was Unsinkable Even After She Had Gone Down.

HEAD OF THE LINE ABOARD

J. Bruce Ismay Making First Trip on Gigantic Ship That Was to Surpass All Others.

The Lost Titanic Being Towed Out of Belfast Harbor.

CAPT. E. J. SMITH,
Commander of the Titanic.

Biggest Liner Plunges to the Bottom at 2:20 A. M.

RESCUERS THERE TOO LATE

Except to Pick Up the Few Hundreds Who Took to the Lifeboats.

WOMEN AND CHILDREN FIRST

Cunarder Carpathia Rushing to New York with the Survivors.

SEA SEARCH FOR OTHERS

The California Stands By on Chance of Picking Up Other Boats or Rafts.

OLYMPIC SENDS THE NEWS

Only Ship to Flash Wireless Messages to Shore After the Disaster.

LATER REPORT SAVES 866.

PARTIAL LIST OF THE SAVED.

Includes Bruce Ismay, Mrs. Widener, Mrs. H. B. Harris, and an Incomplete name, suggesting Mrs. Astor's.

The April 16, 1912, *New York Times*. Details of the sinking are now presented. They support the dire estimate—denied by several other papers—made in the April 15 edition on the basis of early wireless reports.

An anxious crowd waits for *Titanic* survivors to disembark from the *Carpathia* on the evening of April 18, 1912. (Library of Congress)

An injured Harold Bride, the *Titanic*'s second wireless operator, leaving the *Carpathia* on April 19, 1912. (Library of Congress)

The U.S. Senate committee investigating the disaster questions the *Titanic*'s most notorious survivor, Bruce Ismay (hand on chin), chairman of the White Star Line and president of International Mercantile Marine. (Library of Congress)

The independently owned Ottawa *Evening Journal* providing the "Thrilling Narrative" by Grattan O'Leary. Despite the sensational and misleading headline, O'Leary's story was solidly based on fact. (*The Evening Journal* [Ottawa], April 19, 1912)

Stills from a newsreel released after the sinking of the *Titanic*. The ship being shown is actually the *Olympic*, but the newsreel implies it is the *Titanic*. (Courtesy of Kino International)

Still from a newsreel released after the sinking of the *Titanic*. The ship being shown is actually the *Olympic*—note how the name on the tug has been erased lest it give away the ruse. (Courtesy of Kino International)

Poster from the film *Saved from the Titanic* released one month after the sinking.

Four scenes from the 1943 film *Titanic* produced by Nazi Germany.
Clockwise from the top left: the grand staircase; the Marconi cabin;
mayhem in the lifeboats; and the postsinking inquiry. This is the only
Titanic film to deal with the latter; however, the way it is portrayed only
compounds the anti-British propaganda theme that runs throughout
the film. (Courtesy of Kino International)

The bow section of the *Titanic* from the IMAX® production *Titanica*.
The depth of field and illumination of the wreck the film provides are
impressive. (©IMAX Corporation/Undersea Imaging International
Inc. & TMP (1991) I Limited Partnership. Reprinted with the permission of the IMAX® Corporation.)

Paintings from Canadian artist Steve Gouthro's interpretive series, "Vestiges of the Titanic." Although inspired by photographs of the wreck site, the paintings evoke aspects of the tragedy that transcend what photography alone can represent. (Reprinted with permission of Steve Gouthro.)

CHAPTER 8

The Search for Answers

From the 15th to the 19th of April, the primary goal of newspapers covering the sinking was to gather and present all possible information pertaining to *what* had happened. After the *Carpathia*'s arrival and launch of the U.S. Senate inquiry, the burning question became *why*.

Answers gradually emerged, but they were beset with controversy and sometimes contradictory. Not surprisingly, public fascination was relentless. In the New York press, coverage of the story did not leave the front pages of the *Times* until May 3; the *Tribune*, April 29; the *Herald*, April 28; the *World*, May 5; and the *Evening Journal* and *Sun*, May 4. If we also include Astor's funeral and the disposition of his estate, then *Titanic*-related stories lingered in the headlines of most New York papers until May 9.

Although it was the April 19 *Times* that caught the eye of the world, other New York dailies had also seized the moment afforded by the *Carpathia*'s arrival. A brief consideration of what they emphasized might be appropriate here before we consider follow-up coverage based on the Senate inquiry that began the same day.

The *Tribune* went with a headline emphasizing that the collision had occurred at 21 knots. A subheadline noted that the men in first and second class remained calm during the crisis, while Italians in steerage had to be shot to keep order. Needless to say, New Yorkers of Italian extraction did not take kindly to this bit of xenophobic reporting, based as it was on contradictory testimony. In a later article, Colonel Archibald Gracie, a devotee of history and future author of *The Truth about the Titanic* (1913), claimed no one was shot, although a revolver was fired once. Another set of comments had Dr. Washington Dodge insisting that it was two men in first class trying to get into a boat who were shot by an officer who then turned the gun on himself. One of the most reliable witnesses, Lawrence Beesley, did not mention a shooting; his observations were recounted in the *Tribune*, as they had been in the *Times*, but at half the length.

The *Herald* went with a headline citing Astor's heroism in helping his wife and several other female passengers gain access to the boats. Consistent with the excellent visuals the paper had been presenting since the beginning of the week, the front page contained a sequence of drawings by 17-year-old Jack Thayer showing the ship breaking in two before the final plunge. This thesis had few adherents among the survivors at the time and was readily dismissed in subsequent decades. Then, in 1985, Robert Ballard's discovery of the wreck did indeed show the *Titanic* to be in two pieces, affirming the keenness of Thayer's perception. When James Cameron filmed the final plunge in his *Titanic*, the images bore a striking resemblance to Thayer's drawings. Another impressive visual scoop followed on page 2: five photographs taken from the *Carpathia* showing the lifeboats coming alongside and survivors being taken aboard.

The article chronicling Astor's gallantry was followed by one on the less laudable comportment of Ismay. The tenor of the piece suggested that no matter how he obtained his place in a boat, he should not have. In an interview with one of the *Carpathia*'s officers, who wished to remain anonymous, the man claimed to have observed Ismay during the passage to New York "demanding" food and "forcing" two dollars on the steward who brought it to him. In a more positive vein, the paper noted that Ismay had declared his support for the inquiry and his willingness to answer formally all questions. The last notable personality whose behavior was discussed was Captain Smith. He was said to have remained at his post while shouting commands through a megaphone; the widely cited incident of his rescue of a child was not part of the *Herald*'s commentary.

A photograph of the *Carpathia* docking graced the front page of the *World*, along with estimates of the death toll and the contention that "Nearer My God to Thee" was the musical finale. This song was also deemed to be *the* one by the *Herald* (the *Times*, however, on the basis of the testimony of its star witness, Harold Bride, leaned toward the Episcopal hymn "Autumn," with its haunting line, "Hold me up in mighty waters").

Today, the story of the band—or bands, since there was a quintet led by Wallace Hartley as well as a trio for the Café Parisien—and the final song is often pondered when the sinking is discussed. Walter Lord, in a sequel to his best seller *A Night to Remember*, *The Night Lives On*, devotes an entire chapter to it. In my own research travels, I have been told of a monument to the *Titanic*'s bandsmen in Broken Hill, New South Wales, Australia, at least 600 miles from the sea. There has even been a novel devoted to their story, Norwegian author Erik Fosnes Hansen's *Psalm upon Journey's End*, which will be discussed in the next chapter.

As to the final song, several schools of thought prevail. Survivor Eva Hart, in a 1990s television interview, insisted it was "Nearer My God to Thee" and that hearing the hymn in later years always gave her chills. Doubters argue that, although the hymn might have been played earlier on that fateful day, it is unlikely that such a somber piece would have been selected during the evacuation since the purpose of the band playing was to keep people's spirits up. Proponents of this view favor an upbeat popular selection, such as "Songe d'Automne." Walter Lord seems inclined in this direction. He disqualifies the hymn "Autumn" on the grounds of its obscurity and the fact that hymns are usually known by their first lines, not by the titles of the melodies on which they are based; in the case of the rarely performed "Autumn," the lines would be "Guide Me, O Thou Great Jehovah." He also invokes further evidence against the favorite of *Titanic* movies, "Nearer My God to Thee," by noting that it has three different melody possibilities, two used in Britain and one in the United States. How could both American and British survivors claim with certainty that this was the piece they heard?

After dispensing with discussion of the final song, the *World* focused on the personalities who made the voyage, mentioning the noble behavior of Isidor and Ida Strauss, owners of Macy's, who died together rather than be separated. The paper's coverage of the actions of Ismay surrounded him with a question mark. On one hand he was quoted as saying that White Star would do its utmost for the survivors and their families and that he welcomed the Senate inquiry. On the other hand the paper noted that he "snapped back angrily" at reporters who asked if he left in the first boat, claiming instead to have been in the last. A few pages late, several sailors (the name Jack Williams is mentioned) stated that they saw Ismay leave on the first boat, a claim that the later inquiry would in no way support. Adding to the loss column of its Ismay scorecard, the *World* noted how he, along with other employees of the line, had their plans for an immediate departure from New York thwarted by Senator Smith.

Ismay's case was presented more matter-of-factly in the *Sun*, although readers probably still ended up thinking the worst. The coverage also included the requisite barrage of interviews with survivors willing to recount their experiences. This was prefaced by the most detailed assessment to appear in any New York paper regarding the actual landing of the *Carpathia*, replete with descriptions of the confusion and sadness that reigned.

All New York newspapers on April 19 mentioned the inquiry that would begin that same day. However, only Hearst's *Evening Journal*, taking its mandate as an evening publication seriously, included extended testimony—a brief summary appeared in the evening edition of the *Sun*. The proceedings, initially held at the Waldorf-Astoria, would be moved to Washington, DC, on Monday the 22nd.

The disaster's most notorious survivor presented events from his point of view, one that Senator Smith would have cause to challenge in the days to come. According to the *Evening Journal*, Ismay opened with a lament for the loss. He then went on to note that although he knew of the presence of ice, he was just a passenger and had no say regarding navigational decisions. In defense of White Star, he insisted that the ship was not trying to set a record; in defense of himself, he restated the circumstance of his departure in what he claimed was the last boat. Reporting this testimony was a good beginning for the *Journal*'s remaining *Titanic* coverage but not enough to erase the pain caused to so many by the false rescue stories it ran initially.

The inquiry generated enormous interest, and not just because of the statements made there and the personalities involved. The flamboyant and relentless way Senator Smith conducted it became an international cause célèbre and led to divided attitudes among New York newspapers. The *Times*, initially supportive of the proceedings, soon turned negative. The reason was obvious. In the midst of enjoying global accolades for being the disaster's publication of record, the paper became implicated in the very events being reported when Senator Smith linked its coverage to the corporate high-handedness he was seeking to expose regarding White Star and Marconi.

Probing the culpability of White Star meant subjecting its managing director, Bruce Ismay, to an avalanche of scrutiny. However, if we look at the tragedy dispassionately, it can be seen as one in which nature and culture rather than specific individuals played major roles: Shakespearian in terms of the drama and values that were played out, un-Shakespearian given the absence of strong central characters who can be singled out as responsible for determining the course of events.

Yet the public, then as now, could not abide a tragedy wrought of human failure in which there were no distinct personalities upon whom to lay direct blame. Ismay, therefore, became the personification of the British Board of Trade and the navigational practices of White Star.

By April 20, Ismay's initial testimony at the inquiry was widely reported. The paper that made the most of it was the *World*. "ISMAY IS GRILLED" ran the headline, with a large portrait underneath. What Ismay had said while testifying was simply not enough for the populist-leaning paper. A reporter followed his every move and noted that Ismay was pacing, smoking, twitching nervously, and barely able to hold himself together—behaviors that must have led readers into assuming some taint of guilt. Ismay heightened the negative aura surrounding him when he consented to be interviewed by the *World* reporter. Although declaring that he was just a passenger and that his conscience was clear, he also remarked that the hearing had been unfair, especially to him. Several days later he wisely retracted the statement. Other issues besides the sinking appeared to have been at stake in the paper's accusing portrayal of him, such as the worth of U.S. popular democracy compared to British hereditary privilege. The reporter waxed explicit on this contrast: "His whole makeup denotes a life of ease rather than one of strength, as if he were accustomed to having his own way because it is given to him rather than because he wins it."

Two days later the headline read, "ISMAY PUTS RESPONSIBILITY ON DEAD CAPTAIN." Since there was a modicum of sympathy for Captain Smith—the April 20 *World* had quoted someone claiming to have witnessed the child rescue incident—to render such an accusation undoubtedly aroused more public ire. But as might be expected, the text of the accompanying article did not quite match the implications of the headline. Rather than blame the captain for the tragedy, Ismay merely restated how the skipper, not he, was responsible for the speed and route the ship followed and that, as far as he understood it, the decisions made were quite normal under the circumstances.

Even the *Times*, less prone to sensationalizing, realized that Ismay-bashing was the theme of the week. The paper's April 21 summary of the hearing cited a wireless message from the *Carpathia* urging White Star to make the *Cedric* ready to spirit Ismay and the other company survivors back to England as soon as possible. Its signature of "YAMSI," a coded name that used a simple letter reversal and fooled no one, served to make his actions all the more suspicious. Ismay's explanation only made matters worse: that he was concerned for the welfare of his crew lest they "get into trouble" while in the United States. The paper further compounded his image problem by citing an earlier interview in which he described the inquiry as "brutally unfair."

The subsequent witnesses called to testify were mostly crew. They were suspicious regarding the direction in which the senator might lead them and were as a result somewhat retentive. Another factor that must have weighed on their minds was the possible repercussions that might follow statements made at the inquiry, when they would later have to face their employer, White Star, as well as the British press after the voyage home.

It was widely felt among White Star employees that Senator Smith was not a man knowledgeable enough to conduct such an investigation. A Midwesterner from Michigan, his maritime knowledge was minimal, but he took nothing for granted. Although some of the questions he asked about seafaring practices reflected a landlubber's ignorance, they often yielded information that enlightened a U.S. public uninformed in such matters. The more knowledgeable British public was fueled by a press that derided him constantly and often referred to his conduction of the inquiry as a "farce." No doubt the senator's dramatic style and populist sentiments repeatedly grated against their traditional reserve. However, over the past several decades the weight of *Titanic* scholarship, even in Britain, has tended to regard the senator and his inquiry with increasing respect. Flamboyant he may have been, but conscientious and thorough as well. No one has done more to redeem this episode in U.S. history than psychologist and historian Wyn Craig Wade. His book, *The Titanic: End of a Dream*, first published in 1979, contains an extensive profile on the Michigan senator and a detailed account of the hearing.

While the British press questioned the legitimacy of the senator's "farce," their U.S. counterparts took a suspicious attitude toward several witnesses from Britain. It was felt that their discomfort with the proceedings would prompt them to reveal less than they knew. As the lead-off man, Ismay probably set the tone for this attitude, but it was later exacerbated when the person took the stand whom many considered to be the one most informed to comment on the disaster: Second Officer Charles Lightholler.

When Lightholler was queried he told the amazing story of his own survival. At one point the senator asked when he left the ship. The response was that he did not. In a quick retort that Lightholler must have appreciated the senator asked if the ship left him. "Yes," was the reply. Most of the other questions addressed navigational practices and lifeboat capacity and procedure. Nearly all New York papers intimated that getting answers from him was like pulling teeth. When safely home, Lightholler would repeatedly denounce the aims and leadership of the investigation.

It did not help Lightholler's cause to be preceded on the stand by Captain Arthur Rostron of the *Carpathia*. In terms of seamanship, Rostron's wisdom and actions during the disaster seemed the embodiment of informed heroism. It earned him a Congressional Medal of Honor. The press inevitably weighed Lightholler's testimony against Rostron's and found it evasive and imbued with suspect judgment. The question of judgment was most apparent when the issue was broached as to why Lightholler lowered boats with so few people in them. The response—that he did not want to overload the tackle and was not sure the ship was doomed in any case—was cited in a number of papers, most notably the April 20 *Times*. Nevertheless his words were deemed less than convincing.

The issue of Lightholler's judgment emerged several days later. On April 24, the headline in the *World* read, "LOOKOUT SWEARS GLASSES WOULD HAVE ALLOWED HIM TO SPOT BERG." The reference was to binoculars, not eyeglasses, and to Frederick Fleet, who spotted the berg from the crow's nest on the fatal night and then relayed his observation to the bridge. In testifying before the hearing, he stated that he could have spotted the ice earlier and in time to avoid it had the crow's nest been supplied with binoculars. It was an intriguing hypothesis, and the press made the most of it. Such a small, innocuous item, the presence of which might have prevented the so-called at the time "disaster of the century"! Thoughts come to mind now—perhaps they did in 1912 as well—of the famous proverb inspired by the fate of Richard III at the Battle of Bosworth, whereby the absence of a nail leads to the loss of a horse's shoe, then of the horse, the battle, and eventually the kingdom.

Why were no binoculars issued to the lookouts? Ironically, they were, from Belfast to Southampton, and to lookouts on most other White Star vessels. For the *Titanic*'s transatlantic voyage they were recalled and assigned to officers on the bridge. Fleet and the other lookouts requested them back and were refused. The officer denying them was Lightholler. Would they in fact have made a difference? When questioned about the incident, Lightholler shrugged it off, claiming that an overreliance on binoculars can be a liability in maintaining a sharp vigil. Other experts, such as Admiral Peary (the renowned polar explorer, who must have had some familiarity with icebergs), disagreed. His opinion on the issue was voiced in an interview in the April 24 *World*. My own familiarity with binoculars suggests that this question can only be answered with a knowledge of the type of binoculars available. A powerful binocular that functions well in daylight might not necessarily work well under low-light conditions—the dark, moonless night of April 14, for example. Generally speaking, the lower the power and wider the aperture, the better a binocular's light-gathering capability under dark sky conditions. It would indeed be interesting if among the *Titanic*'s salvaged artifacts the binoculars that Fleet requested were to turn up.

Another larger and more controversial story soon eclipsed the binocular episode. It was foreshadowed in Fourth Officer Joseph Boxhall's testimony on April 22. In some papers that evening and in others the next day, amid his reported comments on ice, navigation, and lifeboat evacuation, we find the unsettling observation that he had spotted a ship approximately five miles from the *Titanic*. Boxhall, who had binoculars, saw both her port and starboard lights and tried to signal her using a Morse lamp. There was no acknowledgment of his call nor response to the distress rockets he was periodically firing. Subsequent witnesses corroborate his story. Since it was assumed that any such ship would have certainly responded, the incident remains puzzling, but it was soon supplanted in the press by commentary on other issues.

Then came news from Boston. The Leyland liner *Californian* had docked there on the 19th, and rumors were spreading among the crew that some of them had seen a distant ship and rockets the night the *Titanic* went down. Captain Lord, in a press statement (in New York it appeared in the April 24 *World*) attributed such talk to the crew's overactive imagination. The next day the *Boston American* dropped a bombshell—a legitimate scoop for a Hearst paper at last—by printing the statement of Ernest Gill, an assistant engineer on the *Californian*. Gill recounted seeing a ship's lights that night as well as rockets indicating "a vessel in distress." He also told of overhearing conversations about the incident among several officers in the morning. The day after this statement he was whisked off to Washington, along with Captain Lord and several crewmen. Although Gill had been paid $500 for his story (a precedent already set by Bride and Cottam with the *Times*), Senator Smith found it convincing enough to have all those involved testify formally. In reporting the story, the *Times* made explicit mention of the $500 paid to Gill. The paper was still smarting from the negative feelings aroused by its payoff to Bride and Cottam and wanted to emphasize that it was not alone in engaging in such a practice.

Gill's statement was read to the committee, and he was questioned. Both seemed credible. Captain Lord was next. He mentioned the distant ship and that an effort had been made to contact her with Morse lamp. Then shortly after he had retired for the night, he was informed that a rocket might have been spotted, whereupon he asked the duty officer to keep signaling in Morse code. Eventually the ship in question disappeared and was assumed to have sailed away. The *Californian*'s wireless operator, Cyril Evans, was then called. Although asleep during the sinking, he told of hearing talk about the rockets the next morning. He also answered "No" to a question that hovers over the *Californian* incident to this day: did he know why he was not called to his station by the captain when the first rocket was sighted?

Press coverage of Captain Lord was unsparing and public reaction swift. He became scapegoat of the moment, easing for a time the burden of criticism from the shoulders of Ismay. The incident was also one in which the British Board of Trade inquiry, although approaching its investigation quite differently, would concur with the U.S. Senate assessment.

Of the many issues raised at the inquiry (far more than can be considered here), the *Times* exclusive with Marconi's wireless operators was one that made the press itself part of the very chain of events it was mandated to cover. When these interviews were initially published, the importance of the two operators in the disaster scenario became unquestionably clear. But since their accounts had been a *Times* exclusive, other papers seemed not to have given the men the coverage they deserved—until Senator Smith put them on the stand, along with Marconi and his chief New York engineer, Frederick Sammis.

In the April 21 *World*, there was extensive critical commentary on Bride's statement to the committee and his exclusive to the *Times*. To further cast him in a negative light, the paper cited his repeated denunciation of the wireless operators aboard the U.S. Navy's *Chester*. A subheadline then informed readers that Uncle Sam's operators were equal to the best, and a substantial article marshaled evidence to prove the contention. The *Herald* of the same day built its case against the *Times* by discussing Sammis's Marconigram urging the operators to keep their mouths shut and to hold their stories. These journalistic critiques were only possible because the senator had done his wireless homework and asked probing questions.

When Smith put Marconi on the stand, the inventor denied arranging for an exclusive, despite the evidence. He also claimed that the messages were sent only because he was not averse to his operators accepting payment for any stories once their duties were discharged—from whom this payment might derive was, he insisted, of no concern to him. But Smith's research had already uncovered Marconi's liaison of several years with the *New York Times*. To the paper's readers and rivals, this must have come as no surprise—as noted earlier, a Marconi section regularly supplied the paper with European news, and when the inventor elected to speak out on this or that issue, the *Times* was often his venue of choice.

Throughout his interrogation of witnesses regarding the wireless collusion incident, Senator Smith was more concerned with exposing the Marconi Company's corporate machinations than he was in indicting the journalistic ethics of the *Times*. Rival papers tended to follow the opposite course. Marconi was a hero whose questionable judgment in this instance merited no more than a slap on the wrist, although the April 24 *Evening Journal* rendered a harsher verdict. The *Times*, on the other hand, was a competitor that had transgressed. Accusations of profiting from a tragedy were particularly vehement from the camps of Pulitzer and Hearst.

The *Times*' reaction was twofold. First it sought to defend actions that had yielded the exclusive, and then it waged a campaign to discredit the senator. In the April 26 issue an extended commentary argued that Bride, injured and having lost all his belongings (violins resound between the lines), gave the interview only after his duties had been discharged. The commentary continued by vehemently challenging Smith's contention that the Bride story was an attempt on the part of the paper to keep news of the *Titanic* away from the rest of the world in general.

Rather than defend Marconi directly, the paper went on to reprint statements given at the hearing in which he defended himself from Smith's accusations. The senator's probing questions and occasionally caustic responses to Marconi's answers were, of course, omitted. The discussion came to a close by indirectly challenging Smith's competence to lead such an inquiry, citing criticisms that had appeared in the British press. The *Times* was particularly derisive of Smith's questions to Fifth Officer Lowe regarding the composition of an iceberg. They had been posed earlier to Boxhall, and the exchange showed that

Smith was clearly aware that debris other than frozen water might be involved (especially in the side that might have been in contact with land). The *Times*, however, preferred to convey the impression that he was oblivious to the obvious.

In the days that followed the *Times* increased its Smith-bashing. Editorials continued to question the senator's competence in maritime affairs and to malign his methods. The April 29 issue reported, on the basis of shaky evidence, that fellow senators on the committee insisted he abandon the investigation or they would resign. It is not difficult to construe this story as another effort on the part of the *Times* to deflect the mounting criticism to which it was being subjected, especially since the article that followed contains a denial that the paper had behaved conspiratorially and monopolistically in securing the Bride interview. Ironically, the *Times* had supported Smith before he exposed its collusion with Marconi. In going on the attack, the paper also wanted to convey a sense that other members of the press shared their view of the senator's ineptness. Several late April subheadlines cited British newspaper accounts decrying the hearing and its chairman. The accompanying *Times* articles—one suspects the cleverness of Carr Van Anda—bemoan the bad impression of the United States the hearing was imparting to the rest of the world.

This anti-Smith campaign was obviously too self-serving to win many supporters among the public or rival papers. The *Times* would eventually abandon its efforts to discredit him, but only after one sarcastic last volley. A subheadline on the front page of the May 1 issue read, "LONDON OFFERS SMITH A JOB." The article describes how an English music hall had invited him to lecture on navigation and safety at sea, for a price he could name. The impression conveyed was that the offer was taken seriously since his formal decline was reprinted.

Smith's concluding statement regarding the inquiry took place before the Senate on May 18. With flowery rhetoric that avoided holier-than-thou moralizing, he found the British Board of Trade overly lax in its shipping regulations (especially those pertaining to the number of lifeboats on giant liners) and White Star less than diligent, given its failure to both test available lifesaving gear and to establish drills and stations. On the personal side, Captain Smith should have been more vigilant given the conditions; the same went for Captain Lord of the *Californian*. The senator concluded by calling for more stringent regulations for commercial shipping as well as for wireless—Marconi was spared the embarrassment of being mentioned by name in the second instance.

The U.S. press response was overwhelmingly positive; the British press was mixed, but mostly negative. Perhaps the most laudatory coverage was in the Hearst papers. They included a personal letter of congratulations from the Hearst himself—perhaps so gracious a response concealed a sense of relief that at no time during the inquiry did Smith raise the issue of irresponsible reporting in the days prior to the *Carpathia* docking. Even the *Times*, with the hatchet for Smith finally buried but probably not forgotten, conceded that his summation, although not informed by maritime expertise, was well founded in every instance.

PART THREE
Imagining Disaster

Our intellect has created a new world that dominates nature, and has populated it with monstrous machines.

—Carl Jung

CHAPTER 9
Responses and Renderings in Literature

As the furor over the *Titanic*'s demise subsided in the press, commentary on the event resurfaced in essays, poetry, and film. Later decades would see the topic broached in fiction, music, theater, and more recently in visual art, radio, television, and a seemingly endless number of websites. Through these various media, the status of the disaster has been transformed from a devastating news story, tinged with unanswered questions and the assumed accountability of various agencies, to an inclusive metaphor for technological hubris and cultural extravagance. What began as an accident of history has become one of its enduring moral lessons—a real-life counterpart to high tragedy in literature. The works of Sophocles, Shakespeare, and Melville seem as appropriate to understanding the implications of what happened as do the conclusions of any purely historical study.

The emergence of the *Titanic* disaster as one of the dominant moments in Western cultural history can be seen to have taken place in three phases bounded by the following years: 1912 to 1954, 1955 to 1984; and 1985 to the present.

The first phase began with a series of responses to the event by several luminaries of the literary world, among them George Bernard Shaw, Sir Arthur Conan Doyle, Joseph Conrad, and Thomas Hardy. Cinema also entered the scene at this point and would be a factor in how we have come to regard the *Titanic* in every decade of the past 100 years. The 1930s saw a formidable rendering of the tragedy when Canadian E. J. Pratt embraced it in a lengthy narrative poem. The final event of note in the first phase occurred in 1953 with the release of the Twentieth-Century Fox production *Titanic*. Although those first three decades following the disaster saw nothing to rival the *Titanic* mania that came later, interest was consistently maintained despite, or perhaps in part because of, the greater horror of two world wars, the Holocaust, and Hiroshima.

The second phase began with the 1955 publication of Walter Lord's remarkable book, *A Night to Remember*. It soon inspired an adaptation for television and prompted that medium's continued interest in the *Titanic*. Three years later Rank Productions of Great Britain released the movie *A Night to Remember*. It still stands as the definitive cinematic telling of the story and one of the finest examples of the ever-popular disaster film genre. The 1960s saw the humble beginnings of the Titanic Historical Society, and the next decade ended with the lavish made-for-television drama *S.O.S. Titanic*, along with speculation that it might be possible to find the wreck. The 1980s opened with *Raise the Titanic* and three failed attempts to locate the wreck.

In 1985 Robert Ballard's successful expedition to find the *Titanic* began the third phase. This discovery set the agenda for events to the present. They include later expeditions to salvage the wreck, leading to the artifact exhibitions; the opening of an inquiry into the *Californian* incident based on new evidence as to the position of the *Titanic* in 1912; the giant-screen films *Titanica* and *Ghosts of the Abyss*; James Cameron's *Titanic*, in its original and 3D versions; the World Wide Web; and all the commemorative events of 2012.

This rich legacy of representation begins in the aftermath of news coverage of the sinking. By the third week of May 1912 the press firestorm had abated. The U.S. Senate inquiry had been over for almost a month, and the British Board of Trade's version was in the throes of folding its tent. Testimony had been given by eyewitnesses, maritime experts, and those with both credentials. Journalist had editorialized endlessly, as had the general public in countless conversations.

The tragedy was without precedent, not in terms of loss of life but in how it illustrated the convergence of so many factors. The old adage about truth being stranger than fiction must have seemed appropriate. After the two inquiries, there was a sense that the loss of the *Titanic* was not just a devastating accident whose painful memory would eventually subside; it created a scar on the very soul of Western civilization. One element that made it so unsettling was the way the cast of players in the drama was deployed. Technology and nature played the leads, with individual personalities assigned supporting roles—a reversal of the way major historical events were usually played out. Never had Emerson's observation that "Things are in the saddle and ride mankind" rung so true.

The tragedy had exhausted the efforts of journalists to chronicle its full implications, and historians were no better equipped for the task. Yet almost immediately, and in every decade since, artists working in various media and genres have added their impressions, the literary tradition being a recurring source in this regard. Writers whose expertise is in tragedy, fate, and individual responsibility have contributed provocative insights. One of the first such commentaries was an essay by George Bernard Shaw in the *Daily News and Leader* on May 14, 1912. It put him on a collision course with another powerful literary voice of the time, Sir Arthur Conan Doyle.

Shaw called his piece "Some Unmentioned Morals," and in it he accused both the press and public of failing to face directly the reasons for and consequences of the tragedy. Instead of a profound outpouring of sympathy for the victims and a dispassionate reflection on the circumstances of the sinking, what had come to the fore was misinformation and false heroism couched in "outrageous romantic lying." Employing a baroque and often sarcastic style, Shaw claimed that British reaction to the event was underscored by a hidden agenda of face-saving and national pride. Too much, he insisted, had been attributed to fate and not enough to negligence.

Shaw went on to question the wisdom of "women and children first," although not its nobility, and then scornfully noted how it was violated in the boat of Lady Duff Gordon, which had 10 men and two women. Obviously no fan of Captain Smith, Shaw resented vehemently the depiction of him as cool and brave in the crisis, depictions that he claimed evoked the image of Nelson; had the captain done his job properly he would have remained anonymous. The officers were also critiqued, not for acting ignobly but for being all too human and then later portrayed as heroic. He cites the case of Lowe versus Ismay in this context, whereby the Fifth Officer, when supervising the loading of a lifeboat, was given some unwelcome advice from the managing director of the line, whom he promptly told to "go to hell."

Leaving no popular image of the ship sacred, Shaw made reference to news stories of the band playing "Nearer My God to Thee." Obviously informed by later testimony from the hearings, he noted that what was played were upbeat ragtime tunes to avoid panic. While this was going on vital information was being held from the passengers, especially foreigners in third class. Their alleged unruly behavior was, for him, exaggerated by the press in an effort to highlight the allegedly more admirable reactions that came from those of English descent.

A week later in the same paper came a biting challenge from Conan Doyle. He chastised Shaw for accusing everyone of lying while basing those accusations on false assumptions. If Shaw had thoroughly assessed the situation, instead of selecting evidence to confirm his prejudices, he would have noted how the lifeboat that left after the one cited had 65 women and five men. Needless to say, Conan Doyle was doing some selection of his own since the actual ratio of male to female survivors was just over one to three.

With respect to Captain Smith, Shaw was accused of confusing public sympathy for an honored seaman with approval of his navigational decisions; one mistake should not undo an otherwise illustrious career. Conan Doyle went on to note how the captain gave up his life-belt and eventually swam with a child to a boat that he himself refused to enter. This event became one of the enduring *Titanic* legends, and, although never verified, it appeared in a widely seen news cartoon. As for the alleged comparisons of Captain Smith to Nelson, this point prompted Conan Doyle to offer £100 to the Fabian Society (the socialist group in which Shaw played a prominent role) for any convincing journalistic evidence of it.

The incident of Lowe versus Ismay was regarded by Conan Doyle as an act of courageous defiance that put duty ahead of the privilege of rank. He went on to note that reliable witnesses saw foreigners rush the boats, only to be stopped by an officer's pistol shots. And regarding the band playing to avert panic: was this not a wise decision, and should they not be honored for carrying it out? He concluded by minimizing the chauvinism that outraged Shaw, arguing that much would be lost if such expressions of courage and duty were not lauded. He acknowledged Shaw as a "genius," but one who used his talents to condemn, misjudge, and compound the anguish of the situation.

Shaw followed with a lengthy rebuttal. Exuding bravado, he argued that no sane person who had carefully studied his text could disagree with it. He deemed Conan Doyle's criticism a "romantic warmhearted protest." The great playwright then suggested that the great novelist look into his very own novels for authentic cases of heroism, not to the fabrications of the press. The £100 was refused on the grounds that he did not want to unduly deprive a friend. For Shaw, any praise for Captain Smith, whom he contended took a major gamble and lost, diminishes the dignity of those captains who do their duty with thoroughness and vigilance. If the *Titanic* had been a military ship, would he not have been subject to a court martial? The rebuttal ended by noting that ultimately the great moral loss following the disaster remained the substitution of "aspiring achievement" for "sensational misfortune."

Several days later Conan Doyle closed out the exchange with a brief rejoinder. He denied suggesting that Shaw had lied, only that, despite his brilliance, a clear lack of judgment was evident along with an insensitivity to the feelings of those involved. What neither of these two literary titans probably realized at the time was that the issues over which they crossed pens would continue to be debated for over 100 years.

A literary figure far more knowledgeable in maritime affairs entered the arena of commentary when Joseph Conrad aired his views in the May 1912 issue of the *English Review*. His eloquent and highly charged essay, "Some Reflections on the Loss of the *Titanic*," was informed by 20 years of service as a seaman, mate, and master and by an assiduously gathered collection of newspaper accounts of the disaster.

Conrad's essay expressed an almost mocking attitude toward the U.S. Senate inquiry. It was viewed as rife with misguided enthusiasm and persistent attention to irrelevant details, such as the number of explosions that came from inside the ship as she was going under. Conrad asked why the senators did not pursue in this manner the many accidents that occurred in the U.S. railway system. The senators' incompetent performance turned a high drama worthy of Shakespeare into something more resembling one of the Bard's comedies. These views echoed the way much of the British press regarded Senator Smith's investigation. They also reveal a rarely seen nationalistic side of Conrad. Especially telling in this regard was his contention that since the *Titanic* was a British ship wrecked in international waters, the surviving officers should not be accountable to the United States or any other foreign government. No mention is made of the fact that the ship was actually owned by International Mercantile Marine, an American trust headed by J. P. Morgan.

Any solace the British Board of Trade might have taken from these remarks would have been quickly overridden by subsequent criticism directed at them. Conrad noted that here was an organization of alleged expertise that was complacent, ill informed about the design implications of new ships, and susceptible to being pressured by commercial interests. Its greatest oversight in this regard was the regulation basing the number of lifeboats a ship carried on her tonnage, a carryover from a time when the normal maximum for a ship was 10,000 tons—less than a quarter the size of the *Titanic*.

Conrad went on to suggest that the sheer size of the *Titanic*, which some experts thought was a safety feature, making her a giant lifeboat, was a liability in that it necessitated handling her more delicately than most smaller vessels. To back this contention, he cited an incident he observed several years earlier in Sydney, Australia, whereby a ship half the size of *Titanic* gently drifted to her berth and virtually destroyed it. He also noted that the steel plating on giant liners simply could not be made as proportionately strong as would be the case for smaller vessels.

Another aspect of the tragedy with which Conrad had little patience was the argument by some of the builders that the ship would have survived had she collided directly with the iceberg—a view that implied the seamanship was not as informed as it could have been. True, he noted, the *Arizona* a few years earlier had survived such a collision, but she was less than 5,000 tons and could not, according to Conrad's estimate, have been traveling faster than 14 knots. The "modern blind trust in material and appliances" and commercial pressure to make ships more appealing to the highly affluent created an unwieldy monster. She was too large for her purpose as an efficient medium of transport and, because any free space was assigned to more pleasurable pursuits, inadequately equipped with lifeboats.

In contrast to Shaw and Conan Doyle, who stressed negligent navigation, Conrad's emphasis was on the unseaworthiness of the vessel and the shortsightedness of those who brought her into service. For Conrad, the *Titanic*'s course and speed did not, per se, represent an unusual risk. Could we therefore surmise that his failure to broach this issue, as most others had done, indicates this former seaman's loyalty to his maritime brethren? His lament over the way seamen had been forced to modify their routines because of commercial pressures suggests as much. The essay hints that seafaring will always have an element of risk associated with it but that a properly prepared vessel is adequate to most situations. The case of the *Duoro* is mentioned, a ship one-tenth the size of the Titanic, which was rammed and sank in 15 to 20 minutes. Nevertheless all 10 lifeboats were launched, and every passenger, except for one who refused to leave the ship, was saved; the captain and most of the crew perished. Conrad's moral was that technology can fail, and so can men, but that men, when given a chance, can prove to be "truer than steel"—especially, he noted in an ironic afterthought, the kind of steel used for the bulkheads of modern giant liners.

Conrad's reputation and maritime knowledge led to widespread discussion of his statement and a few challenges. He responded in the journal's next issue by refusing to retract his criticism of the U.S.

Senate's investigation, adding that its motivations, if not its methods, were laudable. The rest of his commentary was given over to a technical dissertation on ship design. In reiterating his point about the inadequacy of hull plate thickness he made a colorful comparison to the Huntley and Palmer biscuit tin, showing the latter's clear superiority in strength-to-size ratio. (Over the years the phrase that has come down is something along the lines of, "The *Titanic* was ripped open 'like a Huntley and Palmer biscuit tin,'" a rather different analogy from Conrad's.) Given the impossibility of making hull plates as relatively thick and strong as Huntley and Palmer's tin, several ways were suggested for making a ship's transverse bulkheads as watertight as possible. The first was to downsize luxury appliances and limit the number of passengers. As in his previous essay, Conrad again leaned toward solutions that would use what we would today call appropriate technology. He added to the list of interior design ideas the use of mechanical cranes instead of hand-operated davits for the lifeboats and also proposed that such boats be equipped with small motors.

Two years later Conrad would face a different challenge when, in the *Illustrated London News,* he was asked to reflect on the collision between the *Storstad* and *Empress of Ireland* in the Gulf of St. Lawrence. The incident sank the latter in just over 15 minutes, taking a thousand lives. Navigational error, not ship technology, was the culprit. Conrad did not hesitate to address this question, and his response showed considerable sympathy for both captains.

Prose was not the only medium the literati employed when reflecting on the disaster. On May 14, 1912, the same day Shaw's essay appeared in the *Daily News and Leader,* Thomas Hardy stepped on the stage at Covent Garden and recited the evocative strains of his poem "The Convergence of the Twain." Traditionally regarded as one of his lesser efforts, a recent reassessment by Joan Cullen Brown regards it as a "brilliant tour de force" ideally suited in style and tone to its subject. Perhaps it is no coincidence that her evaluation postdates the discovery of the wreck and comes at a time when we know more about the ship than ever before.

The title of Hardy's poem suggests a coming together of disparate phenomena. He views the disaster through a wide-angle lens that avoids both sentiment and condemnation. Notably absent is the familiar narrative of the voyage as a rudely interrupted celebration of La Belle Epoque with its associated litany of names. Instead, the first half of the poem surveys the physical aftermath of the collision, the *Titanic* interred on the North Atlantic seabed. The images are haunting, pushed toward us slowly, as if we were drifting into this netherworld where

> Dim moon-eyed fishes near
> Gaze at the gilded gear

Hardy's portrait of the wreck describes a still magnificent structure, now "Deep from human vanity," or shorn from the life that created it. The impression is of an enormous corpse being turned first into a skeleton, and then to dust.

> Over the mirrors meant
> To Glass the opulent
> The sea-worm crawls

In stanzas I to V Hardy takes us to a place that, since the 1985 discovery of the wreck, millions of us have now glimpsed in a variety of media. Few words have been written since his which so effectively match the visual evidence.

In stanzas VI to IX, we are taken back in time just prior to the collision. Hardy again rejects the standard view, which has the magnificent ship ramming an inert iceberg. Both the iceberg and the *Titanic* are said to derive from the same "Immanent Will." They are regarded as complementary elements in a cosmological, but not necessarily religious, grand scheme. Culture has given this "creature of cleaving wing" for which nature has "Prepared a sinister mate." The two share billing in the drama and are seen as "twin haves of one August event," fated to converge "By paths coincident."

The use of symmetrical imagery is further extended when Hardy balances his description of the iceberg seemingly growing in size as it looms toward the ship with the description of the ship as it might have appeared from the iceberg. This point of view is very cinematic— 35 years later we find the collision sequence in *A Night to Remember* partly filmed this way. The poem ends with the collision, which is referred to as a "consummation," suggesting both destruction and rebirth. It "jars two hemispheres," again a linking of the destinies of nature and culture, as well as a way to signify the global impact of the event.

"The Convergence of the Twain" is a remarkably rich work, eerie and powerful. It reflects a trend in late Victorian Romantic literature to regard nature as an awesome and potentially malevolent force.

Darwin's view, in which nature is characterized by a struggle for existence, certainly for Hardy overrode the tamer notions of Rousseau and Wordsworth. He extended that struggle to include culture challenging nature as a result of human hubris. In the final reckoning, however, nature is all inclusive and must have the last word, in this case voiced at the end of stanza V by the "moon-eyed" fishes surveying the wreck, who inquire: "What does this vainglorious down here?"

High verse about the *Titanic*, as penned by Hardy and later by E. J. Pratt, is not the only verse. In the popular culture of various folk traditions, the sinking has been the subject of numerous rhymes and ditties, the most famous of which are perhaps the many versions of the campfire song "It Was Sad When That Great Ship Went Down." It seemed that for a time almost anyone who had an interest in poetry thought they could also write a piece about the *Titanic*. An abundance of popular verse flooded the nation. In a delightful anthology, historian Steven Biel has assembled many examples.

At first glance, a seemingly unlikely contributor to *Titanic* versification is the African American oral tradition. "*Titanic* Toast" and "De *Titanic*" are two notable examples. "*Titanic* Toast" is an oral poem with internal dialogue. Over a dozen versions have been transcribed by researchers, and many others no doubt exist. During the early 1970s, Bruce Jackson published a brief compilation, and at the end of the decade Wyn Craig Wade brought the poem to the attention of *Titanic* researchers. Although virtually unknown to whites, "*Titanic* Toast" has been celebrated by millions of African Americans in the decades since 1912. A "toast" is performed without musical accompaniment but in a very dramatic and rhythmic manner; in this sense it can be seen as a forerunner of rap. Although numerous variations of the poem exist, the overlap in content is high so that reasonable generalizations can be made regarding the dominant themes.

The hero of the poem is named "Shine," a seemingly odd choice since this term was occasionally used by whites as a pejorative label for a black male, yet ironically appropriate in that Shine would be the one to outwit white culture during its supreme moment of folly. He works in the hold, probably as a stoker, sees the damage created by the collision, and tries to inform the captain, who ignores him. Shine then utters several profanities, dives overboard, and starts swimming to New York. He does this in front of the *Titanic*'s millionaires, in some versions "a thousand millionaires," who offer him a fortune to come back and save them. He refuses.

In all variants of the story there is also female temptation: a rich man's daughter, the captain's daughter (who is usually depicted as pregnant and unmarried), or a thousand whores. They come up on deck and offer themselves to Shine in an effort to lure him back to the ship to save them. Marriage proposals from some of the wealthy women, usually the captain's daughter, are often part of the bargain. Shine does not yield. In some versions, another black man named Jim (a black Everyman to Shine's trickster persona?) joins Shine in the swim to New York but succumbs to the allure of the females and returns to the ship and inevitable death. This temptation sequence is intriguingly reminiscent of one in Homer's *Odyssey*, also in its original form an oral narrative. From their rocky sea-swept perches, the Sirens use beguiling vocals and the promise of sexual rapture to lure Odysseus and his crew. Some men, like Jim in *"Titanic* Toast," succumb and perish.

Shine swims with boundless energy toward New York, outdistancing (depending on the version) either a shark or a whale—sometimes both. Occasionally the route is circuitous and he winds up in Los Angeles first, but eventually he always gets to New York and receives news of the fate he escaped. Nearly all versions end with Shine inebriated and often in the company of women. This could be interpreted as a return to normal life, with its basic pleasures, sense of social place, and newly acquired wisdom regarding the vulnerability of white civilization.

"Titanic Toast" is unusual in the "toast" genre in that it works with an overt theme of black/white racial opposition. The moral lessons that reside in the poem seem straightforward. Neither the white man's money nor his women are worth the risks involved in getting them; therefore they should not be coveted. The appearance of the captain's unmarried, pregnant daughter suggests that even white nobility can transgress. In rejecting her Shine is rejecting soiled goods and learning that white skin and purity are not synonymous but only another myth of the oppressor. Finally, as different as *"Titanic* Toast" is from accounts of the sinking in the poetic renderings of "high culture," there is convergence on one fundamental point: arrogant overconfidence in technology can pose a threat to people of all social backgrounds.

One of the ironies of *"Titanic* Toast" is that there were no blacks on the *Titanic*, nor is it likely that there could have been, given attitudes of the time. This restriction is central to the song "De *Titanic*," which was performed and perhaps composed by Leadbelly. It was eventually collected and published by John Lomax during the 1930s. The song pivots on the refusal of the *Titanic* to accept as a passenger the great heavyweight boxing champion Jack Johnson, who up to that time had defeated all white challengers:

> Jack Johnson wanted to get on bo'ad;
> Captain Smith hollered, "I ain' haulin no coal."

Although the incident is fictitious, we do know that despite his fame and money, Johnson was often refused access to the venues of white society; one such refusal was passage on a ship, thus giving "De *Titanic*" a partial basis in truth.

The lyrics go on to describe the fate of the *Titanic*, replete with a citation of the singing of "Nearer My God to Thee." After the sinking Johnson eventually receives news of it and realizes was that denial of his passage was a blessing in disguise. He dances in celebration. This leads to a concluding moral implying, as in the case of "*Titanic* Toast," that what the white man has is not always worthy of envy:

> Black man ought to shout for joy,
> Never lost a girl or either a boy.
> Cryin', "Fare thee, *Titanic*, fare thee well."

Although the African American oral tradition kept the *Titanic* alive as a subject for poetic reflection, the ship would not reenter the high-art world of poetry until 1935. That year saw the publication of "The *Titanic*" by E. J. Pratt, a 30-page epic often regarded as the pre-eminent narrative poem by the most renowned poet in twentieth-century Canadian literature.

Pratt (1883–1964), whose first initials are intriguing identical to those of Captain Smith (Smith was often called "E. J.," but Pratt was usually addressed as "Ned"), had a background that allowed him to have a special link to the story of the *Titanic*. He was born and raised in a Newfoundland fishing community where maritime lore was a staple of everyday conversation. As an adult he became an ordained Methodist minister like his father. Marginal in this profession, as in his social and geographic origins—Newfoundland would not become a part of Canada until 1949—he sidestepped taking up a parish and pursued a doctorate in religious studies. During his academic sojourn he absorbed enough literature in the natural sciences and humanities to become a cosmopolitan intellectual. From 1920 to 1953, Pratt taught English literature at the University of Toronto and was often regarded as Canada's unofficial poet laureate. American and British editions of his work have led to a modest but enthusiastic following, especially in New England, where his seafaring themes are much appreciated.

That Pratt himself deemed "The *Titanic*" a singularly important work in his overall output is attested in later interviews and in the dedication to his father. No doubt he could have written about the disaster earlier in his career since the event is a rich source of metaphor and he had always been on intimate terms with its circumstances. By waiting to write it until mid-career, he was able to bring to the task both stylistic maturity and extensive experience in writing about maritime themes. In numerous Pratt poems leading up to this one, the ocean and her many moods are staples. Turbulent, dangerous, widow-making waters are often described in a manner that indicates a debt to those Romantic poets who had depicted nature in tempest. Pratt's word images of storm-tossed seas also evoke the visual renderings of nature in paintings of the nineteenth-century British romanticist J. M. W. Turner.

Five years before Pratt wrote "The *Titanic*," a major crisis at sea prompted a poem that became an unintentional dress rehearsal for it. In "The *Roosevelt* and the *Antinoe*" he described the perilous attempt of the former to rescue the latter in January 1927 during one of the fiercest storms in North Atlantic history. The poem tells how the *Antinoe*, a British grain freighter heading to England from New York, was ravaged by snow, sleet, and wind. She lost her lifeboats and her steering and navigational capacities. Listing badly, she sent an intermittent SOS and was located with a direction finder by the *Roosevelt*, then lost and found again by dead reckoning when her wireless gave out. The *Roosevelt* persisted in the rescue attempt in what at times seemed like a futile struggle that claimed the life of two of her crew. All 25 crewman were taken from the foundering *Antinoe*. This heroic rescue also repaid a Homeric debt since Captain Tose of the *Antinoe* had directed a similar rescue 10 years earlier. In researching the poem Pratt did not limit himself to newspaper accounts but traveled to New York to read the logs of both ships and to interview several crewmen.

In "The *Roosevelt* and the *Antinoe*" humanity, reduced in technological means and against all odds, prevails over the cold indifference of nature. Exactly the reverse takes place in "The *Titanic*." The poem chronicles the ship from her launching on May 31, 1911, to her destruction on April 15, 1912. It is written, as are most of Pratt's longer poems, in an ornate style that bespeaks a debt to the Romantics and even Shakespeare. A superficial reading might lead to the impression that the style is anachronistic, but Pratt is so adroit at meshing older language use and form with contemporary themes that the result is accessible as well as compelling. Conceptual influences include Hardy, Conrad, and Melville. Details regarding events during the voyage seem to have been drawn from survivor Lawrence Beesley's 1912 memoir, *The Loss of SS Titanic*, probably the most consulted account prior to Walter Lord's *A Night to Remember*.

In the poem, as the ship is completed she becomes the epitome of boastful achievement. The scene then shifts to Greenland, where Pratt describes how nature crafted and launched the iceberg that sank the *Titanic*—a theme that has been explored more recently in Richard Brown's *Voyage of the Iceberg*. Pratt also notes how an omen of the disaster to come occurs as the *Titanic* is leaving Southampton and her suction pulls the *New York* loose from her moorings, resulting in a near collision. This moment of doubt, however, is soon forgotten as we become caught up in the wonder of a vessel that blends power and elegance. Several pages follow in which two distinct themes play off one another in a counterpoint of irony: the sumptuous menu for first-class passengers and the wireless messages warning of ice ahead.

Wireless held a particular fascination for Pratt. He claimed that one of the great moments of his life occurred when he participated in a high school field trip to Marconi's wireless station near St. John's, Newfoundland. In 1901 he met the inventor, whose presence seemed almost god-like. Shortly after the encounter Marconi succeeded in bridging the North Atlantic with his wireless. One headline following the triumph impressed Pratt then and again later when he was composing "The Titanic": "No More Losses at Sea." Fate would conspire against this form of hubris as well by allowing disaster to take place so close to the scene of Marconi's success and by creating one of history's most famous "so near yet so far" scenarios when the *Californian* failed to respond.

Midway through the poem, two pages are given over to a description of a poker game and the ensuing conversation among several first-class passengers. Metaphoric implications soon reveal themselves. What seems like a winning hand turns into quite the opposite. A moment later one of the players orders soda and ice. The response is shattering and provides the first indication in the poem that *the* moment has arrived:

Ice: God! Look—take it through the port-hole—Look!

The scene then shifts to the bridge, where the sighting is repeated. Queries and speculations among the crew follow the collision. They seem similar to what we find in most accounts unless the poem is heard rather than read, thus making apparent Pratt's superb ear for conversational rhythm.

Although the *Carpathia*'s rescue of the *Titanic*'s survivors is not part of the poem, the valiant and dangerous commitment to get to the ship as soon as possible is told in a manner that echoes the heroism celebrated in "The *Roosevelt* and the *Antinoe*." And as the end of the *Titanic* draws nigh, one scene follows another with cinematic swiftness. The band plays. Lifeboats leave—some orderly, others in confusion. Millionaires maintain their composure. As the ship rises for her descent, boilers and bulkheads break apart. When she finally vanishes, Pratt ignores the chaos of those dying in the water and the terror of the survivors in life-boats awaiting rescue. Instead he turns his attention to the iceberg and concludes with a serene portrait of it drifting on a silent sea.

The lengthy account of the disaster, which Pratt rendered into poetry, would subsequently become the domain of prose as novelists began entering the world of *Titanic* commentary. The immensity of the event, and the gaps between its "facts," allowed for the injection of fictional possibilities. In 1938 the German writer Robert Prechtl published *Titanic*, and within two years British and U.S. editions became available. The disaster had not gone unnoticed in previous fiction, but until Prechtl's effort there was no sustained attempt to make it the centerpiece of an extended prose narrative. Perhaps it took 25 years for the event to recede sufficiently into the annals of history for it to become an appropriate vehicle for the intermingling of real and hypothetical personalities in the creative development of subplots.

Prechtl's novel has never enjoyed a wide following. It remains, despite recent interest in the *Titanic*, a rarely mentioned and hard-to-find source. The text is both ponderous (368 pages) and excessively deliberate. The author is at least honest regarding the latter, stating in the preface how the facts of the disaster must be carefully trans-posed to a qualified fictional context to be truly understood. Instead of providing the reader with characters whose lives we can follow intimately, the first two-thirds of the novel interweaves real and fictional characters into a series of theatrical vignettes. The conversations provide an intriguing glimpse into ideas in the air at the time. Most are voiced by the renowned passengers, especially John Jacob Astor. Technology is at the forefront of these exchanges, followed closely by religious and social issues.

Astor's economic machinations are considered in several lengthy digressions on prevailing social conditions circa 1912. He also figures in a scheme to buy the White Star Line from Bruce Ismay, who in turn is committed to winning the Blue Riband for the fastest crossing, which will up the value of the line's stock and save it from potential bankruptcy. Occasionally discussion gets around to the rivalry with German commercial shipping, which the arrogant robber barons on board insist must be defeated at all costs. These themes would later surface in German director Herbert Selpin's 1943 film *Titanic*, which seems to have been influenced by Prechtl's novel, although the credits indicate no acknowledgment.

The last third of the story occurs postcollision and deals with the evacuation of the ship. Several new characters are introduced, and the theme of British arrogance and overreaching is replayed. Captain Smith is not given a sympathetic portrayal. Amid the numerous chaotic scenarios aboard the ship during her final moments is an incident of murder followed by a rape described with such startling explicitness it is hard to imagine that it was written in the 1930s. We also find a consideration of the valor exhibited by the Marconi operators, as well as the *Californian*'s unresponsiveness and the *Carpathia*'s sprint to the rescue.

Time and again Prechtl's facts are wanting or deliberately fabricated, as in the instance of Astor's desire to buy White Star and the widely held misconception that the ship was trying for a record crossing. However, in fairness to Prechtl, *Titanic* scholarship then was not as it is now. Artistic license aside, his effort is still a worthy one, although by the final chapter the lack of personalities we can identify with, celebrate, or mourn diminishes the success of the book as popular fiction.

Seventeen years after Prechtl's effort, the drama of the *Titanic* was vividly told in a nonfiction best seller, Walter Lord's *A Night to Remember*, which will be discussed in the next chapter. It does everything a good novel does and more, and has become a hard act to follow for any writer engaging the *Titanic* in fiction or otherwise. By the end of the 1980s, however, the discovery of the wreck created a new wave of information and interest pertaining to the sinking and its historical context. This occurred at a time when the public's curiosity regarding the Victorian and Edwardian periods was being stimulated by motion pictures and television dramas—most recently in the award winning PBS miniseries Downton Abbey (2011–2012), which begins with an extended reference to the *Titanic*. At least four noteworthy novels emerged from this renewed interest: *Titanic: A Novel*, by Tony Aspler; *No Greater Love*, by Danielle Steel; *Psalm at Journey's End*, by Erik Fosnes Hansen; and Cynthia Bass's *Maiden Voyage*.

Aspler, who is Canadian and therefore heir to the literary tradition of E. J. Pratt, used the sinking of the *Titanic* as the extended finale for a melodramatic adventure and social commentary. His themes include class conflict, the rampant acquisitiveness of the robber barons during the waning years of classical capitalism, and the transference of industrial wealth from Britain to North America.

The novel's protagonist is Henry Blexil, butler to Lord Rutherford and occasional pugilist in the mold of John L. Sullivan. When Lord Rutherford goes bankrupt because of what appears to be bad investments—in reality he was swindled—Henry's services are transferred to the family of his former employer's business associate, the brash and unscrupulous American railroad magnate Thadeus Tarr. From his underclass vantage point, Henry witnesses Tarr's brutal suppression of a coal miner's strike in West Virginia and the various machinations that keep Tarr perpetually on the short end of his dealings with archrival J. P. Morgan. (Morgan also controls International Mercantile Marine, which in turn owns the formerly British-owned White Star Line, and therefore the *Titanic*.)

One evening at the family's summer estate, strained relations between Henry and Tarr are bent past the breaking point when the latter catches his butler *in flagrante delicto* with Nicole Linely, the live-in chaperon and companion to Tarr's wife, Cornelia. Nicole happens to be Tarr's live-in mistress, and as we later learn, she had served J. P. Morgan in that capacity as well. Henry's involvement with Nicole leads to his termination by Tarr. During his departure he comes upon the aftermath of a mysterious murder, then briefly returns to Tarr's Fifth Avenue mansion, where he discovers documents implicating the millionaire in several corrupts schemes, including the one that bilked Lord Rutherford. This information is given to a *New York Times* reporter, who will search for corroborating evidence. The reporter in turn gives Henry a contact at White Star, which leads to a job as wine steward on the *Oceanic*. Wine figures in several effective scenes throughout the novel, no doubt a reflection of Aspler's authorship of several books on the subject.

Henry's career leads to a new love interest, Kitty Boyer, a stewardess whom he rescues from harassment with his pugilistic prowess. He also embarks on a persistent quest to amass further evidence against Tarr on both sides of the Atlantic. Henry and Kitty eventually seek and acquire a posting on the Titanic. By coincidence Tarr and family are also destined to make this maiden voyage. They will be staying in the suite of J. P. Morgan, whose failure to make the trip, usually attributed to illness in historical accounts, is here attributed to his conflict with Tarr. The final 200 pages use revealing details of the voyage as a backdrop for dramatic developments in the plot. Encounters and conversations are created between the lead characters and the Duff Gordons, the Astors, Mollie Brown, and Benjamin Guggenheim. There is also a pivotal scene at the captain's table where Henry is forced to serve Tarr.

The shipboard intrigue includes some crucial wireless transmissions regarding Tarr's business practices as both Henry and antitrust legislators close in on him. Not surprisingly, a visit to the Marconi cabin includes a discussion about the nature of the medium with one of the operators, Harold Bride. Another conversation of interest takes place between Lightoller and Captain Smith over the possibility of an encounter with ice. The exchange discusses such things as the way a lack of wind-induced ripples breaking against the base of a berg might make a potential sighting difficult and how this situation could be compounded if the blue side of such an obstacle were facing the ship.

As might be expected, the climatic moments of the plot and the fate of the *Titanic* run parallel courses before Tarr is undone and Henry and Kitty manage to survive. What happens to some of the fictional characters also reflects the fates of several actual passengers. One of the more humerous lines in the novel comes as chaos engulfs the ship. Tarr, defiant to the end, snarls, "I pay a fortune for this and the goddamned ship sinks." Less humorous is a sexual encounter with murderous results, reminiscent of the one that occurs at the same point in Robert Prechtl's novel.

Aspler's book seems not to have found a wide audience. The next English-language *Titanic* novel would. In 1991, Danielle Steel, obviously following post-1985 *Titanic*-related news stories with interest, published *No Greater Love*. Her story takes place in the world of first-class passengers and centers on Edwina Winfield, whose life is both shattered and then remade by the tragedy.

Twenty-year-old Edwina is the eldest child of Bertam Winfields, the self-made publisher of a San Francisco newspaper and gentle and generous patriarch to a family of six children. Returning from England on the *Titanic*, the Winfields, along with Edwina's betrothed, the dashing young Charles Fitzgerald, are given a rude awakening shortly before midnight on April 14. When accounts are reckoned the following day on the *Carpathia*, the entourage has been whittled down to Edwina and her five younger siblings. Her mission is clear almost immediately: to put her own life on hold and manage the surviving brood to adulthood. In undertaking the challenge she becomes a quintessential Danielle Steel heroine: someone who exudes feminine grace in conjunction with high-tensile resolve.

The novel's first 100 pages will appeal to anyone interested in the disaster and unfamiliar with conventional accounts; the author has done her homework. As real and fictional characters intermingle, so do hard facts pertaining to the ship and the voyage. We also see the vessel turned into a veritable Edwardian loveboat—not surprising given the author's penchant for the romance genre. Bertram and wife Kate have a fulfilling marriage. Edwin and Charles seem bent on the same marital course. As both couples drift through the ship, they encounter John Jacob Astor cooing with his young bride Madeleine, Benjamin Guggenheim appearing surreptitiously with his mistress, and Ida and Isidor Strauss, at the end of their natural lives, still inseparable as they face this unnatural end.

The aftermath of the disaster takes Edwin from the U.S. Senate inquiry through a life of noble self-sacrifice. The novel chronicles how she keeps her family together and tries to reconcile this choice with the possibility of romance and a more conventional life of her own. To reveal the extended details of the novel is unnecessary. Suffice to say that memories of the *Titanic* haunt the Winfields; the *Lusitania* makes a cameo appearance; and there is a concluding segment where the once-fateful voyage is retaken 11 years later on the *Titanic*'s sister ship, the *Olympic*, with romantic implications. Throughout the novel, the changes wrought by the disaster on a single family serve as a reminder for what it actually did to numerous people who were on board and psychologically to an entire generation.

Just prior to the 1997 release of James Cameron's extravaganza, two *Titanic* novels caught the attention of readers on both sides of the Atlantic. The first was Erik Fosnes Hansen's *Psalm at Journey's End*, originally published in Norwegian in 1990 and available in English translation in 1996. That same year also saw the release of Cynthia Bass's *Maiden Voyage*. Not surprisingly in the aftermath of *Titanic* saturation resulting from Cameron's film, subsequent novels have been hesitant to tread those increasingly familiar waters.

Hansen's *Psalm* is one of the most internationally popular novels to come out of Scandinavia prior to Stieg Larsson's Millennium trilogy. It tells the story of the *Titanic*'s bandsmen, but not exactly. Although details of the fateful voyage and the band's role in it are accurately told, the seven musicians in name and background are completely different from the ship's actual quintet headed by Wallace Hartley.

Hansen does not make this clear until the postscript, where he notes that the story of the actual bandsmen has been and will continue to be told elsewhere. The novel is complex, as it goes into the back-stories of the individual musicians, each of whom hails from a different European country. The occasional awkwardness of the prose perhaps results from the translation of Norwegian idioms or the fact that the novelist was only 25 when he wrote *Psalm*, his second novel. Despite this, his insights into character are profound.

As most readers will probably be aware beforehand, the primary characters introduced to them are doomed. A deep sense of melancholy surrounds each one, along with the Europe they inhabit as fin de siècle change and the coming specter of the Great War darkens a mood to which the celebratory launch of the *Titanic* endeavors to provide a counterpoint. The lives of five of the seven bandsmen are told using back-stories that reveal pained personal circumstances followed by the unlikely happenstance that brought them together on the ship of dreams.

Jason, the violinist bandleader, was fascinated at a young age by an illustrated Bible depicting the Ark during the deluge surrounded by drowning people, one of several examples of foreshadowing in the novel. A victim of school bullying, his parents died of disease in India, where his father was serving as a doctor. Subsequently raised by his aunt and uncle, his life takes another turn for the worse when the girl-friend he made pregnant commits suicide by drowning. Abandoning his pursuit of medicine, he wanders the streets destitute until a friend convinces him that the sea might be his salvation. Jason then parlays his talent as a musician into a career as a ship's musician.

Alex, also a violinist, is overwhelmed by the grim poverty in prere-volutionary Russia and falls in with a con artist who when arrested declares Alex to be the mastermind. He manages to escape to London aboard a Swedish freighter, where he encounters Jason. His back-story is told via a long and almost apologetic letter to his brother.

Spot, the pianist, is German, a musician who had yearned to be a composer. Blessed with talent for the former and cursed with lack of inspiration for the latter, he sinks into a psychological abyss and is eventually abandoned by his wife and child. David, the youngest, at 18, is an Austrian Jew whose father's musical store is vandalized by anti-Semites. His world collapses and he flees to London when he loses the love of his young life to an older rival, an actor from Berlin whose most famous role is Mephistopheles in Goethe's *Faust*. Petro-nius, the Italian double bass player, joined a marionette theater as a youth and became betrothed to the owner's daughter. After she left him to marry another, his negligence resulted in a fire that destroyed the theater and killed its owner. He fled with a circus, where he subsequently honed his musical craft.

These accounts are interspersed with events aboard the ship and its cast of actual historical characters: purser McElroy's comings and goings; Thomas Andrews, the ship's builder, whom Hansen refers to a father to the ship and uncle to the crew, checking on everything from soup to bolts; and Captain Smith, the regal overseer of all. The source for the events and personalities described is the work of Walter Lord, yet occasionally an error or oversight slips through, easily recognized by those "Titanicologists" Hansen refers to in his postscript. For example there was no black stoker in the hold, and Bruce Ismay, described inaccurately as boarding with his wife and three children, is then accurately shown surreptitiously entering a lifeboat on his own.

The bandsmen die with the ship as they evidence a grudging sense of duty rather than the nobility that has become so connected with the *Titanic* myth. The strength of the novel, however, resides not with its tale of the ship and her fate but with Hansen's recounting of the lives of the principle characters before they board. Conditions of the poor in London are described through the eyes of Jason and David in almost Dickensian terms. Conditions in the European countries from which the other protagonists hail evidence a keen sense of social history writ small and personal. Of all the *Titanic* novels considered here, *Psalm* says the least about the ship itself but the most about the culture of her time.

Maiden Voyage by Cynthia Bass is a very different kind of novel. It focuses on one character, is told in the first person, and points toward a social movement, female suffrage, for which the sinking of the *Titanic* raised intriguing questions. Bass employs the voice of a male narrator looking back at a period in his youth that culminated with a voyage on the ill-fated ship. His name is Sumner Jordan; the "Sumner" derives from a homage to the strident abolitionist Charles Sumner; his mother is an ardent suffragist. Sent from his home in Boston to visit his estranged father in London as a reward for participating in a poetry contest, 12-year-old Sumner's coming of age includes hobnobbing with literati such as James Joyce and Ezra Pound; a sexual awakening through a masturbatory experience inspired by surreptitious glimpses of his father's mistress; and a passionate crush on a young American suffragist, Ivy Earnshaw, who was stirring up London with her opinions.

The trip home is in first class aboard the ship that young Sumner describes as "the first born child of marine engineering and art." The usual cast of characters is encountered. Sumner even gets a chance to play with the wireless under the supervision of Jack Phillips. Still, he feels lonely, and his interest in the voyage is neither here nor there until he spots Ivy on the dance floor. The Oedipal theme is clear enough. Not only does Ivy seem like a younger version of his mother, she knows and admires her. With the prodding of a bon vivant, womanizer, and Annapolis dropout, Pierce Anderson, Sumner makes the acquaintance of Ivy, but only after Pierce forces his hand through jealousy by feigning interest in her himself.

The evacuation of the ship following the collision creates its own drama among the three of them. None want to get into a lifeboat: Ivy because she resents the preferential treatment given women; Pierce because he simply feels his life is already a loss; and Sumner because he has a desperate need, inspired by his namesake, to be heroic in some way, especially after failing to come to Ivy's aid when she was besieged by a mob in London and carted off by the police. Ivy and Pierce realize that the only way to get Sumner into a boat is to force him to go with Ivy by heeding the call for women and children. Pierce will also be saved despite his death wish. An officer, sensing that Pierce might have some maritime expertise, puts a gun to his head and forces him to take charge of a boat.

Wracked with guilt at having survived, Sumner's life is made more complicated by the friendship that springs up between his mother and Ivy and the fact that his youth impedes him becoming a romantic companion to the young suffragist. At this point in the novel Bass uses her characters to unleash a debate that emerged historically in the aftermath of the sinking. Are suffragists hypocritical if they demand gender equality on all counts but accept unequal and privileged treatment to save their lives during a crisis? And is it not the very men who regard women as children who act first in sacrificing their own lives? Bass highlights an issue often ignored in accounts—including the current work—of the *Titanic* disaster and its aftermath. Some suffragists even marched to protest the privileged position given to women during the sinking.

In her take on the event and some of its consequences, Bass weaves a compelling narrative. A minor quibble might be the precociousness of 12-year-old Sumner. That he would claim to experience "a shudder of bliss" when writing a line of poetry sounds a bit far fetched, although scenes describing his sexual urges ring true enough. Although young

Sumner did keep a detailed journal, no time period is given as to when his adult self penned the account. We do learn in an afterward that he served as a flight instructor during World War I, when he would have been 18 or 19. Deemed too old and American to serve in the Royal Air Force at the outbreak of World War II, he again became a flight instructor when a pilot shortage allowed him to fly combat missions during the Battle of Britain—a hero at last.

Maiden Voyage inspired me to write the following postscript to it, inspired by a question put to me on several occasions when I have given talks on the *Titanic*. If the call was "women and children first" in 1912, what would happen today in similar circumstances? A bizarre example can be given that recalls an observation once made by Karl Marx about how events in history that occur first as tragedy can recur as farce.

On August 4, 1991, the French-built and Greek-owned cruise ship MTS *Oceanos* was severely damaged by rough seas and sank in the Indian Ocean off the coast of South Africa. A breech in her hull had flooded the engine room, and both the main and auxiliary power sources were severed as she began to sink. In response, the crew, along with Captain Yiannis Avranas, abandoned the ship and her passengers in such a hurry they failed to close the lower deck portholes, the standard procedure in such a situation. They also left the passengers and entertainers to figure out how to launch the remaining lifeboats, which eventually became intractable because of the listing of the ship. Fortunately the South African military, in one of the most spectacular rescues ever attempted at sea, deployed 16 helicopters to rescue what remained of the 571 passengers, all of whom survived. Video footage—available on the internet—taken by both passengers and rescuers is riveting. Avranas's response to the furor surrounding his dereliction of duty was that, when it is time to abandon ship, "it doesn't matter what time I leave. Abandon is for everybody. If some people want to stay, they can stay." Those who would judge Captain Smith of the *Titanic* harshly should pause to remember the *Oceanos*.[1]

---

[1] It took the 100th anniversary of the *Titanic* tragedy for history to repeat itself with respect to the Oceanos. As of this writing there is an ongoing investigation and litigation regarding the *Costa Concordia*, which ran aground and partially sank with 4,100 on board off the coast of Italy on January 13–14, 2012. Once again accusations of negligence have been raised (this time leading to manslaughter charges). Captain Francesco Shettino's lax navigation, and the fact that he and most of the crew left the ship with passengers still on board, contributed to a maritime tragedy that will not soon be forgotten.

CHAPTER 10

The Sinking in Cinema

The first major big-budget film to be made about the *Titanic* never was. In 1938, David O. Selznick, with his magnum opus *Gone With the Wind* still in production, tried to lure Alfred Hitchcock from England to the United States to direct pictures for him. Foremost on Selznick's mind was a film version of the *Titanic* story, to be based on screenplay by Wilson Mizner and Carl Harbrough. It would use the ship as a backdrop for the story of a con artist renouncing his evil ways upon meeting the right woman. This kind of theme, the redemption of an immoral person, had become frequent in Hollywood at the time as a result of censorship imposed by the Hays office in 1934. Selznick envisioned expanding the screenplay to create a balanced production, part melodrama, part spectacle.

In retrospect, it seems obvious that this is not the kind of project that would have offered Hitchcock's directorial style the possibilities he thrived on—a psychological rather than a romantic or technological dénouement; besides, the outcome could not be other than obvious, leaving the "master of suspense" without his requisite suspense. According to his biographer Donald Spoto, Hitchcock nevertheless tried to ingratiate himself to Selznick by claiming that he, too, had entertained the idea of a picture about the *Titanic*; however, his private conversations suggested otherwise. He mocked the limited possibilities of such a film, in one instance noting that a good way to shoot it would be to begin with a close-up of a rivet while the credits rolled, and then to track slowly back until after two hours the entire ship would fill the screen and "The End" would appear. Selznick had no inkling of this attitude, and as late as July announced that production would begin the following January. Hitchcock was quite flippant when interviewed about it and, according to Spoto, told one reporter, "Oh, yes. I've had experience with icebergs. Don't forget I directed Madeleine Carroll."

Selznick was so serious about the project that he entertained the idea of buying the defunct liner *Leviathan* to use as a set. His plan called for the ship to be brought from New York to California via the Panama Canal and then be given a face lift to make her look like the *Titanic*. Plans for the film were eventually dropped or displaced by other projects. It has never been clear as to why. Simon Mills has suggested there was discomfort in Britain, especially in British shipping, with the idea of a film dredging up one of its darkest moments. We can also surmise that with the world on the edge of a catastrophe—although some Hollywood moguls were more concerned with how Hitler's actions might effect their European film distribution—filming an earlier one might be ill advised. (Fortunately for posterity, Hitchcock's first film for Selznick was *Rebecca*, which won a best-picture Oscar.)

Several years later, temporarily free from Selznick's constraints, Hitchcock did get a chance to make a film involving a maritime tragedy. In *Lifeboat* (1944), he eschewed the possibility of filming the ship in the story actually sinking or using a cast of thousands. Instead, he created an intimate portrait of a handful of diverse survivors adrift in a sea of uncertainty after their ship had been sunk by a German U-boat, which also succumbed in the attack. The film, although excellent, was intended to serve as war propaganda. Ironically, several critics at the time argued that this function backfired because the German captain pulled aboard by the survivors was a bit too clever and complex. Creating a stereotypic villain would never be Hitchcock's style.

In the decades following the abandonment of a Selznick–Hitchcock *Titanic* film, seven major screen narratives about the disaster were produced, four as motion pictures and three as television productions. The first cinematic rendering was the 1943 German film *Titanic*; it would followed in 1953 by a Hollywood offering with the same title; later that decade the British film *A Night to Remember*, based on the best seller of the same name by Walter Lord, was released in 1958; and 1997 saw James Cameron's *Titanic* become a box-office sensation, followed by its re-release in 3D in 2012. Often overlooked in discussions about cinematic recreations of the ship and her fate are three very different television productions. In 1956 *Kraft Television Theater* rendered *A Night to Remember* into a teleplay broadcast live; a made-for-television movie, *S.O.S. Titanic*, appeared in 1979; and in 1996 the popular miniseries format gave rise to *Titanic*. As a minor theme, the *Titanic*, either directly or by implication, has appeared in numerous other films, such as *Cavalcade* (1933), *History Is Made at Night* (1937), *The Unsinkable Molly Brown* (1964), *Time Bandits* (1981), and *Ghostbusters II* (1989). Before assessing the major films and television productions of the sinking, it should be noted that they had precursors, therefore giving the story of the *Titanic* an appearance on screen in every decade from 1912 to today.

Immediately after the disaster, a variety of newsreels were fabricated using footage of the *Titanic* before she started across the Atlantic, coupled with shots of her sister ship, the *Olympic* (in some cases with her name scratched out of the film to create an impression that she is the actual *Titanic*), and the use of various models, sometimes resembling a toy boat in a bathtub, to recreate the sinking. Narrative cinema was not very far behind when, on May 14, exactly one month after the collision with the iceberg, the Eclair Film Company released *Saved from the Titanic*, starring Dorothy Gibson, a period actress, model, and actual *Titanic* survivor. It was a case of art imitating life—sort of. Although only a few stills remain from the film, we do know that Miss Gibson cowrote the screenplay and that considerable license was taken with her story—despite her wearing the same dress that graced her on that fateful night—which in the film featured a rescue by and romance with a gallant naval officer.

The cinematic potential of the sinking was not lost on the fledgling but soon to be formidable German film industry. The Germans, perhaps wisely, waited for the completion of both inquiries before beginning production on *In Nacht und Eis* (*A Night in the Ice*, or some variation thereof, since no English version is known to have been released). Produced by Continental Kunstfilm and directed by Mime Misu, it was long thought to have been lost. In 1995 Simon Mills assiduously researched the film's background and aspects of the narrative based on the censor's certificate. Then in 1998, with the television documentary *Beyond Titanic* (produced by Van Ness Films in conjunction with Fox Television and the Arts and Entertainment Network), for which I served as a consultant and on-camera commentator, in production, a colleague told me that he had heard on BBC World Service that a collector in Germany had discovered a *Titanic* film thought to have been lost. I knew immediately this could not be the infamous 1943 Nazi-commissioned *Titanic*, for which various versions were available. Following up this information, I verified the film as the aforementioned *A Night in the Ice*, but had no idea of its condition or if it could be viewed without restoration, and almost as an afterthought I let the *Beyond Titanic* producers know of its existence. To my surprise, I received a phone call several days later saying that they had secured a copy and were delighted to be able to use excerpts from it in the documentary.

The film is in three reels, giving it a running time of approximately 40 minutes, and is a fine production for its time. The tilted set, inundated by water, is made all the more dramatic when we see Jack Phillips, with water almost up to his knees, still trying to transmit his distress call. Of course, despite the film's title, it had to be shot in the daytime because of its complexity and the limitations of 1912 movie technology. In addition to the Berlin studio, an actual liner, HAPAG's *Kaiserin Auguste Victoria*, was used for some of the sequences. The external scenes, using models, seem dated and are far less effective than the interior shots above and below decks.

Although a 1913 Danish film *Atlantis* is not literally about the *Titanic*, it is as close a facsimile as it is possible to imagine and therefore merits at least passing mention here. At just under two hours it is also one of the first full-length feature films in cinema history. The special effects are convincing, even by later standards, and *Atlantis* enjoyed worldwide success—possibly diminishing any potential in that regard on the part of its German precursor—as did the Danish film industry until the great upheaval of World War I. The film's central theme, following what was well known about the *Titanic*, was the divide between social classes: a middle-class doctor is torn between two women, an immigrant in steerage and a wealthy actress in first class. The large cast and period decor and costumes—of course not "period" at the time—are impressive. What the ship actually strikes is never made clear. During the evacuation scenes, I can only speculate that it was either an elaborate set with one side facing the camera or an actual ship (although much smaller, of course, than the *Titanic*), partially submerged in shallow water, from which the survivors' lifeboats depart.

With the coming of sound at the end of the 1920s, British International Pictures deemed the time right for a *Titanic* picture of their own. They recreated the tragedy in *Atlantic* (1929). Directed by German cineaste Ewald André Dupont, Euro-marketable versions were shot in English, German, and French; a silent print with intertitles was also released for those cinemas not equipped with synchronized sound projection. The film did not use the actual title of the ship that inspired it so as not to further taint the White Star Line, which was still operating at the time. Nevertheless, the company was more than mildly upset by the project. Despite changing the name of the ship, anyone in the know would realize that any vessel's name that ended in -*ic* belonged to that company; someone really in the know might recall the loss of over 500 lives in White Star's *Atlantic* almost 50 years earlier. White Star's early fears about the film came to pass, given responses to the version released in Germany. The film intimated that the British shipping industry, via the *Titanic*, was out to recklessly set a record in order to best the Germans, when in 1912 Cunard's *Mauretania* already had that record. It was the German ship *Bremen* that would wrest it back, and Germany's maritime safety record was far from perfect despite boasts in the press in response to *Atlantic*.

Based on Ernest Raymond's play *The Berg*, *Atlantic* was a studio production, with the lifeboat sequences shot using a docked liner. The film did not have a successful run and earned mixed reviews. According to Morduant Hall, who reviewed it in the *New York Times* on October 6, 1930, passable production values were overwhelmed by an atrocious and overly melodramatic script; a similar opinion has been expressed by film historian Tony Thomas. In the English-language version I screened, the dialogue evidenced the limitations of the early sound era: slow paced and stilted, with the limited mobility of the actors doubtless a result of fixed microphone positions. The special effects were adequate for their time, although in the collision sequence the iceberg resembles a battering ram. The film also begins the venerable if debatable movie tradition of using "Nearer My God to Thee" as the final song. At the end of the credits we find an interesting name, given the Hitchcock comment cited earlier: Madeleine Carroll. I assume she did not play the iceberg.

If a major film about the *Titanic* was inappropriate for Anglo-American audiences in the tense prewar years, and unthinkable during them, Joseph Goebbels thought German audiences might be receptive to just such a film; it could effectively couch anti-British propaganda in a lavish escapist spectacle. He recruited Herbert Selpin for the project, whose considerable and successful experience included three films in which maritime themes figured prominently. What resulted was a series of events surrounding the production that provided a drama almost as heart-wrenching as the one depicted in the film. Three decades later, David Stewart Hull, in his revealing study of the films of the Third Reich, examined what had happened in the making of *Titanic* and in so doing interviewed Selpin's widow.

It seems that Selpin was initially enthusiastic about the project and the directorial challenge it would pose despite being forced to collaborate with a hard-line propagandist screenwriter, Walter Zerlett-Olfenius. Problems arose when Zerlett-Olfenius was sent to the port of Gotenhafen, now Gdynia, to work on background footage with the second unit crew while Selpin remained in Berlin filming the major scenes. Zerlett-Olfenius did nothing to expedite the film's production, deferring instead to naval officers who were more interested in carousing than assisting the film crew, although they were obliged to cooperate by the propaganda ministry. When Selpin found out, the incident compounded disagreements he had already had with his screenwriter over the way the propaganda element was disrupting the artistic continuity of the film. The director went into a tirade, criticizing his screenwriter's competence and the man's worshipful and deferential attitude toward the naval officers, who were also criticized for their failure to cooperate. Taking this as an insult to the Third Reich as well as himself, the outraged screenwriter went straight to the SS, and the incident was brought to Goebbels' attention.

When summoned before Goebbels, Selpin did not recant. The enraged propaganda minister ordered the director arrested on a charge of treason. Goebbels then found himself in a dilemma over what to do next. His previous meddling with the German film industry had led to a scandalous tragedy in which Joachim Gottschalk, one of the most popular matinée idols of the time, was badgered mercilessly to divorce his Jewish wife. He constantly refused, whereupon Goebbels ordered her deportation to the camps. On November 6, 1941, minutes before the Gestapo arrived, Gottschalk killed his wife, their child, and himself. The German public was heartbroken, the film community outraged.

After pondering Selpin's case, Goebbels decided that the risk of further scandal must be overridden by the goals of the Reich. On July 31, 1942, Selpin was forced by prison guards to hang himself. The official cause of death was listed as suicide. Evidence confirming what many knew to be murder surfaced in a 1947 trial. Zerlett-Olfenius was given a five-year prison sentence for his involvement in Selpin's death—a sentence that was never served; rumor had it that he escaped to Switzerland.

Titanic continued filming with Werner Klinger as director. There was tension on the set. Those on the set were tyrannized by a decree that Selpin's name could not be mentioned. When the film was finally completed, Goebbels faced another problem. Selpin's death was public knowledge, and the terror he had so effectively depicted on screen had now come to German shores with the start of the allied bombings. A German release of the film was out of the question, but to recoup the enormous production costs it premiered in occupied Paris at the end of 1943 and had a short but successful run. Only after the war could Germans view the film, but British protests pulled it from the western zones, where it remained unavailable until the 1960s. East Germans had continuous access to the film since the anti-British theme was ideologically correct and could also be interpreted as anticapitalist.

The film is a fascinating mix: part lavish spectacle, part terror-filled docudrama. As real and fictional characters intermingle, generous liberties are taken with historical facts. An archvillain is created in the person of Bruce Ismay (Ernst Fürbringer), who exudes greed and arrogance in every scene in which he appears. In trying to save his corrupt company from bankruptcy and to ensure enormous profits, he bribes and coerces the captain into steaming full speed via the dangerous northern route in order to set a record and earn the Blue Riband. Much of the film also involves a greed-meets-greed rivalry between a financially scrapped Ismay and Astor (Karl Schönböck) as they speculate on the stock market, with Astor hoping to get control of White Star.

To give German audiences a sense that they were not detached spectators to the events of the film, appropriate characters were introduced. A Teutonic first officer, Petersen (Hans Nielsen), warns the captain about the questionable course the ship is following and is duly chastised. The film also depicts the fate of German steerage passengers, who demonstrate more nobility during the crisis than the English on board. One of the most intriguing passengers is a "Baltic" (probably Russian) aristocrat, Sigrid Olinsky (Sybille Schmitz), who is assumed to have unlimited wealth and is courted in this regard by Ismay, while she in turn tries to court Petersen, with whom she has had a past liaison. He spurns her and her wealth-driven lifestyle, only to find out during the crisis she has lost her fortune and is the better for it. Rather than taking a spot in a lifeboat, she helps steerage women and children until Petersen orders her to join them.

As chaos erupts, the British aristocrats try to bribe their way into the boats. The panicked crowd scenes are emotionally effective and for a moment override the silliness of the anti-British message. The propaganda, however, is not limited to that tragic night. Dismissing Ismay's bribes, Petersen tells him not to worry and that a lifeboat place will be secured for him so that he can be held accountable at the later inquiry. Petersen also survives. After the ship's demise he is hauled aboard a lifeboat after he swims to it with a child in his arm.

At the British Board of Trade inquiry he gives a complete accounting of events, for which the movie serves as a kind of flashback. Ismay is exonerated and blame is placed on the captain (Otto Wernicke) as Petersen looks on incredulously.

For many years the film has proved difficult to track down. When I first started my *Titanic* research almost 20 years ago and was living in Montreal I managed to secure a copy dubbed in French. Anyone now wishing to see the film can secure a Kino DVD of an excellent print with English subtitles. So effective was the film in recreating aspects of the disaster that segments from it were lifted without credit (spoils of war, I assume) and spliced into *A Night to Remember*.

Little controversy would surround the next film called *Titanic*, released in 1953 by Twentieth-Century Fox. In a sense Selznick was right when, 15 years earlier, he had championed the dramatic possibilities of such a picture. Unfortunately his timing was off, and the opportunity would be realized by another producer, Charles Brackett. The cautionary lesson of *Titanic* situated itself more comfortably in the post-war recovery years than it would have in the gloom-enshrouded late 1930s. There was a new mood of optimism, yet it was tempered by just enough Cold War tension to remind people that disaster might only be an air-raid siren's blast away. Another reason for Hollywood's interest in a *Titanic* film at this time was competition from television. Movie attendance was in decline; therefore the big screen had to offer what its competitor could not, and during much of the 1950s this meant grandiose spectacle and sexually charged melodrama. *Titanic* has both.

Titanic—this title won out over *Nearer My God to Thee* and *Passenger List*—was directed by Jean Negulesco, who would later regard the film as one of his best. It was scripted by Charles Brackett, Walter Reisch, and Richard Breen, who would together go on to win an Oscar for best original screenplay. It premiered on the appropriate date of April 14 and had a renowned cast that included Barbara Stanwyck, Clifton Webb, and Robert Wagner. The film succeeds well as a period melodrama and is more than adequate in its depiction of the sinking. Nautical events serve as a backdrop for the personal histories and aspirations of the main characters (exactly the reverse formula would be employed in *A Night to Remember*). *Titanic*, therefore, is not so much the story of the ship as it is a window into the stories on the ship.

The primary narrative centers on the marital breakup of Julia and Richard Sturgess, played by Stanwyck and Webb. After 20 years of marriage and two children—a daughter, 17, and a son, 13—Julia realizes that difference in social class can never be overcome. When she married Richard she was a homespun girl from Michigan with basic U.S. values. He swept her off her feet with his aristocratic charm and the era's equivalent of a jet-set lifestyle. As their children prepare to enter adulthood, Julia sees them becoming pampered snobs. Before it is to late, a withdrawal from caviar and a dose of apple pie is called for. She spirits them off to the United States without telling her husband, a scenario partly inspired by the fate of the "Titanic orphans," Lolo and Momon Navratil, who were taken aboard by their father without his wife's knowledge. After he went down with the ship they were returned to their mother in France.

Richard eventually finds out about Julia's plan and in Cherbourg buys a ticket from a Basque who is emigrating with his family—an unlikely scenario since the voyage was far from being sold out—and agrees to look after the family until the man can follow on the next boat. When Richard eventually finds his brood a war of wills ensues. Both children, he insists, must return with him on the next passage. The daughter, Annette, played with effective haughtiness by Audrey Dalton, will not have it otherwise. Julia concedes that battle but will not let go of son Norman, played by Harper Carter with just the right amount of naïveté and exuberance. To dissuade Richard, Julia unleashes a secret only she knows: the boy was not sired by him but is the offspring of an encounter with an emotionally sympathetic stranger during an early estrangement in the marriage. Richard reacts to this by agreeing to support the boy financially but disavows all other involvement. His behavior toward Norman turns colder than the iceberg looming on the horizon, much to the boy's dismay.

These intrigues unfold amid elaborate sets and the comings and goings of people we now indelibly associate with the voyage—Astor, Straus, Widener, and others. For some reason, instead of Molly Brown there is a similar character played by Thelma Ritter named Maud Young, who attributes her fortune to Montana lead mines, whereas it was Colorado gold in the case of Molly Brown. Several members of the crew also appear at regular intervals, among them Captain Smith (Brian Ahearne) and Lightholler (Edmond Purdom), but unlike *A Night to Remember* we find no Ismay or crew of the *Californian*.

Titanic avoids probing into the various controversies surrounding the sinking, but it does provide a minimal overview of the events leading up to it. This intent is announced in the opening credits where, after a spectacular sequence showing the formation of the iceberg, a credit appears claiming that the scenes of the crew navigating the ship are based on transcripts from the U.S. and British inquiries. For most *Titanic* aficionados there are not enough such scenes, but they suffice to frame the primary melodrama. So do the special effects in the finale, although one suspects, from the movements of the actors, that the tilted deck is more the result of the camera angle than set movement. In the print I screened there was another "effects" anomaly: the ship is shown grazing the iceberg with the starboard side of her hull; the next shot, an underwater view, show the reverse.

The film's primary course, however, is personal rather than nautical. It chronicles the way each member of the Sturgess family is changed by the voyage. Annette starts out with an arrogance derived from her spoiled upbringing. She rejects the advances of Gifford Rogers, a musically inclined student athlete from Purdue, wildly overplayed by Robert Wagner. He of course wins her over in due course, and she comes to realize that the best things in life are not necessarily a soiree at the Rothschilds' and a titled husband. But it is Richard who undergoes the most pronounced transformation, from charmingly arrogant to selflessly heroic, after he receives news about the plight of the ship from Captain Smith. Not only does he safely usher his family into a lifeboat, making amends to Norman en route, but he also delves into steerage to retrieve the Basque children and their mother. British audiences, nostalgic for a time when nobles were noble, must have appreciated this. Julia does. She realizes that Richard has fiber in his being after all and that the marriage was worthwhile even if tragedy must end it now.

The most interesting and unpredictable fate that befalls any character happens to Norman. He begins the voyage wearing short pants, then after several days argues for full-length trousers. He earns his new status legitimately in the closing sequence when he cedes his place in the lifeboat to a distraught woman and goes to find his father. They reaffirm their love and join in the singing of "Nearer My God to Thee" as boilers explode and the ship goes under.

Several subplots play off against the primary story. The most effective one involves a priest, played by Richard Basehart, expelled from his order for alcoholism—an affliction induced by the pressures of serving a destitute parish. In a moving encounter, the distraught wife meets the defrocked priest on the deck the night before the sinking. The scene suggests the adulterous rendezvous 14 years earlier that led to the conception of Norman, but this time the intimacy is spiritual and it is Julia who does the consoling. The exchange helps both characters shed their self-pity. When the crisis comes, the ex-priest ignores the "ex" and sacrifices his own life by going down into the hold to give counsel to the men trapped there. (Basehart would go on to survive his next movie shipwreck three years later as Ishmael in John Houston's *Moby Dick*.)

Titanic is a fine melodrama. Contemporary audiences, now habituated to variants of the genre in made-for-television movies, whereby adultery and the death of a child are no longer shocking themes, might be unimpressed. In the 1950s, however, nothing like it could appear on the small screen. As both "adult" drama and spectacle it provided a worthy alternative to network fare. One element of the film endures, besides its availability in home video formats: a 28-foot, one-ton model of the ship that was used in the film now sits in front of the maritime museum in Fall River, Massachusetts.

For many people, among them Belfast-born film producer William MacQuitty, *Titanic*, the movie, did not have enough of *Titanic*, the ship, in it. Her story begged to be retold with the nautical events given center stage. A remarkable book facilitated the realization of this dream.

In 1955, a young advertising copywriter and part-time historian named Walter Lord (no relation to Captain Lord of the *Californian*) published *A Night to Remember*, a succinct 150-page account of the disaster. Lord did extensive archival research and wrote to and interviewed survivors. The book that emerged was an immediate success and created a surge of interest. This was partly the result of a readiness on the part of the public to engage in some midcentury reflection and to look back at events that had defined the previous five decades. Television evidenced this trend with program such as *The Twentieth Century* and *You Are There*, both hosted by Walter Cronkite—the latter series even did an episode on the *Titanic*.

Lord's book, however, owes more to his literary skills than it does to the climate of cultural receptivity circa 1955. The text interprets and envelops historical facts with a prose more typical of a compelling novel. Lord was one of the few, although certainly not the first, to write this way. The practice is far more common today and is sometimes characterized in literary circles as postmodernist, one criterion for this label being the dissolution of boundaries between previously discrete literary categories, in this case documentary historiography and fiction.

Before MacQuitty could seize on Lord's book as a basis for his film adaptation, it became the source for a little-known but remarkable television production. In 1956 *Kraft Television Theater* turned *A Night to Remember* into a prime-time drama broadcast live. This would be the first of three major television adaptations of the story, but the only one using Lord's book as a source. *Kraft Television Theater* was a weekly anthology drama series that aired on NBC—perhaps not coincidentally the network's head was David Sarnoff, whose initial rise to prominence was closely linked to his relay of wireless information about the *Titanic*. Direction was by George Roy Hill, who became better known as a film director in the 1970s. Noted actor Claude Rains provided the narration. With 100-plus actors and over two dozen sets, including water tanks and a tilting stage, the production, which was broadcast on March 25, was one of the most elaborate live dramas ever presented on U.S. television.

During this era, known as the Golden Age of Television, experimentation was not uncommon. *A Night to Remember* was one that worked. It begged to be broadcast again, but since a restaging was out of the question for logistical and financial reasons, and videotaped productions would not become the norm until the next decade, a kinescope had to suffice. This is a version of the production filmed in 16 mm format from a studio monitor (not the soundstage) so as to faithfully record what the at-home viewer saw. Fortunately, a copy of the kinescope is available for screening at the Paley Media Center (formerly the Museum of Television and Radio) in New York, which is where I accessed it.

Before the term *docudrama* was coined, this program set a worthy standard for the genre. Claude Rains's commentary adds continuity and a wider sense of context, given the limited sets and visual options of a live telecast. The acting is excellent, and the teleplay, adapted by George Roy Hill and John Wheaton, maximizes the possibilities of a live, small-screen (as it indeed was at the time) production. At times the makeshift, flimsy sets are obvious, but it must be remembered that the program's format called for a different production each week. The challenge of creating the grand staircase, bridge, engine room, wireless cabin, and various spaces for each class of passenger on such short notice and with a 1950s television budget must have been daunting.

The ending, unlike most film versions of the story, avoids using the legendary *Titanic* anthem "Nearer My God to Thee," opting instead for another contender for the legendary final song, the Episcopal hymn "Autumn." The final plunge is not shown by using an external shot of the ship but suggested through clever manipulation of the interiors in the closing sequence: Thomas Andrews, the *Titanic*'s builder, sits forlornly at a table in one of the lounges as the ship lists and crashing sounds are heard; the camera pans away from him and then back to what must have been a quick and clever replacement of the actor with a dummy as a chandelier comes down on the figure and the shot dissolves into one whereby the screen fills with water. Just prior to this finale, we get a plug for the network and its head via the insert of a photograph of Wanamaker's department store, with the narrator telling us that during the sinking David Sarnoff was there and receiving the SOS, thereby taking a few liberties with what actually happened.

This impressive telecast was one of the last of its kind. It aired from New York at a time when the television industry was shifting its base to Los Angeles. Methods of production were also changing. At the time of *A Night to Remember*, the proportion of live telecast versus the use of film for prime-time drama and comedy programs was about 50–50. By the end of the decade, the live format would be almost completely superseded, leaving behind a creative legacy the medium has rarely equaled in subsequent decades.

The same year Lord's book was rendered into a television drama, William MacQuitty had a review of it brought to his attention by wife Betty. He immediately knew it could provide the basis for a film unlike any other. At the age of six in 1911, MacQuitty had witnessed the launch of the *Titanic*. During World War II, as a maker of documentary films, he had pondered the possibility of a movie about the sinking, but no specific strategy had come to mind. Lord's book seemed to provide a perfect narrative framework. MacQuitty quickly optioned the rights to it and gave its author a share in the film. This did not go down well with MacQuitty's employer, the J. Arthur Rank Organization. The company argued that such a film had already been done by Hollywood and that the story of the ship, as well as book titles, were in the public domain. MacQuitty countered by noting how Lord had researched his subject for 20 years and had created the kind of plot structure that was necessary for an effective and accurate film. Despite the prohibitive cost of such a project, he was persuasive enough to get the go-ahead and brought Lord on board as a consultant.

Roy Baker was hired to direct, Geoffrey Unsworth was put in charge of photography, and Alexander Vetchinski served as artistic director. The task of transforming Lord's text into a viable screenplay was given to Eric Ambler, who, starting with the *Cruel Sea* (1953), developed such a feel for nautical narrative that he went on later to script the *Wreck of the Mary Deare* (1959) and *Mutiny on the Bounty* (1962). MacQuitty also decided to shoot in black and white using the conventional aspect ratio rather than in wide-screen Technicolor Vista Vision, the format of his previous film, the *Black Tent* (1957). This displeased the distributors, but it was the right aesthetic choice. Black and white, with its play of light and shadow, has a dream-like quality that can evoke universality and suspend disbelief more easily than color. This can often impart a sense of timelessness to a well-made drama, giving it a documentary quality—color films, no matter how well shot or scripted, frequently suggest the decade in which they were made. Despite these contentions, I should add that in the 1953 film *Titanic*, director Jean Negulesco wanted to use color, but financial constraints precluded the option.

Considerable credit for the film's enduring power must go to producer MacQuitty. However, to say it is "his" film goes against the grain of an influential and controversial strain of film criticism known as "auteur theory." It posits that a film, if it can be considered a work of art, derives its qualities from the guiding hand of an author, or auteur: the director. This view arose to counter earlier notions that regarded movies as a collaborative form of mass entertainment, perhaps "art" and perhaps not, at least not in the sense of a painting, novel, or symphony.

If one subscribes to the auteur theory—my own view is that the director's role, depending on the film, can hover between that of a conductor and a composer—then *A Night to Remember* is arguably a case of the producer as auteur. The unique look of the film, the choice of settings, and the decision to avoid major stars so as to background the characters and foreground the ship were all MacQuitty's. He was on the set constantly, making sure everything was just as he wanted it. Lord was impressed, as were several *Titanic* survivors who were brought onto the set, Edith Russell and Lawrence Beesley, with Joseph Boxhall, the ship's fourth officer, acting as a technical consultant throughout the shoot.

Further authenticity was achieved when MacQuitty purchased from the *Franconia* some lifeboats that were similar to the *Titanic*'s. Finding a real ship's exterior to use for the evacuation scenes proved more difficult since various maritime administrators were reluctant to have any of their vessels, even incognito, associated with the disaster. Luckily, MacQuitty was able to secure the partially demolished *Asturias*, which had her starboard side still intact. The film's interior scenes and model shots were done at Pinewood Studios and the lifeboat sequences on Ruislip Reservoir. Conditions were cold throughout most of the shooting. As a result the cast's breath and real shivering are visible, adding further accuracy to the look of the picture.

Although not considered an actor's picture, the leading player, Kenneth More as Second Officer Lightholler, would be associated with the role throughout his career; in 1960 he played the lead in *Sink the Bismarck*. Captain Smith, played by Lawrence Naismith, was so true to character that the real captain's daughter was overcome by the resemblance when she visited the set. Among the actors in the film, at least two have become better known since: David McCallum, who played wireless operator Harold Bride, can still be seen in syndicated reruns of the 1960s television series *The Man from U.N.C.L.E.*; and Honor Blackman, cast as a concerned wife and mother in first class, went on to be the original Emma Peel in the *Avengers* television series and Pussy Galore in *Goldfinger* (1964). Coincidentally, her costar in the *Avengers*, Patrick Macnee, played *Titanic* builder Thomas Andrews in the 1956 television version of *A Night to Remember*.

The film premiered in London on July 3, 1958, where it was a critical and popular success, winning numerous awards. In the United States, critical reaction was also favorable, but public acceptance was slower in coming because of the absence of major stars. MacQuitty spent a month doing radio and press interviews to drum up interest. The Rank Organization even brought over several *Titanic* survivors for the New York premier. The managing director of Rank, John Davis, thought it was a great film and wrote a letter to the producer stating so; he followed this with a decision not to renew MacQuitty's contract.

In addition to its artistic merit, *A Night to Remember* was the first in a several-decades-long tradition of disaster film epics. It is clearly the best in the genre, but it suffered a critical neglect, which now appears to be changing, when it was associated with films such as *The Poseidon Adventure* (1962) and *The Towering Inferno* (1974). As a British production the film also tended to be overlooked in historical assessments of that nation's cinema because it does not fit into the categories that have traditionally typified Britain's film industry: the adaptation of literary classics, historical-military epics, suspense-mystery thrillers, or social realist dramas. Hopefully, with current interest in docudramas on the rise in academic film studies, *A Night to Remember* will be assessed in ways commensurate with its merit.

The docudrama nature of the film is obvious from the outset. Historical footage of the launch is spliced to a dramatic recreation of the christening—"creation" might be a better word since White Star did not practice this ritual. However, this is one of the film's few deviations from known facts about the sinking, if we let the use of "Nearer

My God to Thee" still be an open question. The opening scenes go beyond Lord's book in ways that help contextualize what will follow. Instead of beginning on the ship, we see the convergence of some of those who will make the trip: Lightholler traveling by train to his posting while conversing about the *Titanic* with his wife, and passengers in each class of accommodation making their way to Southampton by various means.

During the voyage numerous personal stories are glimpsed but never told in full, save the one pertaining to the ship. As we move through the 30 interior sets built from the *Titanic*'s original plans we glimpse passengers in each class engaging in various activities. The crew, in almost cinema vérité style, is observed serving the passengers as well as tending to the operations of the ship. Nautical updates are frequent, more so that in any other *Titanic* film. Discussions on the bridge reveal the ship's course and the captain's expectations; scenes of the *Californian* appear early and warn of conditions ahead; and conversations in the wireless cabin allow us to eavesdrop on a place where information about both the vessel and her passengers converge.

Moving through the numerous scenes is Lightholler. While Captain Smith, Bruce Ismay, and the ship's builder, Thomas Andrews, appear at regular intervals, Lightholler's appearances total more than all of theirs combined. He is the key figure in the film, serving almost as a narrator in character. It is an egoless role. Kenneth More plays "Lights" as the embodiment of an experienced seaman caught in unimaginable circumstances who responds with astute maritime instincts and unswerving reason. Lightholler is commanding but not heroic in the conventional sense—he is instead a dispassionate and totally competent officer. This is not the kind of role that yields Oscar nominations. Nevertheless More is nothing short of perfect, and it is easy to understand why it is the most remembered performance of his career.

More than half of the two-hour production takes place after the collision. The action is relentless but also meticulously paced, giving the suggestion of real time. Skillful editing and meticulous continuity make the format successful and contribute greatly to the emotional exhaustion that follows a screening of the film. As the end nears, we see a montage of shots depicting the breakup of various parts of the ship and the pandemonium among the great variety of passengers. The extras are convincing. So is the captain as he surveys the chaos and tries to orchestrate what must be done. His reaction to the unresponsive ship in the distance (which the film, following the book, unequivocally assumes to be the *Californian*), is "God help you." This line is not in Lord's text, nor is a crewman's prefatory remark, "Bastard must be asleep." These scenes understandably outraged the *Californian*'s ex-captain, Stanley Lord, who was 80 in 1958, and prompted further efforts to clear his name, a cause that still has its devotees.

After the ship founders, attention turns to the scenarios in the lifeboats. As the camera sweeps effectively from boat to boat and from one selected passenger to another, the issue of whether to save those dying in the water is debated. We hear only fragments of conversation, as befits the shattered world the survivors represent. Again, Lightholler is the recurring presence, commanding an overturned boat and organizing the ragtag fleet. (To facilitate performing in those cold, wet scenes, Kenneth More wore a wetsuit under his uniform.)

The film's finale takes place aboard the *Carpathia*. As she passes over the debris field left by the *Titanic* we see a haunting recapitulation of what was so meaningful only hours before: the accoutrements of passengers in each class of accommodation, musical instruments, unoccupied life jackets, and lastly all that remains to identify the ship: a life preserver with her name on it.

The next *Titanic* film, *S.O.S. Titanic* (1979), is the second dramatization her story made for television. Most movies made for the medium are hastily produced affairs, simple competent efforts that often deal with social or personal issues—critics occasionally refer to the genre as the "disease-of-the-week movie." When a more expensive historical theme is envisioned, the format usually shifts to the miniseries, as in *Titanic* (1996), which allows for more sponsor exposure and hence greater network revenues. *S.O.S. Titanic* is an exception to the one-off made-for-television movie format. It was an expensive and historically detailed offering produced for a single evening's telecast on the *ABC Sunday Night Movie*.

The film is a U.S.–British coproduction, more British in the production, more American in terms of funding and the actors who get the most screen time. Billy Hale directed from a script written by James Costigan. Costigan spent a year researching the project, and his teleplay is largely based on accounts from the period, understandably avoiding the Walter Lord treatment that was the basis for MacQuitty's film two decades earlier. A major source was *The Loss of SS Titanic*, by Lawrence Beesley, played in the film by David Warner. Other notable cast members include David Janssen, Susan St. James, Helen Mirren, Ian Holm, and Cloris Leachman as Molly Brown, a character who in 1957 she played in "The Unsinkable Molly Brown," an episode of

Telephone Time, a half-hour weekly drama series on CBS. The story was reprised in the more famous 1964 musical film of the same name starring Debbie Reynolds.

Shooting took place in Long Beach, California, on the freshly repainted *Queen Mary*; at Shepperton Studios in London; and in various parts of the North Atlantic. The broadcast did not draw the large audience hoped for, and, given the film's length (three hours with commercials), it has not aired often in subsequent years. It was been available in various home-video formats, but the running time is just 105 minutes. Interesting footage that adds to the mood, if not the storyline, of the film has been deleted, and the opening and closing sections have been altered. The original cut begins with an evocative and beautifully photographed scene of the *Carpathia* locating and taking onboard survivors, then flashes back to the start of the voyage, eventually rejoining the *Carpathia* in the finale. The home-video release puts all *Carpathia* footage at the end.

S.O.S. Titanic tried to tell its story televisually and in a manner that avoids obvious overlap with earlier versions produced for the cinema. It was the first *Titanic* feature to employ color; the muted tones effectively highlight the period decor and costumes. The script succeeds in presenting us with a panoply of interesting characters whose lives we observe in both dramatic and undramatic moments. At times the camera seems to roam at random, stopping for the occasional voyeuristic glimpse. It could be something mundane, such as the making-up of a room, or titillating, as in a deliciously wicked peek into the beauty salon in first class, a scene absent in the home-video version. These are conventions of prime-time soap operas, with their intimate, character-driven scenarios. Details of the ship's navigation and the comportment of her officers were left to the precedent set by *A Night to Remember*.

Concepts used in the film are also reminiscent of the *Upstairs, Downstairs* television series (in which a major character perished on the *Titanic*) that aired on PBS's *Masterpiece Theatre* in the 1970s. For example, we move back and forth between each category of accommodation. In first class, Astor (David Janssen in his last role) wonders whether his young bride loves him for himself or for his bank account; in third class, Irish immigrants reflect on the New World while they dance and court; and in second class, Lawrence Beesley and Lee Godwin (Susan St. James) have an almost passionate attraction for one another. This couple is pivotal to the film, both in terms of their on-screen time and for the way they represent a generic middle class, observing and discussing the lives of those above and below their station. The two actors give an admirable performance.

The eventual collision sequence is more suggestive and less breathtaking than in big-screen precursors but is subtly effective despite the budget constraints and reduced scale of a made-for-television production. As the ship starts to founder, events center on the fate of the by now familiar passengers rather than the destruction of various parts of the vessel and the crew's reactions. The *Californian* incident is avoided, which further distances the film from comparisons with *A Night to Remember*; however, both films deal with the survival of the White Star's managing director, Bruce Ismay (Ian Holm), depicting him as somewhat calculating in an effort to abscond with his life. In *S.O.S. Titanic*, he surreptitiously enters a lifeboat as Captain Smith (Harry Andrews) watches disdainfully from the bridge.

With the ship in her death throes, the band plays, but they are not featured as prominently in those last moments as they are in other films, nor do we hear "Nearer My God to Thee." Instead, the soft strains of "Rock of Ages" (a hymn not on candidate lists for the final song) waft over the cacophony, providing an equally effective substitute. Elsewhere in the film the band is more noticeable. Period songs fill enough scenes to put the production on the verge of being a musical.

The concluding scene, as in *A Night to Remember*, takes place on the *Carpathia*. As Beesley looks out at floating debris from the wreck, he notes that we will never again look at the world in the same way. This echoes Lightoller's final words in the previous film, in which he reflects on how the last vestige of certainty had collapsed. More trenchant is the comment by Madeleine Astor (Beverly Ross), which constitutes the last line of dialogue. When told the tragedy was "God's will," she responds with "God went down with the *Titanic*." This became a widespread blasphemy following the sinking, perhaps a corollary of the ship having been declared earlier to be a vessel that God himself could not sink. History had finally caught up with Nietzsche's philosophical pronouncement about the death of God voiced a generation earlier.

In 1996, one year before James Cameron's *Titanic* would take the world by storm and possibly put an end to the idea of anyone making another feature film about the *Titanic* in the near future, the CBS miniseries *Titanic* was broadcast. Interestingly, with NBC having done the live production of *A Night to Remember* in 1956 and ABC releasing the made-for-television movie *S.O.S. Titanic* in 1979, all of the three original major networks had now become players in the saga of the great ship. One can only wonder what Cameron thought of the CBS broadcast, coming as it did while his magnum opus was in the midst of production. Adding to his dilemma was the lack of public interest in the miniseries and the mixed critical reception it received. It is hard to ascertain if the producers of this program were trying to scoop Cameron. Motivation could just as easily have come from the surge in *Titanic* interest over the previous 10 years following the discovery of the wreck.

The television *Titanic*'s three hours–plus running time is close to that of the movie released the following year. However, interspersed as it was with myriad commercials during the original two-part, four-hour airing, it is easy to imagine the casual viewer losing interest. Having seen the broadcast version and the home-video release, the film is far more viewer friendly when experienced in the latter format—the protracted commercial breaks in the former disrupt continuity in the multiple story lines. Perhaps surprisingly, the miniseries has star power that surpasses Cameron's theatrical version, which put most of its money on screen, that is, in the production itself. George C. Scott, Eva Marie Saint, and Catherine Zeta-Jones headline a large cast, a triumvirate that any television drama would be hard pressed to match. This Canadian–American coproduction was filmed in Vancouver and directed by Robert Lieberman, with a script by Ross LaManna and Joyce Eliason. The ghost of previous *Titanic* films doubtless hovered over the production, and by necessity parts of it had to cover familiar ground, but other aspects point ahead to the star-crossed lovers scenario central to Cameron's film.

As in *A Night to Remember*, and unlike Cameron's *Titanic*, we get ample coverage of the *Californian* and the developing scenario in the wireless cabin—the ice warnings and personal messages. We also get some heart-wrenching moments on the *Carpathia* following the sinking, which are more protracted than in *S.O.S. Titanic*. However, the latter remains the superior film for its subtlety, balance, and understated performances. The CBS television *Titanic*, like its precursors on the big and small screens, has its moments of philosophizing, but for every profound observation we get one that seems trite or perhaps too obvious to need stating. Passengers in each class of accommodation get their requisite exposure time, and the outspoken Molly Brown (Marilu Henner) appears throughout and comments often enough to function like a chorus. The intertwining of real and fictional characters, a mainstay of any *Titanic* film, is just as apparent here. As to the film's historical inaccuracies, they are too numerous—but not too extreme—to mention and have been documented on the web.

Amid the comings and goings of the large cast, three primary stories drive the film, two in first class, one in third class; this contrasts with *S.O.S. Titanic*'s emphasis on the perspective of two protagonists in second class. A young thief in steerage, Jamie Perse (Mike Doyle), falls for a Norwegian immigrant, Aase Ludvigsen (Sonsee Neu), who will inspire him to mend his ways—a theme similar to the Selznick-Hitchcock *Titanic* film that was never made. However, before the boy discovers virtue, he is coerced by a diabolical steward, Simon Doonan (Tim Curry), into robbing passengers and staterooms. Curry's performance as an over-the-top villain—he later rapes Aase—anticipates the Billy Zane character in Cameron's epic. In first class, Isabella Paradine (Catherine Zeta-Jones) is returning to her husband and daughter when she meets her former lover, Wynn Park (Peter Gallagher), and after much reluctance on her part they resume their affair. Also in first class, in a story based on actual characters, Hudson and Bess Allison (Kevin Conway and Harley Jane Kozak) are traveling with their two small children and a nurse, Alice Cleaver (Felicity Waterman), who unbeknown to them was institutionalized for three years for throwing her baby from a train after being abandoned by her lover (this part of the story is fiction since it was another Alice Cleaver who killed her baby).

In the chaos of the ship's final moments, Doonan escapes by disguising himself as a woman and winds up in the same lifeboat boat as Aase. When she recognizes and attacks him he throws her overboard, whereupon one of the crewmen dispatches him with an oar, and Aase is picked up by another boat. Meanwhile Jamie has fallen unconscious into a boat while working the davits. The two are later reunited on the *Carpathia*. The outcome is less clear-cut for Wynn and Isabella. She realizes she loves him (her child was actually sired by him) and sends a telegram to her husband indicating her wish to leave the marriage, but unbeknown to her it goes down with the ship before it can be sent. Wynn convinces her to get into a lifeboat, saying that he will follow in another—a similar scene occurs with a married couple in *A Night to Remember*. When she discovers his body on the *Carpathia* her entire world collapses, only to be partially resurrected when she is greeted dockside by her husband and child. The Allisons are not so fortunate. In the confusion nurse Alice, who throughout the voyage had premonitions of disaster, grabs one of the children and gets into a lifeboat. The Allisons, with the other child in hand, frantically search for the one that is missing and who they still believe to be onboard. All three go down with the ship.

In contrast to this television *Titanic*'s multiple subplots, James Cameron's risk—and almost everything about his film was a risk—was to go with one central story that superseded all others and featured two relatively unknown leads. The film is too well known to merit a detailed synopsis here; however, a few things should be pointed out regarding the making of it and its position in the *Titanic* film pantheon. The project, although building on Cameron's success with the *Terminator* films (1984, 1991), and *Aliens* (1986), was nonetheless regarded as ill conceived. His previous foray into oceanic cinema, *The Abyss* (1989), did not do nearly as well as expected. Other projects not of his making also provided an ominous warning. *Raise the Titanic* (1982) had been a notorious money loser; the same was true for *Waterworld* (1995); and the lack of interest in the television *Titanic* did not augur well for anyone planning to bring this warhorse of a story to the big screen.

As the production ran over budget and schedule, and with its lack of "bankable" stars, a number of film commentators in the popular press began referring to it as "Cameron's folly." At the time, I saw no reason to disagree, so when on the basis of having recently published the first edition of this book I was invited to be in the film as an extra, I hesitated and then declined. It would have necessitated a three-week absence from my teaching commitments, which, if the film were to turn out well regarded, might have been justified as the seizing of a once-in-a-lifetime opportunity, but should it be the flop I suspected, my participation might have been viewed as a dereliction of duty.

My initial response to the film was mixed, influenced as it was by a reverence for *A Night to Remember*. And when esteemed film critic Richard Schickel, reviewing it in *Time*, pronounced *Titanic* "dead in the water," Paramount and Fox, the two studios involved, must have felt like the White Star Line owners did when they received news of the sinking. However, the tide would soon turn and never recede. Critical reception, while not as enthusiastic as the popular response (Kenneth Turan of the *Los Angeles Times* was so negative that Cameron felt compelled to engage him in a war of words), was mostly positive, except in the United Kingdom. It was not just the naïve Hollywoodization of history that had UK critics up in arms. The theme of noble Americans, such as Jack Dawson (Leonardo DiCaprio), Molly Brown (Kathy Bates), and Isidor and Ida Straus (Lew Palter and Elsa Raven), versus bewildered British officers, especially Lightholler (Jonny Phillips), Captain Smith (Bernard Hill), and Murdoch (Ewan Stewart), did not play well.

The UK response to the portrayal of Murdoch has been recently assessed by Stephanie Barczewski, who has provided valuable biographical portraits of some of the *Titanic*'s major British figures.

In Cameron's film, Murdoch is shown contemplating taking a bribe from Rose's (Kate Winslet) fiancée, Cal Hockley (Billy Zane), and then in rapid succession shooting a young Irishman trying to get into the boat before turning the gun on himself. Ignoring the initial protest firestorm, the studio, Fox, and Cameron eventually tried to make amends. Fox donated £5,000 to a Murdoch memorial prize fund, and in Cameron's later documentary *Ghosts of the Abyss* (2003), Murdoch's behavior in assisting passengers to get into lifeboats is described as "heroic." Still, we do have information from several surviving passengers that an "officer" did shoot himself but no evidence that this was Murdoch (some claimed it was Captain Smith). Therefore Cameron's initial depiction of the incident is within the purview of artistic license, although it illustrates questionable historical sensitivity. Is it possible that this negativity (mild when compared to Nazi Germany's 1943 *Titanic*) was revenge for the way the British press treated the U.S. inquiry in 1912? Given Cameron's scholarly interest in all things *Titanic*, it is not inconceivable.

Titanic differs from all previous cinematic and televisual incarnations of the story by being explicitly informed by the discovery of the wreck in 1985 and the subsequent filming that led to the IMAX documentary *Titanica* in 1992. Cameron even employed the same ship, the *Kaldysh*, and its *Mir* submersibles for the opening and closing sequences—he used them to make 12 trips to the wreck site himself. He also had the benefit of having as consultants *Titanic* historian Don Lynch and the ship's visual historian, Ken Marschall, who were frequently on the set. Their informative commentary on the DVD special features connects the filmic to the historical and is *the* source for anyone interested in knowing where director and writer Cameron's artistic license necessitated deviating from the *"Titanic* fact book." Harland and Wolff, builders of the original *Titanic*, allowed the production team access to its archive, and blueprints of the actual *Titanic* were used to construct the sets in the film.

An intriguing feature of the DVD is the deleted scenes section with Cameron's commentary. It gives us a sense of what could have been, as well as what wasn't and why. In the latter category are several scenes of somewhat forced humor that would have brought unnecessary levity to the tone of the narrative, such as Molly Brown (Kathy Bates) asking for ice in her glass with the berg looming in a window behind her. Also deleted was an elaborate sequence with Cal's valet, Lovejoy (David Warner, who was also in *S.O.S. Titanic*), chasing Rose and Jack in relentless "Terminator" fashion, which Cameron deemed to be dramatic overkill. On a more neutral level, several scenes of Jack and Rose were cut for reasons of time and because the actors' strong performance in other scenes firmly established their characters.

Also deleted were several scenes that would have made the film stronger historically. Among them was the ongoing situation in the Marconi cabin—beautifully recreated during production, we only get a brief glimpse of it in the release version. A scene of the *Californian* and her attempt to contact *Titanic* was likewise removed. Eliminating these sequences helped reduce the film's running time, but perhaps another factor was at play. To include them would have made the film resemble *A Night to Remember* perhaps more than Cameron wanted. Still, there is a homage of sorts to MacQuitty's earlier film in the casting of Bernard Fox, who in 1958 played lookout Frederick Fleet, in a small role as Colonel Archibald Gracie, and in the inclusion of three near-identical scenes.

The first involves a hysterical woman caught between a lifeboat being lowered and the ship. The second is an almost verbatim recreation of the dialogue among the bandsmen as the ship is going down while they are still striving to play, in which the comment is made that nobody is listening, followed by the response that "they don't listen at dinner but we play anyway." The third has Thomas Andrews (Victor Garber), the *Titanic*'s builder, staring forlornly at a painting, and as the ship lists and passengers flee, he is asked by an anonymous passenger in *A Night to Remember*, and by Rose in *Titanic*, "Aren't you even going to try for it Mr. Andrews?" In the former film he does not respond, but in the latter he apologizes to Rose for not building a more sturdy ship.

Another cutting-room casualty that would have made the film resemble *A Night to Remember* more closely involves several subplots that would have given other characters more screen time. For Cameron to allow two little-known leads to carry almost the entire film without interspersing their scenes with intrigues among the other passengers was a gamble. However, we can assume that when screening the dailies during production, he sensed, as subsequent audiences have, how the charisma of Winslet and DiCaprio could do just that.

The biggest inconsistency in the film, which understandably seems to trouble no one, is that the story is told in flashbacks by old Rose (Gloria Stuart) but we see things that she could not possibly have observed or known about. Most of the character parts are consistent with portrayals in previous *Titanic* films. Kathy Bates emerges as the definitive Molly Brown, but Lightholler does not have the stoically heroic demeanor that resulted in a career-defining role for Kenneth More in *A Night to Remember*. In Cameron's film he is skittish and unsure what to do, especially when he tries to justify sending out lifeboats with so few people, for which he came under scrutiny at both inquiries, so in this respect at least *Titanic* might be the more accurate film.

The Winslet and DiCaprio casting was unusual, not just because they had yet to emerge as major stars—although DiCaprio did have a young fan base following *What's Eating Gilbert Grape* (1993) and *Romeo and Juliet* (1996)—but because of their youth. In the case of DiCaprio, Cameron may have been tapping into a cinematic youth movement in the 1990s described by Philippa Gates as favoring young, boyish male leads who sometimes had a touch of the androgynous— DiCaprio and Johnny Depp being prime examples—in contrast to the more grizzled, hard-bodied heroes of the 1980s. In *Titanic*, it is the more manly character played by Billy Zane who is not only in the supporting role but also the villain. And is it the folly of youth that sank the great ship, as a number of moviegoers have surmised, since the dalliance of Rose and Jack on the foredeck after their tryst in the car is observed by the lookouts seconds before they sight the berg? Cameron's commentary leaves this an open question, but open I think to the assumption that some kind of momentary diversion might have been all that was necessary to waste the precious seconds that might have made a difference.

Until Cameron upped the production budget with *Avatar* (2009), *Titanic* was the most expensive movie ever made. For a film about the largest moving structure built up to its time, Cameron has claimed that it also featured the largest set ever constructed for a motion picture; however, I wonder if anyone took measurements of the massive set of Babylon in the back lot of D. W. Griffith's *Intolerance* (1916). *Titanic* also went on to become the number one box office film of all time, earning 11 Oscars in the biggest sweep since *Ben Hur* (1959). It still might be number one by measures other than financial, having had a longer theatrical run than *Avatar* and more repeat patrons, especially adolescent girls, not to mention its 3D resurrection. The film's cross-generational appeal contributed mightily to its success: a period drama for adults; an action film for teenage boys, which had become a huge film demographic; and a "chick flick" for the type of young females who have made the more recent *Twilight* films (2008, 2009, 2010, 2012) so successful.

Cameron has called his *Titanic* a fairy tale set against a historical backdrop; similarly the 1953 *Titanic* can be seen as a period melodrama placed in such a context, and Selpin's 1943 *Titanic* used the Gilded Age for Nazi propaganda ends. Only MacQuitty's *A Night to Remember* foregrounds the ship and the events relating to it so completely and effectively that it remains *the* definitive *Titanic* film. Finally, it should be noted that Cameron's commitment to the ship and her legacy has extended beyond his blockbuster. Seven years after *Titanic*, he directed and coproduced the documentary *Ghosts of the Abyss*, to be discussed in the next chapter, a 3D production that took us deep into the "ship of dreams," to places that could only be imagined by previous generations.

CHAPTER 11

Resurrection and Preservation

It has now been 100 years and counting, and the *Titanic* is still in the media. The re-release of James Cameron's *Titanic* in 3D, new theories about the sinking, and a variety commemorative events keep public interest alive and pass the legacy along to a new generation. Directly or indirectly, today's *Titanic* "culture" has been influenced by the most important event in the history of the ship apart from her sinking: the discovery of the wreck by Robert Ballard in 1985. Although it has brought some closure to the saga, it has perhaps opened up just has many new questions and sources for speculation. In the two decades prior to the discovery of the wreck, historical knowledge about the tragedy had been accumulating at a greater rate than at any time subsequent to 1912. In 1979 Wyn Craig Wade published *The Titanic: End of a Dream*, a meticulous study of the sinking and its context, emphasizing the U.S. inquiry and the role of Senator William Alden Smith. That same year saw the saw the television docudrama *S.O.S. Titanic* broadcast. What both those events share with each other, and with Ballard, James Cameron, and many others who have researched the great ship, is the assistance of the Titanic Historical Society (THS), based in Indian Orchard, Massachusetts.

The THS remains the single most important chronicler of events and personages relating to the *Titanic* disaster. Other similar organizations have come and gone, and if THS seems less prominent today as *the* go-to source for *Titanic* information than it was when I began my research two decades ago, it is because *Titanic* sites have now inundated the World Wide Web. There is even an *Encyclopedia Titanica*. Facts and reprints of articles are just a click away, but the THS is the

longest running archive of its kind and unsurpassed in informed interpretation of all things pertaining to the great ship. It was founded on
September 6, a date chosen to commemorate the date in 1869 that
saw the formation of the Oceanic Steam Navigation Company Ltd.,
which would go on to develop White Star into a world-renown shipping line. The organization was initially called the Titanic Enthusiasts
of America and started out with just six active (dues-paying) members
and 45 honorary members, most of them *Titanic* survivors. The survivors were contacted through an "information book" compiled by a
film distributor for theater managers who, when booking *A Night to
Remember*, might want to get in touch with survivors for publicity purposes. The book was acquired by Edward Kamuda, son of a former
theater manager and the person most responsible for launching the
THS and navigating its successful course.

Kamuda had his initial interest in the *Titanic* piqued by reading
about it in high school. When the 1953 movie *Titanic* played at his
father's movie theater, curiosity about the disaster was displaced by a
passion to learn as much about it as possible. Subsequent exposure of
the ship's story in print, on television, and in film convinced him that
the memory of the event should be preserved in some kind of system-
atic way. To that end the THS was established, along with an initial
newsletter, *The Marconigram*. Funding came from the pockets of the
active members, augmented by a modest donation from Walter Lord,
an honorary member. Eventually the newsletter, like the organization
itself, underwent a name change. The Marconi Company was still in
business during the 1960s and insisted that the use of its name was
copyrighted; perhaps the company also felt unease at being associated
with the legendary disaster. The publication was thus changed to *The
Titanic Commutator*—often mistaken for "Communicator," notes
Kamuda. A commutator is an instrument used to measure the degree
of list on a ship, a device of some importance onboard the *Titanic* after
the collision. (It is also a term used in electrical engineering and math-
ematics, where it has different meanings, thus adding to the potential
confusion of landlubbers.)

During its first several years, the THS received a modicum of recognition, and the newsletter became a lifeline connecting *Titanic* aficionados. Nevertheless the enterprise remained relatively small. On
September 17, 1966, 21 members convened at the Seaman's Church
Institute in New York for the first general meeting. The following
year, with a total membership of fewer than 200 and few new subscribers on the horizon, it appeared the association and newsletter would

go the way of the great ship whose legacy they preserved. If this was to be the case, the membership decided to bow out in spectacular fashion. The April 1968 issue of the *Commutator* transformed the modest newsletter into an 80-page glossy magazine featuring articles on the *Olympic* as well as the *Titanic*. Maritime organizations around the world took notice, and the THS continued on course. In 1973, the 10th anniversary convention, held in Greenwich, Connecticut, drew 140 attendees, 7 of whom were *Titanic* survivors, and attracted international press and television coverage. Total membership soon exceeded 1,000.

In 1976, the THS presented to Jacques Cousteau a plan to locate and explore the *Britannic*, the *Titanic*'s second sister ship (discussed in Introduction), along with relevant archival material that described what might be found. He followed through on the project, accompanied by THS vice president William Tantum.

Two years later, through the auspices of Tantum, the THS helped British television producer Alan Ravenscroft chronicle several ship disasters, among them the *Titanic* and the *Andrea Doria*, for his new series, *When Havoc Struck*. These collaborations prompted discussion of the possibility of locating and filming the *Titanic*, which in turn led Tantum and Ravenscroft into an association with Emory Kristoff of the National Geographic Society and Dr. Robert Ballard of the Woods Hole Oceanographic Institute. They formed Seaonics International and sought investors for the project. Tantum's death in 1980, however, scuttled the endeavor. Ballard did eventually succeed by other means while retaining the support of the THS, and in 1986 he deposited a plaque on the stern deck of the *Titanic* in memory of those who perished, which was dedicated to William Tantum.

The discovery of the *Titanic* (and later, James Cameron's film) escalated interest in her fate and, as expected, membership in the THS. The modest conventions have expanded into more lavish affairs. The 1995 version is notable in this regard since it was held on the *Queen Mary* in Long Beach, California, and attracted significant media attention. The *Commutator* too has grown. It is now an impressive quarterly devoted also to other great ships besides *Titanic*. The examples of maritime history the magazine provides are a boon to researchers such as myself. The THS is still headquartered in Indian Orchard, Massachusetts, and operates a small but impressive museum of *Titanic* memorabilia. However, *do not* look for anything from recent salvage efforts; the THS has always remained opposed to the looting of what they deem should be an international memorial and, more recently, a virtual museum. It is a tribute to Kamuda and the first coterie of active members that they initiated their project at a time when public fascination with the *Titanic* was subsiding after the media interest generated by *A Night to Remember*. Subsequent decades have only served to vindicate their early insistence that the sinking was one of the defining moments of the twentieth century.

In 1976, with the THS-inspired exploration of the wreck of the *Britannic* prompting serious discussion of the possibility of doing the same with the *Titanic*, a remarkably prescient book appeared: *Raise the Titanic*. It was one of a series of action-adventure novels involving maritime themes written by Clive Cussler. Although the story is far-fetched, the parts that deal with the location of the wreck would shift from science fiction to science fact in fewer than 10 years. Cussler's ability to forecast was not due to any mystic clairvoyance but was the result of his knowledge of undersea exploration and its technologies, coupled with a sense of where they might be headed next. Before considering the novel, I should note that it is not the first case of art anticipating life with respect to the *Titanic*.

In 1898, in an extended short story, or more properly a novella, called *Futility*, Morgan Robertson described the sinking of the largest ocean liner ever built, the *Titan*, which collided with an iceberg a few hundred miles from where the *Titanic* would late do the same. Much has been made of *Futility* by devotees of psychic phenomenon. They often fail to mention that Robertson was a former seaman and a student of maritime developments who, in becoming a pulp fiction writer, applied that expertise to sea adventure stories; also overlooked is his denial, after the events of 1912, of any unique powers for prediction the future. *Futility*'s moralistic tone, implausible situations, and poor character development are nonetheless offset by intriguing information about the ship and her fate.

Comparing the *Titan* and the *Titanic*, respectively, in just a handful of categories, we get the following: 800 feet in length to 882 feet; 19 watertight compartments to 16; 45,000 tons to 46,328; each voyage was in April; and both ships had triple screws, were alleged to be unsinkable, and were capable of carrying 3,000 passengers, most of whom perished on the *Titan*. Notable differences include the opposite direction of each ship's travel; foggy conditions in the case of the *Titan* versus clear in 1912; and the fictional ship not being on her maiden voyage. Robertson's behemoth also carried auxiliary sails, which leads me to suspect that the *Titan* was in some measure an embodiment of the promise and the limitations of the *Great Eastern* as well as a prediction of some of the design features that might characterize future ships.

Seventy-eight years later, in the novel *Raise the Titanic*, we also see an informed literary imagination creating futuristic vessels, but they now move below rather than above the waves. What brings past and future together in Cussler's tale is a complex Cold War saga that begins in Edwardian times. It involves a powerful radioactive substance, byzanium, with the potential for giving the nation that acquires it global dominance. Since the only byzanium known to exist resides in a vault on the *Titanic*, the plot centers on a race between the United States and the Soviet Union to salvage it by raising the ship.

To bring such an outlandish but compelling action-adventure story to the big screen required both courage and foolhardiness. At $40 million in 1980, *Raise the Titanic*, the movie, became one of the top box-office disasters of all time. It cost and lost more money than the *Titanic* itself, which led British film magnate Lord Grade, who backed the venture, to allegedly reply, "*Raise the Titanic*! It would have been cheaper to lower the Atlantic." The film is badly scripted and largely miscast, a notable exception being Alec Guiness's brief but superb rendering of John Bigelow, a surviving *Titanic* crewman.

Jerry Jameson directed the movie, with William Fry as producer and Martin Sarger as executive producer; the adaptation and script, respectively, were done by Eric Hughes and Adam Kennedy. The cast included Jason Robards, Richard Jordan, David Selby, and Anne Archer. Although universally panned, the film is not without its moments. The underwater footage is impressive, and the surfacing of the *Titanic* was at the time one of the most impressive ocean sequences since the parting of the Red Sea in *The Ten Commandments* (1956). It was done using a 55-foot, $5 million model ensconced in a $3 million, 10 million gallon water tank. The large size of the model gives the look of the ship, and her relationship to the water, greater realism than is normally found in typical ship-in-distress effects sequences, even when using current CGI techinques. Another impressive scene involves the *Titanic* being towed into New York harbor to finally complete her journey. John Barry's musical score here is particularly evocative, as it is throughout the film.

All speculation, fictional or otherwise, about raising the *Titanic* should have been laid to rest after she was discovered to be in two pieces with much of her structure collapsed. This fact, however, did not deter science fiction writer Arthur C. Clark. In his 1990 novel *The Ghost from the Grand Banks*, he described an attempt to raise the stern section in the year 2012 and to tow it to Tokyo. Clark had a long-term interest in the *Titanic* and perhaps felt usurped when it was Cussler who managed to incorporate her into a science-adventure novel. His own effort seems hastily written and falls below the standards he established with his other novels.

The real search for the *Titanic* had almost as much drama as these fictional accounts. It pitted a visionary scientist who tried to keep the media at arm's length, Dr. Robert Ballard, against an eccentric oil entrepreneur and attention-getter extraordinaire, Jack Grimm. The race also involved the rivalry between North America's two leading centers of oceanographic research: Woods Hole in Massachusetts (Ballard's affiliation) and Scripps Institute in California, whose participation was made possible through Grimm's finances.

Although as a youngster Ballard was fascinated by the *Titanic*— hardly an exclusive club—he first gave thought to a more intimate encounter with the ship in 1973. As an aspiring marine geologist fresh out of the navy, he began working at Woods Hole with the *Alvin* group. *Alvin* was a three-man submarine built in 1964 that had proven effective in dives up to 6,000 feet. This depth limitation confined *Alvin*'s use to the continental shelf and adjacent regions. After 1973, a modified titanium hull extended its range to 13,000 feet, which happens to be the approximate depth of the *Titanic*. Ballard did not envision a search for the legendary ship as a singular project. Rather, it offered a chance to extend and test deep-sea search procedures, perhaps ultimately leading to a manned dive to the wreck. Oceanic research would be the major beneficiary, with information at those depths no longer limited to the sonar-driven abstract approach of the geophysicists. As a geologist, Ballard wanted to theorize about things he could actually see.

With the support of William Tantum of the THS, a viable *Titanic* search was planned. Woods Hole showed cautious interest, but a disaster at sea in 1978 involving the loss of expensive equipment being tested for the project led it to withdraw sponsorship. Ballard, Tantum, and the previously mentioned Seaonics International group then sought funding for the project elsewhere. Jack Grimm entered the picture as a possible backer, but his goals, which included salvage, were not consonant with those of Seaonics. When Tantum died in 1980, he did so believing that Ballard would be the one to eventually locate *Titanic*. With the disbanding of Seaonics, Ballard became just as convinced that it would be someone else and reluctantly stepped to the sidelines while Grimm mounted three expeditions.

The flamboyant and confident Grimm attracted the participation of the Scripps Institute and the Lamont-Doherty Geological Observatory.

We have no record of what scientists from these venerable institutions might have thought about his earlier expeditions to find Noah's Ark, the Loch Ness Monster, and Tibet's Abominable Snowman. We do know that they took a dim view of the publicity he was generating for his *Titanic* project, especially the incident involving a monkey named Titan (named after the ship in Morgan Robertson's *Futility*, a literary work Grimm held in almost religious esteem). According to William Hoffman, who would later chronicle the second Grimm expedition (from the outset Grimm sought to immortalize his exploits in print and on film), the monkey was, at the appropriate moment, supposed to point to the spot on the map where the *Titanic* would be found. Not being primatologists, the scientists involved said, in effect, "either the monkey goes or we do," to which Grimm retorted, "Fire the scientists." Sanity eventually prevailed, and the monkey remained ashore.

Guided by Grimm's historical knowledge, the first expedition took place in July and August 1980. It employed a low-resolution sonar system, useful for detecting large topographic features but lacking the sensitivity to make reasonably certain that a *Titanic*-sized object might be a ship. Bad weather continually impeded the small research vessel, the *H.J. Fay*. Another setback involved the loss of the magnetometer, essential to identifying possible targets as being metallic.

The second expedition, which took place aboard the *Gyre* in June and July 1981, tried to rectify some of the limitations of the first. However, Grimm did not believe that hype was one of those limitations. He amplified it in order to attract more media attention and potential investors. With improved sonar, a magnetometer, and video and still cameras, success seemed considerably less than a long shot. Unfortunately for Grimm, instead of using 1912 navigational information to rethink the possible location of the wreck, considerable time was spent revisiting targets identified by the previous expedition's sonar. Each in turn was eliminated in a frustrating countdown. When contractual obligations forced the return of the ship, Grimm managed to finagle a few extra hours of search. Using a video camera and microphone, but not the magnetometer, an image was captured, accompanied by metallic sounds, of what appeared to be a large ship's propeller. Grimm tried to convince the increasingly skeptical media that it belonged to the *Titanic*, but many regarded the claim as another one of what were becoming known "Grimm's Tales." Nevertheless, he did convince backers to fund a third expedition, which took place in July 1983 aboard the *Robert D. Conrad*. Despite an expanded survey plan, the temptation to return to the propeller site again and again was too much to resist.

With bad weather limiting the search, as it had in the past, Grimm was finally forced to abandon his quest.

Meanwhile, back at Woods Hole, Ballard continued his oceanographic research, most notably through the development of an underwater video unit, *Argo/Jason*. *Argo* was a deep-towed vehicle for wide ocean-bottom scanning; *Jason* was a mobile robot on a cable leash, capable of peering into crevices and wreckage. The *Titanic* would become the unit's Holy Grail. Funding was provided by the Office of Naval Research, which had an obvious military interest in the technology. A three-week test of the system was authorized for the summer of 1985. Ballard suggested the *Titanic* as a suitable target, but as far as the navy was concerned it was only an "unofficial" goal of the expedition. To increase chances of finding the wreck, Ballard used his connections to secure the assistance of IFREMER, the French National Institute of Oceanography.

The first part of the expedition started on June 24 when the IFREMER vessel *Le Suroit* left port to begin a sonar search, with any *Titanic*-like discovery to be later surveyed by *Jason/Argo*. After Ballard arrived at the operation, several more weeks of looking produced only elaborate data on where the *Titanic* was probably not located. When the *Le Suroit* part of the mission was over, the French sensed glory slipping away. Ballard had mixed emotions. He was frustrated by the elusiveness of the quarry but relieved that he would have a chance to continue the search visually with his own equipment. On August 12 the torch was passed to the U.S. vessel *Knorr*. She headed to a sector not covered earlier.

A key to finding the wreck, Ballard believed, was in trying to locate the debris field. In this kind of search cameras have an advantage over sonar since they are not limited to finding the main body of the ship. And so it was that shortly before 1:00 a.m. on September 1 a boiler was sighted, which eventually led to the location of the wreck and those first memorable photographs.

Ballard's next challenge was to deal with the media. An inkling of how fast things were moving became apparent when he called Woods Hole with the news later that morning, and they already knew. So did the *London Observer*, which must have gone to press around the time when the debris field was first spotted. The newspaper subsequently ran an inaccurate story claiming the wreck was being salvaged, an accusation that led to protests from the United Nations. IFREMER, already frustrated, became irate when the first pictures they saw of the wreck came from U.S. networks via satellite. Little did the French know that the U.S. networks were miffed as well since the first images shown publically were via a Canadian network that had helped fund the expedition's documentation. In the midst of this maelstrom, an emotionally overcome Ballard was forced to break off one of his many radio interviews, in this instance with NBC's Tom Brokaw, when he realized the *Knorr* was leaving the site before he had paid his last respects.

He returned to the site in July 1986 aboard the *Atlantis II*, with funding from the U.S. Navy and the support of Woods Hole but without IFREMER. This time *Alvin*, the manned submersible, came along. Nine times Ballard visited the wreck, likening the experience to exploring the moon. The pictures taken attest to the epoch-making status of the project at the time, although many more from a variety of sources have been released since.

The knowledge, affection, and respect Ballard has shown toward the *Titanic*, as evidenced in his best selling book *The Discovery of the Titanic*, various articles, and media appearances, has continued unabated to the present. His wish has always been that the great ship be allowed to rest in peace. However, "wrest a piece" became the goal of the IFREMER-led next expedition.

Ignoring legislation passed with presidential approval by the U.S. Congress, which authorized the wreck site as an international memorial, IFREMER returned in 1987 under the aegis of international salvage law. Funded by a consortium of U.S. and European investors, their submersible, *Nautile*, scavenged an estimated 1,800 artifacts from the site. On one of those dives, William F. Buckley, Jr., was invited along and described the experience in the October 18, 1987, issue of the *New York Times Magazine*. Negative reaction to the salvage was immediate, especially from *Titanic* survivors and the descendants of those who perished on the voyage. Most were not impressed by the offer made to them of first choice of purchase of a selected number of artifacts. Even those with no emotional stake in the ship were angered when it became clear that the site had been treated carelessly. For example, the crow's nest was destroyed in an effort to recover the ship's bell, and no archaeological grid indicating the location of the finds seems to have been drafted and made archivally available.

Further U.S. reaction produced the Weicker Bill forbidding the sale or exhibition for profit of salvaged artifacts from the *Titanic*. Interestingly, one of its staunchest opponents was William F. Buckley, Jr., who while not necessarily defending the salvage operation did not feel that what had been taken should be denied access to a U.S.

market. Some of the artifacts were displayed on U.S. television on October 28, 1988, on a broadcast originating from Paris, *Return to the Titanic . . . Live!* Barely remembered today, although there is a wonderful joke about it in James Cameron's *Titanic*, the show needs to be assessed here because at the time it was a hyped media event that turned into a much derided one while attracting more viewers than anything *Titanic* related ever shown on television. Not since the discovery of the wreck three years before had the ship been deluged with such media coverage. The pièce de résistance of the show was to be the opening of a safe recovered from the ship.

This telecast belongs to a genre media scholars sometimes refer to as a pseudoevent: a news story created expressly for the media. On such occasions the audience is supposed to experience the "revelation" along with, not after, the attendant experts. The mystery of the *Titanic* was presented as a kind of deep-sea striptease: aspects of her story were told with the safe lurking tantalizingly in the background. The host, Telly Savalas, conveyed sincerity but seemed haggard, missed several cues, and at one point almost tripped over a chair—an understandable situation given that the hour of the broadcast from Paris was geared to prime-time East Coast North America. What the safe actually revealed was not some jewel-encrusted treasure but a few soggy banknotes and a handful of memorabilia (the safe in Cameron's *Titanic* yielded something more interesting: a portrait of Rose, as well as the aforementioned joke). Later allegations of fraud—it was claimed the safe had been opened beforehand—kept what transpired newsworthy for nearly a week. The press had a field day in criticizing television's attempt to create live news.

In 1993, the French returned to the site under contract to RMS Titanic Inc., a New York–based consortium, now headquartered in Atlanta, that has been salvaging, auctioning off, and exhibiting the ship's possessions ever since. The 1993 haul yielded 800-plus items, which were brought to Norfolk, Virginia, for sorting, thereby challenging the spirit, if not the letter, of the Weicker Bill. A year later, the U.S. Federal Court freed RMS Titanic Inc. from any formal restraint by granting them exclusive salvage rights. To date, seven expeditions have yielded upwards of 5,500 artifacts, enough to mount as many as six exhibitions worldwide at any one time. Strong opposition to the project was expressed by both Robert Ballard and Edward Kamuda of the THS.

Initially, RMS Titanic Inc. claimed that the pieces would not be sold off individually, although they would be exhibited. Eventually, huge profits were made from both options. The first of the many exhibitions, including a permanent one now housed in Las Vegas, took place in 1994 at the National Maritime Museum in Greenwich, England. It attracted controversy. The exhibitions still do, but less so than in the past. The legality of international salvage law has trumped all attempts to make the wreck site sacrosanct. Despite the questionable ethics behind the exhibitions, they do provide an unusual and perhaps unprecedented glimpse of a hundred-year-old era. Having for a long time resisted attending one since I share with many *Titanic* devotees a belief that the wreck site should be a memorial, the prospect of doing this book compelled me to relent. I attended two such exhibitions: the large one in New York, and a smaller version in Kitchener, Ontario, where I was invited to be a speaker, with no stipulation that I support RMS Titanic Inc.'s venture in my talk.

The exhibitions work as a unique window into the era—a freeze-frame of aspects of the cultural life of 1912—not so much because of the artifacts per se but as a result of the broader explanatory context in which they are situated. Many of the objects on display are of course fragments: floor tiles, coins, pieces of furniture, bath valves, containers, cooking utensils, parts of the ship's fittings, and so on. However, where salvage could not provide, facsimiles have been created in their stead. Most notable among them are the ship's telegraph—not the wireless but the pedestal-mounted lever used to change the ship's speed—and the cabin accommodations of different classes of passenger. Throughout the exhibit there are large photographs and charts (such as a passenger list by class of accommodation and subsequent fate) which, along with numerous captions, provide a nicely potted history of what is on view.

Upon entry each visitor is given a boarding pass with the name of an original passenger on it. On my first visit I drew the name of an anonymous immigrant in steerage who perished; the second time I fared better and became Sir Cosmo Duff Gordon, who survived, but whose wife was reputed to have insisted that their lifeboat not go back to pick up those consigned to the freezing water. Exiting through the gift shop, the most affordable of the authenticated relics for sale were pieces of coal about the size of a small grain of rice. I wondered immediately whether RMS Titanic Inc. found them in situ this way, or if they fragmented normal-sized pieces?

One interesting offshoot of the discovery and salvage of the *Titanic* has been the possibility of establishing the near exact position of the ship when she sent her distress signals. This has important bearing on the *Californian* incident. Estimates of the *Californian*'s position relative to the *Titanic*'s can now be ascertained with more certainty than was the case before the wreck was located. In his 1987 book, Ballard engaged the problem, thus fueling a controversy dating back to 1912 that has already yielded several books and will simply not go away.

Ballard's calculation of the likely position of the two ships differs from 1912 estimates, but the distance between the ships remains somewhere between the 5 and 21 mile minimum and maximum debated then. Those on board the *Titanic* claimed the former figure, believing, on the basis of the two inquiries, that the ship they sighted was the *Californian*. Captain Lord and his contemporary supporters, known as "Lordites," have favored the latter distance. If correct this would mean that the mystery ship observed by the *Titanic* must have been a vessel other than the *Californian*.

Other factors to consider include the *Titanic*'s failure to respond to the *Californian*'s Morse lamp, which would have certainly been visible if the two ships were as close as both inquiries assumed. Also, the ship sighted by the *Titanic* was later observed leaving the scene, while we know that the *Californian* drifted the entire night with her engines shut down. Again, the question of a third ship has to be raised. The leading candidate is a Norwegian sealing vessel, the *Samsun*. Hunting illegally and not having wireless, she might have assumed the rockets the *Titanic* was sending up were to signal her position to the authorities and therefore fled the scene. It is also possible that a fourth ship was in the area as well, and that this might have been the one the *Californian* unsuccessfully tried to contact by Morse lamp.

These issues were hotly debated in the 1990s and occasionally reported on in both print and television news. This led to a formal reinvestigation by the British Department for Transport's Marine Accident Investigation Branch (MAIB). Looking into the vast array of data, some of it conflicting, MAIB released its report on April 2, 1992. It is a detailed and compassionate study but not conclusive. Respectful disagreements between investigators are forthrightly aired. One board member believed the ships were 5 to 7 miles apart and visible to each other; another contends it was probably 17 to 20 miles, with mutual visibility unlikely. All agree that the *Californian* observed the *Titanic*'s distress rockets and took no action. They also concur on what Captain Lord should have done: gone to the bridge, called the wireless operator to his post, and readied the engines. More recently, in 2006, Senan Molony published the results of his exhaustive compilation of the documents and testimony surrounding the controversy.

No matter what our views on Captain Lord and the *Californian*, it seems almost certain that a third "mystery" ship was even closer to *Titanic* on that fateful night.

The conclusion of the MAIB report contains a fascinating and convincing guess at what would have happened had Captain Lord responded to the first distress rocket and prepared his ship for a rescue effort. He would have immediately had to verify the *Titanic*'s position, which, as the *Carpathia*, *Birma*, and decades of subsequent reassessment have shown, was about 12 miles east of her transmitted coordinates. Getting to the *Titanic* at night through an ice field would have precluded an all-out sprint. Under these circumstances, the estimated time of arrival would have been, at best, the time of the sinking, and more likely some minutes later. Little could have been done for those not already in lifeboats.

As a non–maritime expert, I would add the following to the MAIB's concluding speculations: even if the *Californian* was the minimum distance and responded as rapidly as possible, thereby arriving, say, thirty minutes before the final plunge, what could she have done? Maneuvering into position to take up and relaunch lifeboats would have been a time-consuming procedure, especially at night; in daylight it took five to six hours of careful rescue work to get all survivors aboard the *Carpathia*. It would also have been time consuming for the *Californian*'s crew to launch their ship's lifeboats and row them to the site. There would have been no time for those boats to be raised by the *Titanic*'s davits. At best they might have been able to pull a few people from the water; at worst they would have faced a risk of being capsized in the confusion. Twenty-eight degree water, in any event, does not give those immersed in it more than a few minutes in which to help their own cause.

The 1992 MAIB report was not the only *Titanic*-related event to catch the public eye that year. In October, the IMAX® film *Titanica* premiered in Ottawa, Canada, and then went on to be shown in IMAX/OMNIMAX theaters around the world, becoming one of the most successful films in the history of IMAX up to that point in time.

Titanica was largely the brainchild of Canadian director and producer Stephen Low. He had originally wanted to film Robert Ballard's 1986 expedition using IMAX cameras, but a combination of circumstances thwarted the plan: lack of a second submersible to provide dramatic footage of the first approaching the wreck; the relatively primitive state of deep-sea lighting systems; and the ever-present difficulty of raising funds. These challenges were eventually surmounted, and an expedition was launched in June and July 1991. Russia's Shirov

Institute of Oceanology made available their research vessel, the *Akademic Kaldysh*. The project became a joint Canadian, Russian, and American venture, committed to marine biological and geological research as well as to filming the *Titanic*.

As the first full-length IMAX feature (as opposed to the previous format based on a series of shorter subjects) *Titanica* runs 95 minutes, plus a 15-minute intermission. One of Low's goals was to make IMAX documentaries dramatically as well as visually appealing in order to attract the mainstream movie-going public. Contributing to the story line are the crewmen of the *Kaldysh*, whose personalities we get to know as we follow them through their assigned tasks. Not leaving the dramatic aspect of the film to chance, important moments in the two *Mir* submersibles (one carrying an array of powerful lights) that were launched from the ship were recreated in postproduction sequences shot in Toronto.

The film's deep-sea visual pyrotechnics are the result of a lighting system that generated the equivalent of 150,000 watts of illumination (as a reviewer of the film I was privy to a press kit filled with production details). Such panoramic lighting made navigating the submersibles less dangerous than in the past. Nevertheless, the venture was not without its hazards since a bulb imploding, due to tremendous water pressure, could have fatal consequences by pulling the glass out of the portholes from the sudden pressure change. In all, 13 dives were made, with the average time per dive being 18 hours, most of it in temperatures near freezing; Low himself logged a total of 40 hours undersea.

The underwater footage is breathtaking in detail and depth of field. The viewer is presented with many different parts of the screen to scan and dwell upon. Shots of the debris field act as a prelude to finding the wreck and provide some of the most evocative moments in the film: a suitcase here, a shoe there, and pieces of coal everywhere—the great ungluing of an era. We also glimpse a toilet and are told they were made of iron for third-class passengers, porcelain for second class, and marble for first class, the implication being that each of these materials sinks in more or less the same way, as did the people who used them.

The film also has a human interest side that centers on the multinational crew. However, IMAX films work best when capturing a natural panorama or detail of technology. (Two years before the first IMAX film was released in 1970, Stanley Kubrick's *2001: A Space Odyssey*, the last film shot in cinerama, anticipated the style that would suit

IMAX. Scenes in *Titanica* of the *Mir* submersibles approaching the wreck are eerily reminiscent of scenes in Kubrick's great film.) Surprisingly, where the IMAX technology used for *Titanica* opened up new and unsuspected visual possibilities was with the projection of still photographs that were used to provide historical background. These images chronicle the building of the ship and the Southampton-Cherbourg-Queenstown leg of the voyage. Plate glass negatives transposed to IMAX film provide a stunning depth of field and a sense that the people in them are about to move.

At judiciously selected moments in the film, between the narrative of the expedition and the archival flashbacks, we meet the grand dame of the *Titanic*, Eva Hart, who was seven when she boarded the ship. For most of the rest of her life she was a personable resource for those interested in *Titanic*. Fittingly, she closes the film. Speaking in a church with a vaulted ceiling that resembles the hull of an overturned ship, she tempers any excessive zeal we might feel for the technology demonstrated in and by the film. We are reminded of what such an attitude led to in 1912 and warned that history is not above repeating itself.

At this point during the 1990s, *Titanic* was certainly in the air, but that interest seemed to be largely documentary. Dramatic reenactments in film seemed to have had their day until James Cameron defied all expectations. One of the consequences of Cameron's film was to significantly influence the box office success of another and very different dramatization of the sinking: *Titanic*, the Broadway musical. It debuted on April 23, 1997, seven months prior to the release of his blockbuster. It seemed as unlikely as Cameron's film to be earmarked for success. Early reviews were mostly poor, and attendance was modest. Things began to change that December, no doubt as a result of the hype surrounding Cameron's film. With music and lyrics by Maury Yeston and a book by Peter Stone, the production went on to win five Tony Awards, including for best musical.

The musical featured a true ensemble cast rather than major stars and had no memorable songs that would outlive the production. How then could it have been so successful? The answer came to me when I saw a performance. The songs, although not catchy, are well crafted; more importantly they mesh perfectly with the book. The narrative themes are simple: celebration of the ship; Ismay urging for more and more speed to set a record (perpetuating a long-held fallacy); a worry about ice; the aspirations of those in each class of accommodation; and nobility in the face of the inevitable. Noticeably absent from the production is the band playing "Nearer My God to Thee," probably to avoid its cliché status in previous films; and despite the large cast of characters, there is no Molly Brown, most likely to avoid association the 1964 film musical *The Unsinkable Molly Brown*, starring Debbie Reynolds, which in turn was based on the 1960 Broadway production by Meredith Wilson.

With the success of Cameron's *Titanic* having generating renewed interest in the ship, which has carried over into the twenty-first century, along with Cameron's commitment to her legacy, he directed the 2003 large-format documentary feature *Ghosts of the Abyss*. He revisited the wreck site with mobile cameras that allowed filming parts of it that had never been seen before. Accompanied by a team of scientists and actor Bill Paxton, who appeared in *Titanic*, Cameron made effective use of 3D technology—a first for Disney, under whose auspices the project was undertaken. Less structured (there are a few recreations of ghost-like passengers) and in some ways less dramatic than *Titanica*, the film still creates an impression that few nature-type documentaries can match.

In 2010, *Titanic II* (not to be confused with the 2002 comedy short of the same name about a young woman obsessed by the Cameron's *Titanic*) also creates an impression, in this instance one of incredulity as to how such a silly film could be made in the first place. The premise of this straight-to-DVD production—although not strictly speaking a *Titanic* film per se hence its consideration here rather than in the prvious chapter—anticipates the commemorative voyages of 2012, only in this case the journey is being made in the reverse direction by a *Titanic* replica with a 50-knot overdrive. The ship is owned by an arrogant young playboy, Hayden Walsh (Shane Van Dyke, who wrote and directed the film). His exgirlfriend, Amy Maine (Marie Westbrook), serves on the ship as a medical assistant. Her father (Bruce Davison) is a captain in the Coast Guard and is concerned that the *Titanic II* has been rushed through its safety inspection. If parts of the vessel look familiar, the cropped and CGI-tweaked exteriors use the *Queen Mary* as a body double, as did *S.O.S. Titanic* and the original *Poseidon Adventure*, to which this film exhibits more than a passing resemblance.

The ship's fate is, of course, inevitable, even though precautions have been taken for all eventualities, save one. Global warming has calved off massive Greenland glaciers. Down they tumble, creating a tsunami of biblical proportions. This is no real danger for ships at sea, or so it is supposed—since at midocean tsunamis are mere undulations—until it is realized that these waves, traveling at "843 miles per hour," are pushing huge chunks of the ice that caused them. (Tsunamis are fast, but this exceeds the speed of sound!) As a result, unlike in 1912, these 2012 bergs are proactive and need not wait for the ship to strike them. The vessel lists and starts to go down by the bow, as did her predecessor. This time there are plenty of lifeboats—the worst place to be, as there is a second round that yields a "mega-tsunami." It dispatches the lifeboats and causes *Titanic II* to overturn, recalling the fate of the *Poseidon* in an earlier film.

Amid the chaos, Hayden turns heroic, disdaining a free helicopter ride off the ship during the first strike in order to find Amy. However, he was never actually a villain per se, although comparisons with Bruce Ismay will be obvious to those in the *Titanic* know—Hayden does order full speed against the captain's (D. C. Douglas) advice, which blows the untried engines, but he does so to reverse course because of the advancing peril. He cannot be blamed for the ship's fate. She was doing nothing wrong and had taken all safety precautions. Perhaps there is a subtle message intended here: that *Titanic* (I) was caught in an unimaginable web of circumstances that defy any blame resulting from hindsight.

After a *Poseidon Adventure*-like journey through water and fire in the overturned vessel, Hayden makes sure Amy gets the last remaining dive suit as the ship goes down. Meanwhile her father dons his own dive suit and leaps from a helicopter to effect a rescue. He drags Amy and Hayden's body into an inflatable life raft as dawn breaks—minus the strains of "The Morning After." Sarcasm aside, the film is what it is, and no one should expect something Cameronesque. It is almost fun but falters because dark sets and muddy cinematography make following the action during the sinking a chore. Understandably, the film would not be what it is without a certain inevitable line, here uttered by the captain as the tsunami-borne berg is about to smash the ship: "Looks like History repeating itself"—not with respect to previous *Titanic* films, however.

CHAPTER 12

Conclusion: The *Titanic* as Myth

In mid-May of 1987, I was in the Philippines traveling between Mindoro Island and Luzon Province on a small, rickety ferry. On December 21 of the same year my memory of that passage turned from pleasant (even though the ferry carried no life preservers) to haunting. At a Greenwich Village newsstand I picked up a copy of the *New York Times*. The headline told of a collision between the ferry, *Doña Paz*, and an oil tanker in waters I had once sailed; 1,500 were believed to have perished. I thought about that same casualty figure with respect to the *Titanic* and would eventually see it in a *Times* headline several years later when I began my research into that most memorable of sea disasters. In 1912, as I have tried to show in Chapter 6, the *Times* got the numbers right. Not so in 1987, but the paper can hardly be faulted, as several of its 1912 competitors can be, for its handling of available reports. Later estimates would put the *Doña Paz* death toll at between 4,000 and 5,000.

Today the *Doña Paz* is largely forgotten, even in the Philippines, except among the families who still grieve for their lost kin. Without doubt, the fate of the *Doña Paz* has fallen victim to our short-term memory of third-world events. Yet even the more recent ferry disasters in Europe, which took hundreds of lives, have slipped from the recall of most of us. The *Titanic* is partly to blame. She wields the memory of her fate with a jealousy that tolerates no rivals.

Although over the past 100 years we have learned much about the circumstances of her demise, a persistent enigma remains: Why is the tragedy still so meaningful to us? What other historical event has generated so many forms of media representation—literary and cinematic—and legions of followers? Facts alone cannot provide a convincing explanation. Indeed the question itself defies closure since the cultural circumstances in which meanings are produced and assessed constantly change. Nevertheless, the problem is worth addressing, even if the resulting answers must remain provisional and reflect a vantage point early in the new millennium following a century of soul searching.

To say that the metaphoric implications of the *Titanic* disaster have given it the status of a modern myth is a contention that would probably gain acceptance among many commentators. Indeed, I have seen the term *myth* used so many times in discussions of the *Titanic* that I have lost count; yet I have not been able to even start a count of commentators who actually define, or at least develop, a concept of *myth* that helps explain why the sinking of the *Titanic* constitutes one. What do we mean, then, by *myth*, and how does the *Titanic* fit whatever conventions we elect to employ in applying the concept? Clearly, the oft-used popular notion of a myth as a false or inaccurate explanation for something is not what we are looking for. Somewhat surprisingly, James Cameron lapses into this usage when he claims that the *Titanic* is no myth because he has seen it. What he has seen, the wreck, is the equivalent of what the Australian aborigines call a *churinga*, in other words a sacred object (not so sacred to RMS Titanic Inc.) that mediates between this time and the dreamtime, where events in the myth(s) actually reside.

Unfortunately there is no easy definition of *myth* but numerous competing and more often than not complementary theories. In the case of the *Titanic*, just about any humanities or social science discipline's understanding of myth has applicability to her story. She is, in a sense, a universal recipient amenable to the efforts of mythographers of almost all persuasions and, as I will try to show, a case study upon which several conceptions of myth can be made to converge.

At a most basic level, when historical events are turned into myths, they reveal a way of thinking that is archaic and universal. All human cultures make sense of their existence in the world through stories, which although not literally true—even though they may have a basis in fact—embody at some level relevant knowledge about the world and often contain moral precepts. For example, the creation myth in Maori oral tradition would probably not be regarded by us as factual, closer though it may be to Darwin's perspective than premodern Western interpretations. However, its literalness is not as important as its literariness: relevant insights about the natural world and Maori life emerge from the events recounted. Similarly, the *Odyssey*—originally part of an oral tradition—has told and still tells of the epic quest that is life's journey, but it also contains, as recent studies have shown, surprisingly accurate information about circum-Mediterranean geography.

No less could be said of various works of literature. The Bible, Greek drama, Shakespeare, and novels such as *Moby Dick* are rich in metaphor, archetypes, and moral lessons. Literary critic Ian Watt has gone so far as to argue for the mythic status of stories such as *Faust, Don Quixote, Don Juan*, and *Robinson Crusoe*. Most of these narratives embody some aspect of the tragic, which gives them a certain relevance when mentioned in the context of the *Titanic*. Her demise is one of the most vivid cases in the history of Western civilization of life reflecting art.

Assessing the mythic connotations of the *Titanic* disaster requires that we go beyond any attempt to objectively ascertain what exactly happened (that would be history). Instead, after establishing how the event has been perceived and interpreted—which previous chapters have tried to do—we go on to consider recurring themes and symbols. In so doing we can apply ideas from a number of traditions of myth interpretation.

In non-Western cultures, myths often reference social as well as natural phenomena. Whether it be about kin or caste, a myth might explain why a given social arrangement is as it is, the obligations that go with it, and their consequences. The myth of the *Titanic* can be looked at this way. It states that individuals in first class had privileged access to lifeboats while those in steerage were held back. Casualty figures clearly affirm this. Preferential treatment continued even after death, as many local memorials to the deceased listed the names in order of social importance, not alphabetically. This led to a questioning of the old imperial order of things. It was also the beginning of a change further hastened by the trauma of World War I, where alphabetic listing replaced social rank.

The above critique can also be seen as tempered by conservatism. Privileged as they were, the rich and famous were not so privileged as to prevent many of them from succumbing. Reversals of the social order occur often in myths. Paupers become princes and vise versa. In the case of the *Titanic*, some notable doyens of the dollar went down with the ship while a number of anonymous immigrants and savvy crewmen were able to finagle their way into lifeboats. The departed's high echelon of Americans included Astor, Guggenheim, Straus, and Widener, and from Canada, Charles M. Hayes (president of the Grand Trunk Railroad) and Markland Molson (the brewery magnate). This has become an enduring theme in many songs and stories about the sinking. As we have already seen, it appears in the African American oral tradition in "*Titanic* Toast" and "De *Titanic*," with their warnings against aspiring to the white man's world. Perhaps over the decades those of us of less means continue to find fascination, and perhaps solace, in this situation whereby the consummate affluence of the notables on board—an Edwardian equivalent of *Lifestyles of the Rich and Famous*—was no assurance against Armageddon.

Myths sometimes involve the projection of anxieties about the world, which psychoanalytical and psychological approaches to the study of myth have tried to address. It constitutes, for example, a major theme in Freud and a minor but significant one in Jung. Playing fast and loose with a Freudian interpretation (he was fascinated by the real-life nightmare of the *Titanic* but did not try to explain it) we could say the *Titanic* disaster represents a case of cultural anxiety resulting from the dominant male order—patriarchy plus technology—being undone by "female" nature. In other words it is a variation on a recurring type of myth that concerned Freud, the *vagina dentata*.

Although ships are, of course, usually referred to as female (the reverse holds in French), they nonetheless represent an attempt by *Homo faber* (man the builder) to overcome the limits nature has imposed on his desire to conquer oceanic space, the great Mother of Waters. Add to the sea's agency an iceberg (having been "calved" or "birthed" are the feminine terms usually employed to describe its origin) slicing away at this male creation, and a case could also be made for an application of Freud's "castration complex." A further inducement to male anxiety is the legendary call "women and children first," especially if we interpret it as nature saving her own.

A Jungian approach might come to similar conclusions without laying the blame on a primordial battle of the sexes. For Jung, the anxiety induced by the sinking might be seen as a manifestation of humankind's overbearing urge to dominate nature. Unchecked reason and technology, he often argued, have created a dangerous split between the human and the natural worlds, leaving us vulnerable to disasters of our own making—the hydrogen bomb was his favorite example. He might have regarded the *Titanic*'s fate as warning against this tendency. Whereas a Freudian approach would see the ship as masculine, Jung, who often made reference to ships, would see it as an archetypal vessel, a symbolic womb, and therefore a *she* who is defiled as a result of the false belief that nature has been mastered by technology.

One of the most intriguing but complex approaches to myth interpretation derives from a tradition known as structuralism. Its most renowned proponent was the French anthropologist Claude Lévi-Strauss, whose many volumes on primitive culture have sought to explain the universal workings of the human mind that underlies all cultures. My own training as an anthropologist during a time when structuralism was in vogue leads me to suspect that it is not without some applicability to the story of the *Titanic* considered as myth.

Structuralism does not assume that the primary purpose of myth is to embody unconscious anxieties, desires, or symbolic archetypes. Myth works instead to mediate contradictions or oppositions relevant to the society in question. According to Levi-Strauss, the formal mental operations through which myth-making takes place derive from an unconscious panpsychic capacity of the human species; however, the symbols used, and their meanings, emerge from social, cultural, and historical conditions. Each element in a myth ultimately relates to every other, not as part of a linear story but as a component in a communication system that poses and seeks to understand a series of questions, many of which relate to the fundamental opposition between nature and culture.

Perhaps the approach can be made more comprehensible by applying rather than merely discussing it. The first prerequisite for a structural analysis of a myth is to highlight the key episodes in the narrative. This enterprise is, of course, subject to the bias of the researcher and could be somewhat arbitrary. Nevertheless, taking the *Titanic* disaster and breaking it down into its familiar and persistent elements, we might get the following "mythemes," to use Levi-Strauss's term:

1. The largest ship ever built embarks on her maiden voyage.
2. She accommodates all social classes and has state-of-the-art aesthetic and technological appointments.
3. The ship is trying to set a speed record (not literally true but a theme in many tellings and therefore part of the myth).
4. Ice warnings are ignored (in actuality they are acknowledged but not acted upon).
5. Collision with an iceberg sinks the ship.
6. Women and children are given priority in the sinking.
7. The rich and famous perish.
8. Nearby ship fails to come to the rescue.

That this does not exactly conform to historical fact is irrelevant; no myth ever does. This is the way the event is most often remembered. Applying a structuralist approach we can posit that the central element on the list, number 4, is the important and pivotal one. It dramatizes the opposition between nature and culture. Numbers 1 through 3 assume the triumph of culture over the limitations of nature, and numbers 5 through 7 dramatize the consequences of that assumption. The question as to whether culture can overcome nature is thus answered in the negative.

Events in myth, as Lévi-Strauss has shown using ethnographic examples, frequently involve the overrating of something and the underrating of something else. Applying this principle to our *Titanic* case study we can posit an overrating of size, speed, and wealth. What could be construed as underrated are the natural elements of weather (that calm, clear conditions posed no danger) and climate (that the time of the year and presence of ice were not an overwhelming concern); perhaps we can add the maiden voyage since these are normally cautious affairs tinged with superstition—attitudes ignored in this instance. Any structuralist analysis of myth would also explore the significance of binary oppositions within the narrative and the tensions that might exist between them. In considering the case of the *Titanic*, these oppositions might include first class versus steerage, the bridge versus the wireless cabin, the *Titanic* versus the *Californian*, and so on.

In a structuralist analysis, myth is therefore a form of discourse that cannot be reduced to a singular meaning or rationale. As a result, other structuralist interpretations of the *Titanic* are possible, but it is unlikely they would stray far from the abiding opposition her story illustrates between nature and culture. If this is an underlying assumption in many myths, as Lévi-Strauss contends, then in Western civilization the fate of the *Titanic* is about as profound an illustration of it as can be found in either history or literature.

Structuralism also posits that a given myth is often formally and thematically related to others, and what is chronicled in one can be reversed in another. I would therefore like to conclude by relating the *Titanic* to several other narratives with which it shares certain elements, most notably the story of Noah's Ark in Genesis. That they are the two most famous ships in Western culture is intriguing enough. Add a structuralist perspective, which assumes that major myths often have countermyths in which events in the first are reversed in the second, and we have an intriguing basis for a comparative assessment. According to the account in Genesis, the Ark was built in response to a cataclysmic flood sent by God to punish a world guilty of excessive corruption, violence, and wickedness. God's original plan was to do away with the entire enterprise, but Noah prompted him to have second thoughts. Here was a man who, in resisting what others had succumbed to, walked in a state of grace and untarnished faith.

God informed Noah of the wrath to come and instructed him to build an Ark of gopher wood, 300 cubits in length, 30 cubits high, and 50 cubits wide. The length of a biblical cubit has been estimated at between 18 and 36 inches. If, for the sake of poetic license, we take the latter figure and agree to not make too much of the comparison, the length of the Ark roughly equaled the *Titanic*'s 882 feet. Her height comes close to the *Titanic*'s 97 feet from keel to boat deck. Noah's vessel, however, measured considerably broader in the beam than the *Titanic*'s near 100-foot width since speed was not a priority. God's oral blueprint also called for the Ark, like the *Titanic*, to have a three-tiered system of accommodation, although the Bible does not specify who or what went where.

Placing his faith in God and avoiding the excesses of the antediluvian era, Noah, along with his extended family and their menagerie, were spared. In the story of the *Titanic*, faith is placed in the conceits of modernity—technology and inevitable progress. In yielding to their excesses, the ship is fatally wounded.

Overweening pride, condemned in the Bible and in Greek tragedy, where it is referred to as hubris, was the *Titanic*'s undoing. The resulting "nautical fall" also recalls another one from literature—Captain Ahab's obsession with the white whale that destroyed the *Pequod* in Herman Melville's *Moby Dick*. And, shifting back to history again, in a case of reach exceeding grasp, the *Titanic*'s lesson appears to have been repeated less than six months after her remains were found when the promise of the *Challenger*—perhaps damaged by ice in her O rings— was likewise claimed by the North Atlantic.

What makes comparison between the Ark and the *Titanic* so intriguing is how each vessel encapsulated the world of her day. Noah brought on board animals, crops, and a small coterie of relatives—a starter kit to rebuild civilization. The *Titanic* had impressive trappings that included a swimming pool, a band, period staterooms, lavish dining areas, a café Parisien, gymnasium, squash courts, and ornate décor— James Cameron's spin on the myth even adds modernist paintings, all of this encapsulated in a state-of-the-art, high-tech package. She was partly a grand hotel, partly a traveling exposition recalling the influential one held in Paris in 1900. In the lexicon of contemporary pop culture, we could describe her as a floating theme park, which in most cinematic renderings also becomes a "love boat."

The concept of a self-sufficient world borne in the womb of a ship is a compelling one. In literature we find a renowned example in the *Nautilus*, the submarine created by Jules Verne in two of his novels, *Twenty-Thousand Leagues under the Sea* and *The Mysterious Island*. Her captain, Nemo, is a technological wizard but also a connoisseur of high culture, especially art and music. Railing against the world for its excessive greed, intolerance, and violence, he creates an alternative one of his own. Eventually he succumbs to some of the same traits he despises, and the *Nautilus* is destroyed; she gets resurrected in the second novel, only to go down for a final time. The idea for such an extraordinary vessel did not spring exclusively from Verne's imagination. In 1867 he was a New York–bound passenger on the maiden voyage of a refitted *Great Eastern*, perhaps the most ambitious sea vessel, relative to its era, of all time.

Like the *Nautilus*, and from more recent fiction Star Trek's *Enterprise*, the *Titanic* has an aura of fantasy about her. She took the bounty of Earth on a voyage that still, over 100 years later, seems more imaginary than real. The trip dramatized how the limits of human achievement could, despite the best laid plans, be highly vulnerable. Her lesson now seems global and apocalyptic. However, even in 1912, as the ship's death throes were being observed by survivors in lifeboats, a number of them describe the scenario as like watching "the end of the world."

A historical assessment might concede that the sinking was one of several events marking the end of an era. But the *Titanic* is not just history; it is also myth because of the ways in which it continues to haunt us. One intriguing thing about James Cameron's *Titanic* is that, with new millennium anxiety, it came on a wave of films that suggested the possibility of one kind of apocalypse or another—*Independence Day* (1996), *Deep Impact* (1998), *Armageddon* (1998), and their kin. Although the YK2 bug may have fizzled, the new millennium brought crises, such as 9/11 and Katrina, which with greater vigilance might have either been prevented outright, in the case of the former, or the worst consequences stayed in the case of the latter. Hindsight with respect to both is like hindsight following the two *Titanic* inquiries in 1912. Recent earthquakes and tsunamis are of a different order; hubris or no, nature had its way.

One of the cautionary lessons of the *Titanic* is that we underestimate nature and overestimate technology at our peril. Could not the ongoing interest in the events of 1912 have a mythic link to the possible destiny of our planet—"Spaceship Earth" as R. Buckminster Fuller used to call it? In Genesis the biblical Ark rescued part of an ancient world from a disaster invoked by God. The *Titanic* has become an ark more appropriate to our contemporary world, her fate warning us to be prudent in the face of both natural and technological uncertainty.

Appendix

THE CONVERGENCE OF THE TWAIN

(Lines on the loss of the "Titanic")

Thomas Hardy

From the *Selected Poems of Thomas Hardy* (London: MacMillan, 1916), 119–21.

I

In a solitude of the sea
Deep from human vanity
And the Pride of Life that planned her, stilly
couches she.

II

Steel chambers, late the pyres
Of her salamandarine fires,
Cold currents thrid, and turn to Rhythmic tidal
lyres.

III

Over the mirrors meant
To glass the opulent
The sea-worm crawls—grotesque, slimed, dumb,
indifferent.

IV
Jewels in Joy designed
To ravish the sensuous mind
Lie lightless, all their sparkles bleared and black
and blind.

V
Dim moon-eyed fishes near
Gaze at the gilded gear
And query: "What does this vainglorious
down here?" . . .

VI
Well: while was fashioning
This creature of cleaving wing,
The Immanent Will that stirs and urges everything.

VII
Prepared a sinister mate
For her—so gaily great—
A Shape of Ice, for the time far and dissociate.

VIII
And as the smart ship grew
In stature, grace, and hue,
In silent shadowy distance grew the Iceberg too.

IX
Alien they seemed to be:
No mortal eye could see
The intimate welding of their later history.

X
Or sign that they were bent
By paths coincident
On being anon twin halves of one August event,

XI
Till the Spinner of the Years
Said "Now!" And each one hears,
And consummation comes, and jars two hemispheres.

THE TITANIC (TRAD.)[*]

It was on one Monday morning just about one o'clock
When that great Titanic began to reel and rock;
People began to scream and cry,
Saying, "Lord, am I going to die?"

Chorus
It was sad when that great ship went down,
It was sad when that great ship went down,
Husbands and wives and little children lost their lives,
It was sad when that great ship went down.

When that ship left England it was making for the shore,
The rich had declared that they would not ride with the poor,
So they put the poor below,
They were the first to go.

Chorus
While they were building they said what they would do,
We will build a ship what water can't go through;
But God with power in hand
Showed the world that it could not stand.

Chorus
Those people on that ship were a long ways from home.
With friends all around they didn't know that the time had come;
Death came riding by,
Sixteen hundred had to die.

Chorus
While Paul was sailing his men around,
God told him that not a man should drown;
If you trust and obey,
I will save you all to-day.

Chorus
You know it must have been awful with those people on the sea,
They say that they were singing, "Nearer My God to Thee."
While some were homeward bound,
Sixteen hundred had to drown.

---

[*](A number of versions exist, sometimes under the title "It Was Sad When The Great Ship Went Down," or "The Great Titanic.")

Bibliography

INTRODUCTION: FROM TRIUMPH TO TRAGEDY

Anderson, Roy. *White Star*. Prescott, Lancashire, UK: T. Stephenson, 1964.

Babcock, F. Lawrence. *Spanning the Atlantic*. New York: Knopf, 1931.

Barczewski, Stephanie. *Titanic: A Night Remembered*. London: Hambleton and London, 2004.

Blom, Philipp. *The Vertigo Years: Europe, 1910–1914*. New York: Basic Books, 2008.

Brinnin, John Michael. *The Story of the Grand Saloon*. New York: Delacorte, 1971.

Cutler, Carl C. *Greyhounds of the Sea: The Story of the American Clipper Ship*. New York: Putnams, 1930.

Davie, Michael. *The Titanic: The Full Story of a Tragedy*. London: Grafton, 1987.

Dugan, James. *The Great Iron Ship*. London: Hamish Hamilton, 1955.

Dunn, Laurence. *Famous Liners of the Past Belfast Built*. London: Adlard Coles, 1964.

Eaton, John P., and Charles Haas. *Titanic: Triumph and Tragedy*. New York: Norton, 1986.

Emerson, George S. *S.S. Great Eastern*. London: David and Charles, 1980.

Guillet, Edwin C. *The Great Migration*. New York: Nelson, 1937.

Kirkaldy, Adam. *British Shipping: Its History, Organization, and Importance*. New York: Augustus M. Kelly, 1970.

Lightholler, Charles Herbert. *Titanic and Other Ships*. London: Ivor Nicholson and Watson, 1935.

Lynch, Don, and Ken Marschall. *Titanic: An Illustrated History*. Toronto: Madison, 1992.

Marcus, Geoffrey. *The Maiden Voyage*. New York: Viking, 1969.

Maxtone-Graham, John. *The Only Way to Cross*. New York: MacMillan, 1972.

McCaugen, Michael. *Steel Ships and Iron Men*. London: Friars Bush Press, 1989.
Pollard, Sydney, and Paul Robertson. *The British Shipbuilding Industry: 1870–1914*. Cambridge, MA: Harvard University Press, 1993.
Robinson, Geoff, and Don Lynch. "The 'Unsinkable' Titanic as Advertised." *Titanic Commutator* 6, no. 4 (February–April 1993).
Tuchman, Barbara. *The Proud Tower*. New York: Bantam, 1986.
Winchester, Simon. *Atlantic*. New York: HarperCollins, 2010.

PART I. WIRELESS WORLD

Aitken, Hugh. *Syntony and Spark: The Origins of Radio*. New York: Wiley, 1976.
Baarslag, Karl. *SOS to the Rescue*. New York: Oxford University Press, 1935.
Baker, W. J. *A History of the Marconi Company*. London: Methuen, 1970.
Booth, John, and Sean Coughlan. *Titanic: Signals of Disaster*. Westbury, Wiltshire, UK: White Star, 1993.
Brooks, Jennie. "The Wireless at Lands End Where the *Carpathia* First Talks." *Titanic Commutator* 19, no. 1 (May–July 1995).
Crowley, David, and Paul Heyer, eds. *Communication in History*. Boston: Allyn & Bacon, 2010.
Douglas, Susan. *Inventing America Broadcasting*. Baltimore, MD: Johns Hopkins University Press, 1987.
Dreher, Carl. *Sarnoff: An American Success*. New York: Quadrangle, 1977.
Harrison, Leslie. *A Titanic Myth: The Californian Incident*. London: William Kimber, 1986.
Kern, Stephen. *The Culture of Time and Space: 1880–1918*. Cambridge: Harvard University Press, 1983.
Lepien, Ray. "The White Star Liner *Republic* (II), Part II, Conclusion." *Titanic Commutator* 19, no. 1 (May–July 1995).
Lewis, Thomas. *Empire of the Air*. New York: Burlingame, 1991.
Lyons, Eugene. *David Sarnoff*. New York: Harper and Row, 1966.
Marconi, Degna. *My Father Marconi*. New York: McGraw-Hill, 1962.
Molony, Senan. *Titanic and the Mystery Ship*. Stroud, UK: Tempus, 2006.
Padfield, Peter. *The Titanic and the Californian*. London: Hodder and Stroughton, 1968.
Sarnoff, David. *Looking Ahead: The Papers of David Sarnoff*. New York: McGraw-Hill, 1968.
Titanic Commutator. "*Titanic* and *Samson*." 29, no. 170 (2005).

PART II. STORY OF THE CENTURY

Beesley, Lawrence. *The Loss of SS Titanic*. London: Heineman, 1912.
Berger, Meyer. *The Story of the New York Times*. New York: Simon and Schuster, 1951.
Cranston, J. H. *Ink on My Fingers*. Toronto: Ryerson Press, 1963.

Davis, Elmer. *History of the New York Times*. St. Clair Shores, MI: Scholarly Press, 1971.

Dupuis, Michael. "And Mind, You're a Nurse." *HerStoria*, Issue 7 (Autumn 2010).

Emery, Michael, and Edwin Emery. *The Press and America*. Englewood Cliffs, NJ: Prentice-Hall, 1988.

Fine, Barnett. *A Giant of the Press: Carr Van Anda*. Oakland, CA: Acme Books, 1968.

Gracie, Archibald. *The Truth about the Titanic*. New York: Kennerly, 1913.

Harkness, Ross J. E. *Atkinson of the Star*. Toronto: University of Toronto Press, 1963.

Hustak, Allan. *Titanic: The Canadian Story*. Montreal: Vehicule Press, 1998.

Juergens, George. *Joseph Pulitzer and the New York World*. Princeton, NJ: Princeton University Press, 1966.

Kobre, Sidney. *The Development of American Journalism*. Dubuque, IA: Brown, 1969.

Lang, Marjory. *Women Who Made the News: Female Journalists in Canada, 1880–1945*. Montreal: McGill-Queen's University Press, 1999.

Lord, Walter. *The Night Lives On*. New York: William Morrow, 1986.

Mott, Frank Luther. *American Journalism*. New York: MacMillan, 1969.

O' Leary, Grattan. *Recollections of People, Press, and Politics*. Toronto: MacMillan of Canada, 1977.

Poulton, Ron. *The Paper Tyrant: John Ross Robertson of the Toronto Telegram*. Toronto: Clarke, Irwin & Company, 1971.

Rex, Kay. *No Daughter of Mine: The Women and History of the Canadian Women's Press Club, 1904–1971*. Toronto: Cedar Cave Publishing, 1995.

Swanberg, W. A. *Citizen Hearst*. New York: Scribner's, 1961.

Swanberg, W. A. *Pulitzer*. New York: Scribner's, 1967.

Titanic Commutator. "Newspaper Headlines of the *Titanic* Disaster." 12, no. 3 (1988).

U.S. Congress, Senate. *Loss of the Steamship "Titanic."* 62nd Congress 2, Document 933 (1912).

Wade, Wyn Craig. *The Titanic: End of a Dream*. New York: Penguin, 1986.

PART III. IMAGINING DISASTER

Aspler, Tony. *Titanic: A Novel*. Toronto: Doubleday, 1989.

Ballard, Robert. "How We Found the *Titanic*." *National Geographic* 168, no. 6 (December 1985).

Barnes, Julian. *The History of the World in 10 1/2 Chapters*. London: Cape, 1989.

Barthes, Roland. *Mythologies*. London: Paladin, 1957.

Bergfelder, Tim, and Sarah Street, eds. *The Titanic in Myth and Memory*. London: I. B. Taurus, 2004.

Biel, Steven. *Down with the Old Canoe: A Cultural History of the Titanic*. New York: Norton, 1996.

Biel, Steven. *Titanica: The Disaster of the Century in Poetry, Song, and Prose*. New York: Norton: 1998.

Boles, Derek. "Catastrophe on Film." *Titanic Commutator* 16, no. 2 (August–October 1992).

Bright, Brenda. "*Titanic* on Film: Fact or Fiction." *Titanic Commutator* 16, no. 2 (August–October 1992).

Brown, Richard. *Voyage of the Iceberg: The Story of the Iceberg That Sank the Titanic*. Toronto: James Lorimer & Company, 1983.

Buckley, William F., Jr. *Happy Days Were Here Again*. New York: Random House, 1993.

Clark, Arthur C. *The Ghost from the Grand Banks*. New York: Bantam, 1990.

Conrad, Joseph. *Notes on Life and Letters*. London: J. M. Dent and Sons, 1970.

Cussler, Clive. *Raise the Titanic*. New York: Pocket Books, 1988.

Dzwa, Sandra. *E. J. Pratt: The Evolutionary Vision*. Toronto: Copp Clark, 1974.

Finney, Jack. *From Time to Time*. New York: Simon & Schuster, 1995.

Fox, Robin. *The Challenge of Anthropology*. New Brunswick, NJ: Transaction, 1994.

Gardiner, Martin. *The Wreck of the Titanic Foretold?* Buffalo, NY: Prometheus, 1986.

Gringell, Susan, ed. *E. J. Pratt on His Life and Poetry*. Toronto: University of Toronto Press, 1993.

Hardy, Thomas. *Selected Poems of Thomas Hardy*. London: MacMillan, 1916.

Harrison, Leslie. "A Titanic Myth: Epilogue, the MAIB Report." *Titanic Commutator* 16, no. 3 (November 1992–January 1993).

Higham, Charles, and Joel Greenberg, eds. *The Celluloid Muse: Hollywood Directors Speak*. New York: Signet, 1972.

Hoffman, William, and Jack Grimm. *The Search for the Titanic*. New York: Beaufort, 1982.

Hull, David Stewart. *Film in the Third Reich*. New York: Simon and Schuster, 1973.

Jackson, Bruce. "The *Titanic* Toast." In *Veins of Humor*, edited by Harry Levin. Cambridge: Harvard University Press, 1972.

Kalman, Tanito. "Morgan Robertson's *Futility*." *Titanic Commutator* 17, no. 4 (February–April 1994).

Kamuda, Edward. "The *Titanic* Artifacts." *Titanic Commutator* 17, no. 4 (February–April 1994).

Levi-Strauss, Claude. *Structural Anthropology*. New York: Basic Books, 1963.

Levin, Harry, ed. *Veins of Humor*. Cambridge: Harvard University Press, 1972.

Lomax, John A., and Alan Lomax, eds. *Negro Folk Songs as Sung by Leadbelly*. New York: MacMillan, 1936.

Lord, Walter. *A Night to Remember*. New York: Bantam, 1956.

MacQuitty, William. *A Life to Remember*. London: Quartet, 1991.

Marschall, Ken. "*Ghosts of the Abyss*: The Outtakes." Pts. I–III. *Titanic Commutator*, 27, no. 163 (2003); 27, no. 164 (2003); 28, no. 165 (2004).

Marsh, Ed W. *James Cameron's Titanic*. New York: HarperCollins 1997.

Mills, Simon. *The Titanic in Pictures*. Buckinghamshire, UK: Wordsworth, 1995.

Parisi, Paula. *Titanic and the Making of James Cameron*. New York: New Market, 1998.

Pellegrino, Charles. *Her Name Titanic*. New York: McGraw-Hill, 1988.

Pratt, E. J. *Selected Poems*. Edited with an introduction, bibliography, and notes by Peter Buitenhuis. Toronto: MacMillan, 1968.

Prechtl, Robert. *Titanic*. New York: Dutton, 1940.

Robertson, Morgan. *Futility*. In *The Wreck of the Titanic Foretold?* edited by Martin Gardiner. Buffalo, NY: Prometheus, 1986.

Ruffman, Alan. *Titanic Remembered: The Unsinkable Ship and Halifax*. Halifax: Formac1999.

Sandler, Kevin S., and Gayln Studlar, eds. *Titanic: Anatomy of a Blockbuster*. New Brunswick, NJ: Rutgers University Press, 1999.

Spoto, Donald. *The Dark Side of Genius: The Life of Alfred Hitchcock*. Boston: Little Brown, 1983.

Steel, Danielle. *No Greater Love*. New York: Dell, 1991.

Sussman, Herbert L. *Victorians and the Machine*. Cambridge: Harvard University Press, 1968.

Thomas, Tony. *The Cinema of the Sea*. Jefferson, NC: McFarland, 1988.

Titanic Historical Society. *25th Anniversary Program*. September 1–4, 1988.

Watt, Ian. *Myths of Modern Individualism: Faust, Don Quixote, Don Juan, Robinson Crusoe*. New York: Cambridge University Press, 1996.

Wells, Henry W., and Karl F. Klink. *Edwin J. Pratt and His Poetry*. Toronto: Ryerson, 1947.

Whale, Derek. "Re-launching 'A Titanic Myth.'" *Titanic Commutator* 16, no. 3 (November 1992–January 1993).

Index

About the Author

Paul Heyer is a media historian teaching in the Department of Communication Studies at Wilfrid Laurier University in Ontario, Canada. His books include *Communications and History: Theories of Media, Knowledge, and Civilization* (Praeger, 1988), *The Medium and the Magician: Orson Welles, the Radio Years* (2005), and most recently the sixth edition of *Communication in History: Technology, Culture, Society* (2010), coedited with David Crowley.